Creating character

Manchester University Press

Series editors: Anna Barton, Andrew Smith

Editorial board: David Amigoni, Isobel Armstrong, Philip Holden, Jerome McGann, Joanne Wilkes, Julia M. Wright

Interventions: Rethinking the Nineteenth Century seeks to make a significant intervention into the critical narratives that dominate conventional and established understandings of nineteenth-century literature. Informed by the latest developments in criticism and theory the series provides a focus for how texts from the long nineteenth century, and more recent adaptations of them, revitalise our knowledge of and engagement with the period. It explores the radical possibilities offered by new methods, unexplored contexts and neglected authors and texts to re-map the literary-cultural landscape of the period and rigorously reimagine its geographical and historical parameters. The series includes monographs, edited collections and scholarly sourcebooks.

Already published

Charlotte Brontë: Legacies and afterlives   Amber K. Regis and Deborah Wynne (eds)

The Great Exhibition, 1851: A sourcebook   Jonathon Shears (ed.)

Interventions: Rethinking the nineteenth century   Andrew Smith and Anna Barton (eds)

Creating character

Theories of nature and nurture in Victorian sensation fiction

Helena Ifill

Manchester University Press

Copyright © Helena Ifill 2018

The right of Helena Ifill to be identified as the author of this work has been asserted by her in accordance with the Copyright, Designs and Patents Act 1988.

Published by Manchester University Press
Oxford Road, Manchester M13 9PL
www.manchesteruniversitypress.co.uk

British Library Cataloguing-in-Publication Data
A catalogue record for this book is available from the British Library

ISBN 978 1 7849 9513 3 hardback
ISBN 978 1 5261 7181 8 paperback

First published 2018
Paperback published 2023

The publisher has no responsibility for the persistence or accuracy of URLs for any external or third-party internet websites referred to in this book, and does not guarantee that any content on such websites is, or will remain, accurate or appropriate.

Typeset by Out of House Publishing

To my parents

Contents

Acknowledgements   viii

Introduction   1

Part I Self-control, willpower and monomania   31
1 *Basil* and *No Name*   33
2 *John Marchmont's Legacy*   67

Part II Heredity and degeneration   95
3 *The Lady Lisle*   97
4 *Armadale*   122

Part III Education, environment and circumstance   153
5 *Man and Wife*   155
6 *Lost for Love*   179

Conclusion   211

Bibliography   216
Index   229

Acknowledgements

I would like to begin by thanking the people who have read this research at various stages of its development, all of whom have been generous with their time and advice. This includes Anne-Marie Beller, Pamela K. Gilbert and Marcus Waithe, with special thanks to Angela Wright for her support and encouragement. My gratitude also goes to the British Society for Literature and Science and the Victorian Popular Fiction Association; I have presented early drafts of several chapters at their annual conferences, and the feedback and suggestions from other delegates have been invaluable. The same goes for the Medical Humanities, Medicine and Literature seminar series at the University of Bristol; the Centre for Nineteenth-Century Studies at the University of Sheffield; the North-West Long Nineteenth-Century seminar series; and the Oxford Literature and Science seminar series, where I have been invited to share my work. I am also grateful to Andrew Mangham, Diane B. Paul and Catherine Delafield for sharing information, ideas and their work with me. My series editors, Anna Barton and Andrew Smith, have been so helpful, informative and patient, that I can only apologise for drawing on the latter quality quite as much as I have. Some of my very early work on Chapter 2 appeared in *Leeds Working Papers in Victorian Studies* ('"She ought to have been a great man. Nature makes these mistakes now and then": Right living in the wrong body in *John Marchmont's Legacy*'), and some material from Chapters 3 and 5 has appeared in my article 'Wilkie Collins's monomaniacs in *Basil, No Name* and *Man and Wife*', in the *Wilkie Collins Journal*; I am grateful to the editors for their kind permission to reprint it here. I would also like to thank my mother, Patricia Ifill, and Louise and Alan Pink, whose houses have acted as writing retreats for me at crucial moments. My eternal thanks as well to Phil Smith, who has always been willing to act as a sounding board, a proofreader, a critic and a cook as necessary.

Introduction

What is SELF? ... the representation of an integral individual human being—the organisation of a certain fabric of flesh and blood, biassed [*sic*], perhaps, originally by the attributes and peculiarities of the fabric itself— by hereditary predispositions, by nervous idiosyncrasies, by cerebral developments, by slow or quick action of the pulse, by all in which mind takes a shape from the mould of the body;—but still a Self which, in every sane constitution, can be changed or modified from the original bias, by circumstance, by culture, by reflection, by will, by conscience, through means of the unseen inhabitant of the fabric.[1]

(Edward Bulwer-Lytton, 'On self-control', 1863)

Caxtoniana: A Series of Essays on Life, Literature, and Manners, by the popular and prolific novelist Edward Bulwer-Lytton, was serialised in twenty monthly parts in *Blackwood's Edinburgh Magazine* between February 1862 and October 1863.[2] In it Bulwer-Lytton offers reflection, advice and opinions on (as the accommodating subtitle suggests) eclectic topics, from the everyday to the philosophical, often both within the same piece. 'On self-control' is one such essay, which uses examples of historical figures to illustrate what Bulwer-Lytton considered to be the true nature of self-discipline. Bulwer-Lytton acknowledges, however, that before he can discuss the control of the self, he must first ask what "Self" is.

This question – 'What is Self?' – was certainly not a new one, but the way in which it interested, preoccupied, and troubled many Victorian thinkers was clearly influenced by their particular socio-historical moment. Both the contemplation of the question and its numerous possible answers were prompted by, and had an impact on, social developments and changes that took place throughout the Victorian period. As in Bulwer-Lytton's essay, the question could arise from the most practical and everyday issues – here the matter of personal conduct. The relevance and context of the question itself changed as social, scientific and religious transformations meant that conceptions and theories of self were contested, altered and created throughout the century. How the self was perceived could radically influence how it was seen to be integrated within its immediate environment and within vaster schemes, both spiritual and secular. So by asking 'What is Self?', the Victorians were asking not simply about individual ontology, but about the multiple complex networks in which they were enmeshed.

Questions of the nature of the "Self" were intimately connected to questions of the extent to which the self was either fixed or malleable, and the forces to which it might be subject. To what extent, it was asked, were humans able to control their actions and desires, to exert free will and thereby be responsible for their own behaviour? Were people at the mercy of their biological composition, their inherited characteristics, their upbringing, their inherent intellect (or lack thereof)? Or were they free, and therefore accountable beings who could make choices and act upon them without constraint? The degree to which individuals could be improved or spoiled not only by their own actions, but by those of the people around them, and by their environment, was also of great importance: what individuals *necessarily* were, and what they *could* be, was vital not only to each person, but to the family unit, wider communities and the nation.

Bulwer-Lytton's own response to 'What is Self?' exemplifies how interrogating the nature of the self inevitably entails some consideration of its creation and development. Whilst not suggesting that the self is a purely physical entity, Bulwer-Lytton defines it in 'flesh and blood' terms of hereditary transmission, the cerebral and nervous systems, and the circulation of blood through the body, all of which may affect the developing 'mind'. He is therefore acknowledging that physiological constitution is a fundamental, formative part of each individual. At the same time this self is modifiable by the influence of external forces such as 'circumstance' and 'culture', and of internal, non-physical forces such as 'reflection', 'will', 'conscience' and 'the unseen inhabitant of the fabric', which we may think of as soul or mind. Ultimately, according to Bulwer-Lytton, that 'complex unity' which comprises 'Self' is alterable and manipulable by those around it and through *self*-modification. It is with such internal and external influences, how the mid-Victorians perceived them and how they were represented in popular fiction, that this book is concerned.

Introduction

As Heidi Rimke and Alan Hunt observe, many Victorians believed, like Bulwer-Lytton, that the various aspects that made up a human personality were modifiable:

> Despite their variant conceptualizations the will, the passions, the soul and the character share the crucial attribute of being suitable objects of governance; they can be worked upon, trained, developed and thus reformed. It is of particular significance to note that the governance of the will can be effected either by individuals themselves or by others; that is, their governance can be both internal and external.[3]

The majority of the mid-Victorian men and women who wrote about the nature of selfhood, including many of those introduced in the following pages, attached great importance to the individual's potential for free will. They held compatibilist views that acknowledged to a greater or lesser extent the many deterministic factors that played on the development of each individual whilst maintaining a belief in the freedom of the willpower to dictate behaviour responsibly. Yet the will itself was something to be cultivated and strengthened; this was crucial because the will was believed to control the passions and regulate the conscious behaviour of the individual.

The raising of people who were capable of self-control, of acting as responsible beings, was often a key concern to those Victorians engaged in the formation of social policy. It was hoped that by employing the correct external determining forces from an early enough age, internal governance could be developed to the point where it could reliably guarantee acceptable personal conduct. Pamela K. Gilbert has demonstrated, for example, how Victorian housing and sanitary reform was based on the belief 'that character is created in the home', and so aimed to make the poorest classes suitable for citizenship by altering their domestic desires and behaviour so as to render them more congruent with those of the bourgeoisie.[4] Left to themselves, the poor were not deemed capable of self-control or self-improvement – their self-determining actions were not to be relied upon, their wills would pursue the wrong desires – and so it was deemed necessary for the State to take a deterministic role in the management of their lives.

Both the above quotations from Bulwer-Lytton and Rimke and Hunt include reference to the influence of what can usefully be called "nurture" on "nature", and of external influences on internal constitution. However, the Victorians who thought and wrote on this subject rarely reduced it to a simple battle between nature and nurture or the internal and the external. The interplay between nature and nurture was acknowledged to be complex and often impossible to disentangle, with the channels of influence working in both directions. The very words that are used to talk about these factors can be tricky. The definition of the word "nature", for example, and what it meant to different Victorians in any particular instance, is debatable: it could be synonymous with "congenital", but it was also frequently observed that nature, or what was natural to a person, could change (or be changed) as a result of behaviour dictated by environmental and social influences. This understanding filtered through all levels of society throughout the period. The morally improving *Chambers's Edinburgh Journal* reminded readers in 1849 that 'habit ... being second nature, is still more difficult to overcome than nature itself', but went on to assert that habit could also have 'corrective properties'.[5] In 1889 the penny periodical the *London Journal* explained to its readers that 'men of great fortune' continue to work, rather than 'resting and enjoying themselves', because 'long habit becomes a second nature' and they would view rest as 'the severest punishment'.[6] Meanwhile, the more highbrow *Contemporary Review* ran articles on topics such as 'the hereditary transmission of acquired Habits' that became 'secondary instincts' that could then be passed on to the next generation.[7] The term "circumstance" also carried various meanings in relation to both nature and nurture; it could mean the conditions of one's birth (from physical health, to inherited features of body or mind, to social class and prospects) or the many environmental factors that could have an impact on one's life (such as upbringing, education, income and so on). Although there is often a tacit understanding of what is intended by such words, they can become slippery when meanings elide, mutate and carry ambiguous or multiple connotations.

Although desirable or detrimental inherent traits might be respectively enhanced or counteracted by external influences, Victorian theorists were aware that there were factors at work that could contradict or overpower any efforts they made to determine the outcome of an individual's development. The inexorable forces of heredity, of inherent constitution, and of social and environmental circumstance could assert themselves in unpredictable and unwelcome ways. The developing personality of an individual was therefore a site of potential danger and vulnerability, as well as opportunity.

Introduction

The sensation novel

Bulwer-Lytton's 'On self-control' is just one example of a popular nineteenth-century author displaying interest in issues relating to determinism. Sensation fiction, the controversial literary genre that dominated the scene in the 1860s, contains numerous representations of deterministic forces that are variously internal and external, naturally arising and socially engineered, complementary and conflicting. Sensation fiction was a genre that engaged with current and provocative issues, including many of those that sparked discussions about determinism and character formation in Victorian society, such as class relations, gender roles, the diagnosis and treatment of insanity, educational reform, and the ethos of self-help. The two leading sensation authors of the 1860s with whose work this book is concerned, Mary Elizabeth Braddon and Wilkie Collins, were both popular and prolific; their widespread appeal meant that readers from all levels of society were exposed to their portrayals of character formation.[8]

Yet the very popularity of the sensation genre generated criticism. With its staple attributes of crime, murder, adultery and bigamy, all taking place in the supposed sanctity of the domestic sphere, sensation fiction was contentious, censured as commercial, plot-driven and cheaply playing on the senses of the reader. Whereas "respectable" literature could be highly valued as 'at once the cause and the effect of social progress',[9] sensation fiction was, as numerous critics have observed, 'seen to be symptomatic of the degeneration, not only of literature, but also of moral values'.[10] In fact it was believed to be not only an effect, but also a cause of moral corruption: 'there were very real concerns that readers – particularly female readers – would be adversely influenced by the amoral characters to be found in these works' (Maunder and Moore, 'Introduction', p. 5). Reviews of sensation fiction were not uniformly damning,[11] but Braddon and Collins regularly received harsh criticism. The *Athenaeum*, for example, described Collins's *Basil* (1852) as:

> a piece of romantic sensibility,—challenging success by its constant appeal to emotion, and by the rapid vehemence of its highly wrought rhetoric … The style of 'Basil' is as eloquent and graceful as its subject is faulty and unwholesome. There is a gushing force in his words, a natural outpouring of his sensibility, a harmony, tone, and *verve* in his language.[12]

Introduction

Similarly, John Dennis writing for the *Fortnightly Review* in 1865 claimed that

> Cleverness, indeed, is perhaps the most striking characteristic of [Braddon's] tales. They are defective as works of art, their moral tone is seldom healthy, they abound with errors of composition and improbabilities of plot; but they display so much ability that the reader willingly overlooks deficiencies, and is satisfied to be excited and amused.[13]

Both reviewers acknowledge the engaging, amusing nature of sensational writing, but these very attributes make it a seductively dangerous form of moral corruption. Such reviews figure sensation fiction itself as a kind of negative determinant, corrupting the populace.

Contrastingly, the critical reappraisal of sensation fiction, which began in the late twentieth century, reframed it, and the journals that carried it, as a genre that served the positive end of educating readers, training them to be discerning and reflective thinkers who would interpret perceptively. Solveig C. Robinson, for example, asserts that *Belgravia* (edited by Braddon) aimed to raise 'readers' tastes', and that 'Braddon drove home the point that *popular* taste didn't necessarily have to mean *bad* taste', whilst Jennifer Phegley argues that family literary magazines such as *Belgravia* 'empowered women to make their own decisions about what and how to read'.[14] From this perspective, sensation fiction is a positive influence.

As well as being morally ambiguous, sensation fiction has often been seen to consist largely of "novels of circumstance", which privilege 'the supremacy of the story', as opposed to Victorian realist fiction's supposedly superior "novels of character".[15] In literary criticism, determinism has traditionally been closely related to realism, particularly with the works of George Eliot.[16] Realism is generally associated with the careful drawing of psychologically nuanced personalities embedded in detailed social networks, whose behaviour leads to logical consequences that are made evident to the reader by an omniscient narrator. Sensation fiction, contrastingly, deals in chance, wild coincidences, the playing out of providential design or the forces of Fate, and is broadly seen as "oppositional" to realism.[17] As Patrick Brantlinger has observed, 'the world of ... the sensation novel is very much one in which circumstances rule characters, propelling them through the intricate machinations of plots that act like fate'.[18]

As part of the disparagement of sensation fiction's 'subordination of character to plot' (Brantlinger, p. 12), Victorian reviewers often dismissed

Introduction

its characters as sketchy, improbable and unconvincing. For example, one critic complained that Braddon's fiction contained 'no real thought, no analysis that is worth the name, no insight into human nature. Everything is shallow and thin. Her men and women are puppets.'[19] Dennis similarly declared that the actions of Braddon's characters were 'marked by the wildest improbability, and it is essential to the plot that they should be', adding that 'in novels of the class represented by Miss Braddon, we look more for an exciting story than for a careful and consistent delineation of character' (p. 512). W. F. Rae, writing for the *North British Review*, dismissed Olivia in *John Marchmont's Legacy* (1863) as 'but a creature of Miss Braddon's imagination ... as unreal as a hobgoblin' (p. 195). Braddon was aware of this perception of her work. Writing to Bulwer-Lytton, her literary mentor, about *John Marchmont's Legacy*, she claimed that she had tried to write a novel in which 'the story arises naturally out of the characters of the actors in it, as contrasted with a novel in which the actors are only marionettes, the slaves of the story', but went on to admit regretfully that 'even my kindest reviewers tell me that it is not so and that the characters break down when the story begins'.[20] H. F. Chorley, one of Collins's most caustic critics, regarded such subjecting of character to plot as a sign of moral and literary laxity: 'Those who make plot their first consideration and humanity the second,—those, again, who represent the decencies of life as too often so many hypocrisies,—have placed themselves in a groove which goes, and must go, in a downward direction, whether as regards fiction or morals.'[21]

Whereas Chorley felt that Collins's prioritisation of plot indicated a subordination of 'humanity' as a theme, reading Collins's and Braddon's fiction in the light of contemporaneous theories of determinism offers an alternative interpretation of their emphasis on plot. Their stories can be read as an acknowledgement of the interplay of determining factors that lead individuals into certain situations (perhaps that of the jilted lover or the disinherited child), and dictate how they will act in those situations (with saint-like resignation, resolute defiance or seditious plotting). Like the works of many contemporary scientists and physicians, Braddon's and Collins's fiction reveals a conflict between a conception of the will as a decisive force and an awareness that a person's personality, abilities and actions are dictated by determining factors over which they have little or no control. This book highlights sensation fiction's attentiveness to the impact of uncontrollable circumstance on the development of the personality, and to the unpredictable external forces that may ensnare and control the individual. Rather than failing to consider humanity adequately, as Chorley claimed, sensation fiction's emphasis on plot can be interpreted as considering the human condition in a manner that acknowledges that a combination of internal and external pressures drive the individual through life, often precluding the possibility of truly independent action.

Supporters of sensation fiction frequently asserted claims to some form of realism in the genre. In a defence of Braddon and her work, George Augustus Sala argued that her novels are 'like dwellers in the actual, breathing world in which we live', and refers the reader to the sensational events related in newspapers and police reports as proof.[22] Brantlinger notes that because they drew on the scandalous, sensationally reported crimes of the day, sensation authors 'could even claim that to sensationalize was to be realistic' (p. 9). Sensation authors employ theories of character formation in the same way that they draw on the news for inspiration: to at once satisfy their readers' craving for what Braddon described as 'strong meat' and to provide some form of realism (Wolff, 'Devoted disciple', 9 December 1864, p. 28). As critics such as Sally Shuttleworth have acknowledged, although they wrote 'from a very different position within the cultural spectrum, and following very different generic rules ... to very different effect', sensation authors often 'drew explicitly on the vocabulary and diagnoses of psychiatric discourse'.[23] For example, the distinctly unladylike, but very thrilling, behaviour of some sensational fictional heroines can be explained in the light of contemporary theories of female biology, and the shocking behaviour of sensational villains is often informed by theories of insanity and criminality.

The 'effect' created by sensation fiction that Shuttleworth mentions is in part a depiction of the self that conflicted with the image of the stable, predictable self, steadily and soberly revealed in realist fiction. This is the dominant critical interpretation of sensation fiction by its founding and foremost critics. It is seen as a genre that 'explicitly violated realism's formal rules of coherence and continuity and the psychological models of selfhood on which those works were founded. Disorder, discontinuity, and irresponsibility are the hallmarks of these feminine texts' (Shuttleworth, 'Preaching', p. 195). Jenny Bourne Taylor writes that 'In sensation fiction masks are rarely stripped off to reveal an inner truth, for the mask is both the transformed expression of the "true" self and the means of disclosing its incoherence.'[24] Lyn Pykett shows how Collins's fiction reveals gender to be 'not something natural and fixed, but produced and subject to change'.[25] More recently, Anne-Marie Beller has shown how the process of detecting the secrets at the heart of sensation plots consistently involves the 'revelation of self-division and incoherence'.[26] Similarly, Kylee-Anne Hingston has read Collins's *No Name* as a novel in which 'stable identities and healthy bodies prove to be illusory', and Lilian Nayder agrees that 'sensation fiction destabilises social categories, treating identity as fluid'.[27]

I acknowledge that sensation fiction provides an unstable, fragmentary, alterable view of the self, but my focus is on how different determining factors are employed to create that view. As the following readings of Braddon and Collins show, they frequently provide clues to the reasons behind their characters' personalities, and lay the foundation for characters' actions by revealing details of family history, upbringing and inherent constitution. As well as drawing on recognised psychological states to explain characters' behaviour, Braddon and Collins often show how those states are brought into being. Maria K. Bachman observes that 'unlike Dickens, who uses caricatured figures for comic or bizarre effect, Collins explores the inner psyches of his mental deviants, examining what it means to be cast as "other" and relegated to the margins of society in Victorian England'.[28] It is important, taking this further, that both Collins and Braddon portray respectable people who *become* deviants; they are not simply looking at 'what it means' to be other, but how one may become that way. Characters in sensation fiction are portrayed equally as enmeshed in biological and social determinants as characters in realist novels.

My readings of Braddon and Collins also qualify the idea that sensation fiction 'highlights the uncertain relation between the outer and inner forms of selfhood' but without the 'possibility, as in realist fiction, of pursuing a course of revelation until the "true" self is unveiled' (Shuttleworth, 'Preaching', p. 196). Whilst in the course of a plot characters may undergo various transformations, there is often, in fact, an initial core of selfhood within each character (itself created by determinants such as hereditary transmission), with potential for development or ruin. Melynda Huskey does acknowledge that there is a 'self "underneath"' the 'public self' of the sensation heroine, but only uses this to point out the importance of 'double lives' in sensation fiction and goes on to emphasise 'the re-creating and revising of female identity as an inexhaustible topos'.[29] Both Braddon and Collins tend to portray characters as possessing a particular set of traits (an original constitution, to use the physiological language of the period) that is then worked on – for better or worse – by circumstances throughout the novel.

Introduction

Braddon and Collins display an alertness and receptivity to the major issues that raised awareness of, and led to engagement with, theories of character formation in the mid-Victorian period. Many of these issues are staples of the sensation genre that have proved popular with modern scholars, such as criminality, insanity, and the role of women in society: critical discussions that touch on character formation tend to do so whilst focusing on these other issues (as in the example of Gilbert above). John R. Reed has written an overview of the free-will debate in Victorian fiction, and some critics, such as Goldie Morgentaler, have explored one particular form of determinism.[30] *Creating Character* takes a different approach by foregrounding the multiple determining factors that are employed by Braddon and Collins, and exploring the numerous functions they can serve, including as a means of addressing other social issues. It also looks at how these sensational representations of character formation are rooted in, challenge and anticipate the ideas of the scientists, physicians and physiologists who were at the forefront of mid-Victorian deterministic thinking.

Victorian notions of character formation

Bulwer-Lytton's decision to describe the self in terms of mental and physical, internal and environmental deterministic forces is typical of many Victorians who addressed this subject either directly or indirectly, but such an approach was not unproblematic for them. Traditional Christian beliefs placed humankind as separate from, and superior to, the rest of the material world. Yet it became increasingly evident, and accepted, that such segregations could not be clearly maintained. In 1876 Thomas Henry Huxley, for example, observed that

> We have almost all been told, and most of us hold by the tradition, that man occupies an isolated and peculiar position in nature; that though he is in the world he is not of the world; that his relations to things about him are of a remote character; that his origin is recent, his duration likely to be short, and that he is the great central figure round which other things in this world revolve. But this is not what the biologist tells us.[31]

Huxley, rhetorically privileging the scientific knowledge of 'the biologist' (which is what, in fact, he was) over 'tradition', challenges the concept of man as a favoured being. In his depiction of the traditional view of humanity, Huxley purposely emphasises a dualist, Christian

Introduction

perspective, in which 'man' refers to the spiritual aspect of each person that is 'in' but 'not of the world', and 'remote' from the physical environment. This physical environment includes the brain and body in which a person's soul or mind was believed to reside temporarily, a discrete non-worldly entity, 'ontologically distinct', as Rick Rylance puts it, and 'remote from the determinations of the body'.[32] As Huxley's speech above suggests, however, new theories and discoveries in biology, as well as (to name but a few) medical, geological and ethnological fields raised contentious questions about the position of man within the world, how he had come to be there and how much he could really be perceived as 'not of the world'.

The revelations of the biologist (and others) provoked a variety of responses, particularly in the periodical press as contributors reassessed (or actively refused to reassess) their views of the world and of themselves in the face of scientific developments. The distinguished Quarterlies both disseminated and contested new scientific theories. Responding to Charles Darwin's *The Descent of Man* (1871), the conservative *Quarterly Review* argued that 'man is the only rational [animal] known to us, and ... his rationality constitutes a fundamental distinction – one of *kind* and not of *degree*', and went on to assert that man is 'also a free moral agent, and, as such—and with the infinite future such freedom opens out before him—differs from all the rest of the visible universe by a distinction so profound that none of those which separate other visible beings is comparable with it'.[33] The article reflects Huxley's description of the traditional view of man, explicitly separating him from the rest of the 'visible' world and awarding him a privileged position, unattainable by other creatures.

Whilst such debate was often conducted in the Quarterlies and upmarket periodicals, other journals also engaged with these deliberations over the nature of humankind and its position in the world. One article in Braddon's middle-brow *Belgravia* (so named as 'bait for the shillings of Brixton & Bow'; Wolff, 'Devoted disciple', 9 August, 1866, p. 138), addresses the 'extreme' views of modern culture, and observes that we 'are even told that Christianity must soon be abolished, and retreat before the superior sciences of sociology and biology'. The article also points out that reformers 'tell us that, having progressed from a brutish and barbarous state, we have our golden age to come', linking the revelations of science to a revaluation of man's level of development and position in the world.[34]

Introduction

Whilst such works as those mentioned above draw a distinction between the traditional Christian and scientific ways of viewing humanity, the divide was rarely so clear-cut, so 'extreme', even for 'the biologist'. The eminent mid-nineteenth-century physiologist William Benjamin Carpenter is one significant example. Carpenter wrote numerous well-respected physiological works, medical textbooks and periodical articles for educated laypersons. Reed identifies some of the problems people such as Carpenter faced: 'at the same time that scientific studies were lending apparent proof to the theory that man was on an ascending plane of progress, they were presenting unwelcome evidences of man's bondage to the earth' (p. 184). Whilst Carpenter did not allow new discoveries and ideas to shake his Unitarian faith, he acknowledged the need to accommodate new physiological evidence about human nature alongside his religious beliefs: 'I cannot regard myself, either Intellectually or Morally, as a mere puppet, pulled by suggesting-strings; any more than I can *dis*regard that vast body of Physiological evidence, which proves the direct and immediate relation between Mental and Corporeal agency.'[35] Carpenter reveals a concern with the possible consequences of new scientific knowledge, and a desire to affirm individual free will, to be more than 'a mere puppet'. Here, he is differentiating between his own beliefs about human nature and those of atheist materialists; like many scientific thinkers of the time, he is attempting to 'tread a tightrope between materialism and automatism on the one side and unscientific metaphysics on the other'.[36] Such delineation was necessary, as Carpenter's own theories offered a 'basically materialist model of brain process'.[37] Carpenter wrote extensively on the reflex action of the nervous system, developed the theory of unconscious cerebration and was influenced by Darwin's theories of evolution – his work was certainly grounded in an understanding of the physical aspects of the human body even as he attempted 'to hold a developmental conception of nervous function and action in balance with dualist assumptions about the existence of the soul and the agency of the will'.[38] Carpenter objected to 'materialist' depictions of man as 'but a *thinking machine*, his conduct being entirely determined by his original constitution, modified by subsequent conditions over which he has no control, and his fancied power of self-direction being altogether a delusion'.[39] He expressed disapproval of literature such as Henry George Atkinson and Harriet Martineau's *Letters on the Laws of Man's Nature and Development* (1851), which, through contentious statements such as 'man has no more power to determine his own will than he has wings to fly', seemed to do away with the concept of autonomous agency.[40]

Introduction

Materialism was often denounced in the periodical press. For example, the *British and Foreign Medico-Chirurgical Review* spoke out against those (such as Atkinson and Martineau) who

> declare that there is no personal Deity, (which is the same as saying that there is no God at all,) that man and external nature are everything, that this world is all, and that we are utterly destitute of all power to shape our own course, but are entirely what our organisation and circumstances make us.[41]

As a scientist who was also a Christian, Carpenter had carefully to negotiate a way between his own faith and the facts that science was revealing to him, and assured his readers that his theories were 'strictly conformable to the highest teachings of religion' (*Human Physiology*, p. 555), and this meant that he needed to assert the existence of free will. A person had to be free to act in a morally independent and responsible manner if he or she was to gain salvation. This free will, however, was reliant on some part of human nature being external from the constraints of the material world. The increasing realisation of 'man's bondage to the earth' during the nineteenth century contributed to the shift towards increasingly deterministic views of humanity (Reed, p. 184). These views emphasised the organisational and circumstantial influences that dictated the development of an individual's personality. Such scientific advances also raised questions about how much humanity had been in control of its progress so far, and how much it could hope to be in charge of its further development.

The mid-Victorian period saw the growth of a number of important scientific theories that precipitated or were a response to a move towards less dualistic, increasingly determinist thinking: 'the scientific world view shifted attention from acts to contexts, from the conscious human actor to the surrounding circumstances, whether in one's environment or one's constitution' (Wiener, p. 162). The publication of Charles Darwin's *On the Origin of Species* (1859) is undoubtedly a defining moment in the century; although the development of humankind was not explicitly referred to, the theory of evolution by natural selection caused many who read *Origin* (or read about it) to re-evaluate Victorian society's place in the universe and to find a new 'scale for the human'.[42] Darwinian theories were swiftly applied to concepts of human social development. Huxley, in 1869, spoke of 'that struggle for existence, which goes on as fiercely beneath the smooth surface of modern society, as among the wild inhabitants of the woods'.[43] In this way the theory of natural selection and the

Introduction

struggle for survival (Herbert Spencer coined the term 'survival of the fittest' in 1864) raised awareness of the influence of both hereditary and environmental factors on the human race. The early 1860s, when sensation fiction was at its peak, were, in many ways a time of progress, but also of tumultuous uncertainty. As Taylor puts it, this was:

> a moment of extraordinary diversity within contrasting and overlapping discourses of inheritance, transmission, and genealogy. Notions of progress begin to transmute into degeneration; the concept of continuous transmission is transformed by adaptation; a unilinear narrative of change combines and clashes with plurality, diversity, and chance, even as organic metaphors and models are overwhelmingly deployed to fix social and sexual identity and to naturalize difference.
>
> (p. 135)

At this time the seeds of later, more decidedly deterministic theories begin to germinate whilst earlier ideas continue to persist, modified in the light of new theories. Sensation fiction drew on old (sometimes out-of-date) and new (sometimes only nascent) notions of character formation, and so an overview of some of the key changes will be helpful here.

There was an overall shift in "moral rule" through the mid-century from a focus on "sin" to one on 'the distinction between the normal and the pathological' (Rimke and Hunt, p. 60), as bad behaviour came to be viewed less in a purely moral light, and more as a sign and result of a poor physical and/or mental constitution. In the early-to-mid-Victorian period emphasis was placed by scientists, physicians and social theorists on both the power of the passions, and the individual's ability to control them through the exertion of willpower – to determine one's own behaviour. This meant that each person was viewed as morally responsible for his or her own actions or, at least, as having the capacity to be responsible. The caveat is necessary because external social influences – an abusive childhood, or defective education for example – were acknowledged to impact on the development of the personality. By the 1860s the need to train the will had come to be seen as crucial in the achievement of self-control and curbing of any wayward impulses. Popular periodicals, often using the metaphor of a horse and rider, encouraged readers to remember that their passions may be unruly but that their will had the power to tame them. The family magazine *Bow Bells* cited the Revd Ward Beecher explaining that 'vanity' and 'pride' may 'bound, and resist, as much as they please, but they can easily be rendered manageable by a determined will'.

Introduction

Beecher adds, however, that this means that 'where there is this strong and brute instinct, you cannot eradicate it, but you are under obligation to control it'.⁴⁴

This belief in the possibility of personal self-control informed social and medical perspectives and influenced legal policies, particularly in relation to two of the staple themes of the sensation novel, criminality and insanity. Martin J. Wiener's extensive study on Victorian conceptions of the criminal shows how early Victorian penal policy was based on the assumption that people were rational and should therefore be able to perceive both the consequences of their actions and the deterrent of threatened punishment. Criminals were understood to be people who allowed their behaviour to be dictated by uncontrolled passions, and crime was seen in terms of 'defective self-management'; the 'remedy' lay in 'reforming and developing the characters of offenders and potential offenders'. These conceptions of human character led to practical measures being taken to create 'a visible force for social surveillance [e.g. uniformed police], a more predictable and systematic hearing process, and a prison system subjecting its inmates to a discipline that would without violence both deter and build character' (Wiener, p. 49).

Closely linked to the management of criminals was the management of the insane. Like the early Victorian criminal, the insane were seen to be victims of their own overruling passions and weakened willpower. For example, John Barlow's *On Man's Power over Himself to Prevent or Control Insanity* (1843) insisted that 'he who has given a proper direction to the intellectual force, and thus obtained an early command over the bodily organ by habituating it to processes of calm reasoning, remains sane amid all the vagaries of sense'.⁴⁵ The Victorian asylum practices of moral management and non-restraint relied on the idea that individuals could, when placed in conducive surroundings, learn to subdue their emotions through the exercise of willpower. The physician James Cowles Prichard, for example, asserted in his successful *Treatise on Insanity and Other Disorders Affecting the Mind* (1835) that 'lunatics' are not only 'susceptible of moral discipline', but that it 'constitutes indeed a very important and essential part of the means of cure'.⁴⁶

These early and mid-Victorian theories about the possibilities and limitations of self-control and willpower inform Part I of *Creating Character*. Collins's *Basil* (1852, revised 1862) and *No Name* (1862), and Braddon's *John Marchmont's Legacy* (1863) all depict the difficulties and dangers attached to attempts to control one's own behaviour in the face of harmful circumstances and inclinations. In these novels characters act

Introduction

in socially unacceptable ways both *in spite of* and *because of* their inherent natures and the situations in which they find themselves. The discussion of these texts also introduces a recurring theme of this book – the depiction of monomania in sensation fiction.

As its name suggests, this particular form of insanity was commonly defined as a condition in which an individual suffered from *one* delusion. The presence of delusion was, for many doctors, a fundamental requirement in the diagnosis of monomania. However, 'by the mid-nineteenth century [monomania] had become a widely used term that could be stretched to mean almost any kind of irrational obsession' (Taylor, p. 47). Monomania could be the result of a number of causes: an insufficient assertion of self-control, a traumatic experience or hereditary transmission. Most medico-historical studies of monomania have centred on French sources, as the condition was first identified and categorised by the French physicians Philippe Pinel and J. E. D. Esquirol.[47] Perhaps the most famous literary monomaniacs are American: Herman Melville's Captain Ahab in *Moby Dick* (1851), and Edgar Allan Poe's delusional obsessives (the narrators of 'Ligeia' (1838), 'The black cat' (1843) and 'The tell-tale heart' (1843) for example). British physicians began to refer to monomania in the 1830s and it quickly made an appearance in the popular press as a condition that could both shock and fascinate readers (which is of course a key reason why it is so suited to sensation fiction). In 1833 *Chambers's Edinburgh Journal*, for example, related 'cases of monomania' in which people experienced strange hallucinations (an invisible guest, a 'vision of a huge dog' and a worm-ridden corpse).[48] The media coverage of controversial cases such as that of Daniel M'Naughton, who suffered delusions of persecution and in 1843 assassinated the Prime Minister's private secretary Edward Drummond, helped to raise public awareness and spurred masses of public debate about the definition and use of insanity in criminal cases.[49] Given the ubiquity of accounts and representations of monomania in mid-Victorian medical circles, in the press and in literature, to the point of becoming 'itself a kind of obsession', the condition deserves more critical recognition.[50]

A number of critics have recognised Victorian literary characters as exhibiting elements of monomaniacal behaviour: Graeme Tytler identifies Emily Brontë's Heathcliff; Diane Mason George Eliot's Latimer; and Ellie Cope Thomas Hardy's Boldwood.[51] Such characters are rarely explicitly described as monomaniacs, but the pervasiveness of the condition in the popular press means that many Victorian readers would have picked up on literary allusions to monomania that readers today may

Introduction

overlook. While some literary critics (such as Tytler and Cope) enter into a detailed discussion of monomania, the definition of the condition, what it meant in the Victorian medical mind and popular imagination, and the heterogeneity of representations of monomania (which was really a broad range of sometimes loosely associated conditions) in Victorian culture have been somewhat overlooked. Critics tend to discuss monomania in relation to only one gender, and as either pathologised obsession or compulsive behaviour.[52] *Creating Character* reflects the diversity of accounts of monomaniacs in Victorian Britain and shows how even in the work of just Braddon and Collins we can find a variety of monomaniacs – they are male, female, obsessive and/or compulsive, amatory and murderous, suffering from *idées fixes* and from hallucinations.

Like other forms of insanity, monomania generated much discussion in the Victorian period about self-management and self-control, and the representation of the condition is one of the key ways in which Collins and Braddon engage with ideas of character formation. Monomania's primary association with obsession allowed writers to figure it as an inner conflict between different aspects of the self; sufferers could be aware of their condition and struggle (often unsuccessfully) to overcome it. The idea of monomania is complementary to the traditional elements of sensation fiction in a number of ways: its emphasis on overpowering emotions and obsessive desires, often described in medical writing as being cunningly concealed by the sufferer, harmonises with the dark secrets and hidden passions of sensation fiction. Both of Braddon's and Collins's most famous works include references to the condition. In *The Woman in White* (1860) Walter Hartright fears that his incessant association of every strange occurrence with Anne Catherick is 'almost like a monomania'.[53] Similarly, Robert Audley in *Lady Audley's Secret* (1862) fears that his compulsion to discover the truth about George Talboys's disappearance may be developing into a monomania, and he is later accused of being a monomaniac by Lady Audley.[54]

Chapters 1 and 2 concern novels that display a much more extended engagement with monomania. Chapter 1 demonstrates two of the many ways in which Collins makes use of monomania in his writing. *Basil*'s melodramatic villain Robert Mannion appears almost supernatural in his untiring pursuit of the eponymous narrator. Collins shows Mannion to be subject to monomaniacal impulses, thus providing a recognised medical condition as an explanation for his outlandish behaviour. The relation of monomania to the idea of character formation becomes apparent as Collins traces the origins of Mannion's condition to a series of perceived social injustices and unfortunate occurrences. However, there is no real sense of Mannion's struggling against this state of affairs, and this is true of the majority of *Basil*'s characters, who are swept along by their own uncontrolled passions and by the forces of circumstance; the result, as circumstance and passions converge, is obsession and monomania. Collins uses the dramatic and emotive feelings associated with the domination of unruly passions described in early-nineteenth-century theories of insanity, in which the environment of a lunatic was paramount to his or her recovery. In *Basil* social conditions are contrived by Collins to increase the monomaniacal feelings of the characters, making the novel intense, oppressive, but also compelling reading. At the same time, the characters are shown to contribute to their own mental deterioration, eagerly throwing themselves into the dramatic and devastating events that constitute the plot.

Like *Basil*, *No Name* depicts a character whose emotions are out of control to the extent of developing monomaniacal tendencies. Unlike Mannion, however, Magdalen Vanstone endures a series of internal conflicts between her "better" nature and her monomaniacal urge. Collins's portrayal of monomania in *No Name* facilitates a contemplation of the different aspects that make up the individual personality, and draws on Victorian theories of will and willpower. Magdalen is actually a very *wilful* character, but her willpower is channelled in the wrong direction as she has never been trained to manage it correctly. Magdalen's struggle against her own overwhelming dominant idea reflects the changes in the nineteenth century concerning the extent to which the individual was viewed as possessing self-control; the will came to be seen as increasingly fragile, manipulable and reliant on physical influences. For example, the renowned mental physiologist Henry Maudsley argued against 'the notion of an ideal or abstract will unaffected by physical conditions', and observed that each moment of consciousness was dependent upon a 'long series of causes', and that it was 'a deliberate fooling of one's self to say that actions depend upon the will, and then not to ask upon what the will depends!'.[55] Collins's depiction of Magdalen's monomania shows a combination of internal and external determining factors in which the influence of upbringing and social surroundings is particularly important. However, her monomania is formidable because of the force of her own personality, and proves resistant to all outside influences. Circumstance brings out the worst in Magdalen, but she has intrinsic reserves of moral strength that are not attributed clearly to heredity or her life experiences, and it is these that save her in the end: it is eventually Magdalen's

Introduction

own better nature that overcomes the destructive aspects of her *own* personality.

Most of the social groups discussed here (the upper and lower classes, criminals and lunatics) were generally seen to be in some sense manipulable; their wills could be cultivated, their defects bred or educated out, or they could be stopped from breeding altogether. When notions of determinism were discussed in relation to gender, things were somewhat different because of the dominant essentialist belief that men and women possessed natural, distinctive traits and capacities that were determined by their biologies. Women especially often found themselves hindered by a general acceptance of the dominance of their reproductive systems. In 1851, for example, one contributor to the *Journal of Psychological Medicine and Mental Pathology* attributed a vast range of medical afflictions in women (including hysteria and moral insanity) to the 'influence of the reproductive organs'.[56] The increasing debates over the rights, education and employment of women often centred on their intrinsic nature and capabilities, and the extent to which they were physically, morally and intellectually different from men. Chapter 2 of this book, on Braddon's *John Marchmont's Legacy*, shows that there was often a blurring of the boundaries between what was seen to be ideal or desirable in women and what was understood to be natural and essentially feminine. This chapter features, like *No Name*, a monomaniacal character with a wilful personality but, unlike Magdalen, Olivia Marchmont is an example of deviant behaviour incited by the *suppression* of natural personality traits. Intellectually brilliant, Olivia is unable to find satisfaction from life as a dutiful rector's daughter and develops a disastrous obsession with her handsome young cousin. Olivia's consequent malevolent actions are read in the light of Victorian medical texts about the nature of women, which often depicted them as volatile and potentially dangerous, and also in relation to Victorian ideas about the ideal woman. Braddon highlights the discrepancies between prevailing images of womanhood and suggests that expecting women to conform to an ideal for which they may not be suited can have destructive consequences. Whilst Olivia's extreme behaviour can be put down to the determinations of her female biology, it is also implied that if her environment had not been so restrictive, disaster could have been averted, and her potential released. Importantly, it is also insistently demonstrated that Olivia's own clashing conceptions of herself, of ideal femininity and of ideal Christian behaviour are equally to blame for her downfall. Whilst Magdalen calls disaster upon herself by pushing beyond gender, social and moral boundaries, Olivia's inability to either conform to, or happily deviate from, the norm has a crippling effect.

Writing that addresses the nature of insanity also inevitably, if implicitly, reflects upon the definition of sanity; tracing what mental processes have gone awry suggests how they should function, and how they should be cultivated. In the Victorian period social conceptions about what was "normal" often became conflated with what was "good": moral, socially acceptable behaviour was seen to be normal, and deviancy was a sign that something had gone wrong at some stage of an individual's development. Gradations and definitions of normalcy and deviancy became increasingly significant as the century progressed, especially in relation to ideas of hereditary transmission that were progressively more influential throughout the century. Although eugenics was largely a late-nineteenth- to early-twentieth-century phenomenon, Francis Galton's 'Hereditary talent' was published in *Macmillan's Magazine* in 1865, and suggested to readers that through the careful selection of a spouse desirable traits could be passed on and enhanced with each generation.[57] Despite the dangerous social policies it would lead to (such as sterilisation practices in America[58]) Victorian eugenics was promoted as a "positive" way of thinking as it aimed to identify, preserve and enhance strengths and desirable characteristics with each generation. Indeed, Galton's initial speculations are naively optimistic: 'what an extraordinary effect might be produced on our race, if its object was to unite in marriage those who possessed the finest and most suitable natures, mental, moral, and physical!' ('Hereditary talent', p. 165).

In contrast to this comparative optimism of eugenics, another concern gained prominence in later decades about indiscriminate breeding between objectionable individuals. Degeneration theories offered a negative spin to both Darwinian theories of natural selection and theories of acquired characteristics (based on J. B. Lamarck's widely accepted early-nineteenth-century theory that organisms learnt traits or skills useful for survival and then passed them on to offspring). Heredity was no longer merely something to be taken into consideration, as it had been earlier in the century, nor was it something to be harnessed for social development, as in eugenicist thought; with degeneration the power of heredity held sway and could destroy entire family lines, threatening (in its most extreme models) the health and progress of society. Maudsley, for example, declared that 'there is a destiny made for a man by his ancestors, and no one can elude, were he able to attempt it, the tyranny of his organization'.[59] Whilst the specific theories themselves varied, the general idea was that once a weakness (physical, mental or moral) entered a family line it would be passed on and enhanced through each generation. Often the only hope for stopping the development of the inherited flaw was the assumption that it, whatever *it* was in any particular case, would lead to sterility and death – the self-destruction of the bloodline.

Daniel Pick identifies 'two different trajectories in the conception of degeneration': a drive to 'isolate a social threat – to reveal, transport, castrate and segregate "noxious elements"', and a concern that 'degeneration lay everywhere'; this led to the question of whether it was 'separable from the history of progress (to be coded as "regression", "atavism" or "primitivism")', or whether it revealed 'that the city, progress, civilisation and modernity were paradoxically, the very agents of decline'.[60] Both ideas of degeneration were reliant on notions of character formation, on whether it was believed that people were being damaged by their environment, or that there was an atavistic threat hidden within the race, which circumstances merely brought out. Such concepts were ideal for exploitation in the sensation novel, a genre that deals in extremes, in modernity, and that shows events escalating towards alarming and destructive conclusions.

The second section of this book emphasises the links between heredity and determinism in sensation fiction that are often overlooked, taken for granted or touched upon only briefly by critics.[61] The form of inheritance that is usually discussed in relation to sensation fiction is financial, owing to the almost ubiquitous plot feature of the disputed, lost, stolen, invalidated or counterfeit last will and testament. Sensation characters frequently murder, marry and commit forgery in order to gain an inheritance that the law says should belong to someone else, and the hero or heroine's reward at the close of the novel is to have that inheritance secured for themselves or their children. Part II discusses two novels in which financial inheritance is still at stake, but in which ideas about biological inheritance (as much as biological inheritance itself) play a key role in determining the depiction of characters and the outcome of plots.

The interplay between "nature" and "nurture" in the formation of the individual is explored in Chapter 3. Braddon's underexamined *The Lady Lisle* (1862) raises questions about the malleability or fixity of the personality: characters in the novel are described and defined in terms of their physical constitutions and hereditary characteristics, and the possibility of altering the development of the individual through upbringing and education is explored and contested. *The Lady Lisle* features a near identical pair of young men from different ends of the social spectrum. The impoverished murderer's son is raised in such a way as to bring out his supposedly inherent negative traits, whereas the heir to the Lisle fortune is given an upbringing that negates his detrimental qualities. Braddon combines education and hereditary degeneracy to segregate the lower classes, and to bring the morally upright middle classes together with the affluent upper classes.

Chapter 4 begins with a reading of Collins's 1855 short story about hereditary insanity, 'Mad Monkton', before turning to *Armadale* (1866), in which a murderous father fears that his sinfulness will be passed down to his son. Collins's imaginative speculations about heredity foreshadow developing degenerationist and eugenicist theories, including the idea that morality was something that could be transmitted through the generations. By applying different "types" of degeneration to different characters (informed by concepts such as miscegenation, atavism and negative heredity), and by offering different reasons for the development of that degeneration, Collins raises questions about class and race. The examination of *Armadale* demonstrates how sensation authors and scientists were drawing on the same fund of social anxiety about the strength and purity of the nation. However, even as Collins explores ideas of hereditary decline, he also uses them to create sympathy with, rather than to reject or isolate, social outsiders. *Armadale* opposes the view that morality is irrevocably hereditary at the same time as it highlights that there would be fearful consequences if it were. This goes against the prevailing drive of degenerationist thinking that 'was at the root of what was, in part, an enabling strategy by which the conventional and respectable classes could justify and articulate their hostility to the deviant, the diseased and the subversive'.[62]

As with theories of biological determinism, ideas about social and environmental influences could be both constructive and disheartening. External circumstances such as social position, education and upbringing are significant determinants. An article in *Belgravia* emphasised the importance of earliest experiences: 'associations, cradle-environing circumstances, are potent to produce an effect everywhere. The groove in which we are to run is ready hollowed for most of us before we cut our earliest teeth.' The article provocatively argues that squires' sons will like guns and Jews' sons will be money-lenders: 'the employers of labour, and those who supply the want, are almost designated from the beginning'.[63] *Temple Bar*'s 'The management of servants' argued that employers should be more lenient on servants who have not only had little or no training, but have been brought up in 'poverty, ignorance, selfishness, vulgarity, and prejudice', which are 'poor nurseries for the infancy and early childhood of servants'.[64] Such lines of thinking meant that the poor and destitute were feared to be criminals and deviants in the making on account of their living circumstances and lack of moral role models. On the other hand, it was believed that if children could be given a correct upbringing, they could be trained from an early age to be upright, responsible citizens.

Although many such articles focused on the management of the lower classes, education was also seen as essential for the middle and upper classes. Huxley was certain that individuals could be given a better chance in the world with a good education, and argued in 1870 that each child was

> a member of a social and political organisation of great complexity, and has, in future life, to fit himself into that organisation, or be crushed by it ... their affections should be trained, so as to love with all their hearts that conduct which tends to the attainment of the highest good for themselves and their fellow men, and to hate with all their hearts that opposite course of action which is fraught with evil.[65]

Huxley's words draw attention to the vulnerability of individual people within a society that is bigger and more powerful than themselves; if they do not comply with its workings (because they have not been 'trained' to) they will be the worse for it. However, it was also understood that, in the same way that hereditary degeneration was not simply a threat to a single family but something that may spread to the nation as a whole, if masses of individual children were receiving poor educations, the consequences for society were not promising. These issues of education and environment are discussed in the final part of *Creating Character*, which covers two novels published at the end of the sensation genre's high-point. In *Man and Wife* (1870), Collins emphasises the influence of society and upbringing on his characters. This is partly because at this point in his career Collins began to turn towards the didactic "novel with a purpose", and in *Man and Wife* he aims to show the detrimental influence of poor education on a whole generation of young men, as well as the destructive nature of the marriage laws. *Man and Wife* depicts the force of external circumstance and social context on characters and shows how their behaviour is dictated by their previous experiences. The novel portrays entire generations, social groups, and the nation as a whole in a state of decline, but that decline is due to poor education and environment, not bad heredity.

The final chapter considers Braddon's *Lost for Love* (1874), a novel that has received little critical attention until now.[66] Like *Man and Wife*,

Introduction

this novel depicts education as a strong determining factor in individual development, and like *John Marchmont's Legacy* it explores themes of female potential and intellect, but *Lost for Love* is far more optimistic in its portrayal of these subjects. In this novel Braddon vouches for women's intellectual capacity and implies that defective education is to blame if this is not fully developed. At a time when women were campaigning for greater rights, including the right to pursue university education, Braddon shows that women are capable of intense intellectual study. However, both of *Lost for Love*'s heroines are educated by, and for, the men who become their husbands, and the conservative notion of woman's role as the helpmate of man is endorsed rather than challenged in the novel.

In the sensation fiction of Braddon and Collins the forms of determinism brought into play are manifold; they portray biological, social and environmental influences as powerful determining factors for a variety of reasons. In his discussion of George Eliot and determinism, George Levine warns readers that although determinism 'informed her artistic vision', they should not be tempted to 'treat George Eliot as a philosopher rather than an artist' (p. 268). Readers of sensation fiction may not be so inclined to regard sensation authors as philosophers, but it is still worth noting that Levine's point is applicable to the following readings of Braddon and Collins: these authors are, first and foremost, crafters of entertaining fiction. The regularity with which they raise questions about nature and nurture suggests that this was a subject they felt would be relevant and interesting to their readers. Eliot takes pains to represent faithfully the determinism that she saw 'working even in the routine actions of ordinary life' (Levine, p. 269). Contrastingly, Braddon and Collins may make assumptions about how character formation works, but they are more willing to pick and choose concepts and theories that will serve their literary purpose at the time of writing. Sometimes the authors interact directly with ideas of character formation; sometimes their views can be inferred from their fiction; sometimes they may be questioning established notions; sometimes they may be drawing on them to provide a "realistic" character background or to promote their own opinions about class, gender and society. For Braddon and Collins, medical, scientific and sociological theories of character formation are fascinating subjects for literary portrayal, and literary devices that can be used in the creation of sensational characters and plots.

Introduction

Notes

1. Edward Bulwer-Lytton, 'On self-control', in *Caxtoniana* (London: Routledge and Sons, 1875 [1863]), pp. 206–14 (pp. 207–8).
2. The subtitle appeared in the initial serialisation.
3. Heidi Rimke and Alan Hunt, 'From sinners to degenerates: The medicalization of morality in the 19th century', *History of the Human Sciences*, 15:1 (2002), 59–88 (p. 62).
4. Pamela K. Gilbert, *The Citizen's Body: Desire, Health, and the Social in Victorian England* (Columbus: Ohio State University Press, 2007), p. 91.
5. Anon., 'The force of habit', *Chambers's Edinburgh Journal*, 294 (August 1849), 105–7 (p. 105).
6. Anon., 'Labour', *London Journal*, 12:290 (July 1889), 47.
7. William Benjamin Carpenter, 'On the hereditary transmission of acquired psychical habits', *Contemporary Review*, 21 (December 1872), 295–314 (p. 295).
8. In one of the most quoted (negative) assessments of Braddon, W. Fraser Rae conceded that she had 'succeeded in making the literature of the Kitchen the favourite reading of the Drawing room'. W. Fraser Rae, 'Sensation novelists: Miss Braddon', *North British Review*, 43:85 (September 1865), 180–204 (p. 204).
9. George Henry Lewes, 'The principles of success in literature', *Fortnightly Review*, 1 (May 1865), 85–95 (p. 85).
10. Andrew Maunder and Grace Moore, 'Introduction', in Andrew Maunder and Grace Moore (eds), *Victorian Crime, Madness and Sensation* (Aldershot: Ashgate, 2004), pp. 1–14 (p. 5).
11. See Laurie Garrison, *Science, Sexuality and Sensation Novels: Pleasures of the Senses* (Basingstoke: Palgrave Macmillan, 2011), p. xiii.
12. Daniel Owen Maddyn, '*Basil: A Story of Modern Life*', *Athenaeum*, 1310 (December 1852), 1322–3. Although sensation fiction was predominantly a phenomenon of the 1860s, *Basil* contains sensational elements and the genre did not simply 'spring into being', as Pamela Gilbert notes: 'there have always been novels with aggressive heroines, novels with sex, novels with crimes, etc.' (Pamela K. Gilbert, *Disease, Desire, and the Body in Victorian Women's Popular Novels* (Cambridge: Cambridge University Press, 1997), p. 80). Maddyn's review anticipates 1860s criticisms of sensation fiction, which was described as unwholesome and diseased. For an overview of the development of sensation fiction in the 1850s (including a discussion of *Basil*) see Anne-Marie Beller, 'Sensation fiction in the 1850s', in Andrew Mangham (ed.), *The Cambridge Companion to Sensation Fiction* (Cambridge: Cambridge University Press, 2013), pp. 7–20.
13. John Dennis, '*Only a Clod*', *Fortnightly Review*, 1 (July), 511–12 (p. 511).

Introduction

14 Solveig C. Robinson, 'Editing *Belgravia*: M. E. Braddon's defense of "light literature"', *Victorian Periodicals Review*, 28:2 (1995), 109–22 (p. 111); Jennifer Phegley, *Educating the Proper Woman Reader: Victorian Family Literary Magazines and the Cultural Health of the Nation* (Columbus: Ohio State University Press, 2004), p. 2.

15 Sue Lonoff, *Wilkie Collins and His Victorian Readers: A Study in the Rhetoric of Authorship* (New York: AMS Press, 1982), p. 18.

16 See, for example, Gillian Beer, 'Beyond determinism: George Eliot and Virginia Woolf', in Mary Jacobus (ed.), *Women Writing and Writing about Women* (London: Croom Helm, 1979), pp. 80–99; Maurice Larkin, *Man and Society in Nineteenth-Century Realism: Determinism and Literature* (London: Macmillan, 1977); George Levine, 'Determinism and responsibility in the works of George Eliot', *PMLA*, 77:3 (1962), 268–79.

17 Although, Janice Allan perceptively notes that sensation fiction relies on the 'appropriation of the representational strategies of realism', and the juxtaposition of realism and sensation, in order to create sensational effects (Janice M. Allan, 'Sensationalism made real: The role of realism in the production of sensational affect', *Victorian Literature and Culture*, 43 (2015), 97–112 (p. 98)).

18 Patrick Brantlinger, 'What is "sensational" about the "sensation novel"?', *Nineteenth-Century Fiction*, 37:1 (1982), 1–28 (p. 13).

19 [?] Williams, '*The Lovels of Arden: A Novel*', *Athenaeum*, 2294 (October 1871), 487–8 (p. 488).

20 Cited in Robert Lee Wolff, 'Devoted disciple: The letters of Mary Elizabeth Braddon to Sir Edward Bulwer-Lytton, 1862–1873', *Harvard Library Bulletin*, 22:1–2 (January and April 1974), 5–35, 129–161 (17 January 1864, p. 19).

21 H. F. Chorley, '*Armadale*', *Athenaeum*, 2014 (June 1866), 732–3 (p. 732).

22 George Augustus Sala, 'The cant of modern criticism', *Belgravia*, 4 (November 1867), 45–55 (pp. 52–3). This was a recurring theme in *Belgravia*: Frederick T. Monro's 'Truth is stranger than fiction' argues that the 'incidents of everyday life' provide the 'fountain from which sensation-writers of the present day draw their inspiration' (Frederick T. Monro, 'Truth is stranger than fiction', *Belgravia*, 9 (July 1869), 103–8 (p. 103)). Numerous critics have explored sensation authors' literary engagement with contemporaneous crimes and scandals: for example, June Sturrock, 'Murder, gender, and popular fiction by women in the 1860s: Braddon, Oliphant, Yonge', in Maunder and Moore, *Victorian Crime*, pp. 73–88; Andrew Mangham, *Violent Women and Sensation Fiction: Crime, Medicine and Victorian Popular Culture* (Basingstoke: Palgrave Macmillan, 2007), pp. 49–86; Kate Summerscale, *The Suspicions of Mr Whicher; or, The Murder at Road Hill House* (London: Bloomsbury, 2008).

23 Sally Shuttleworth, '"Preaching to the nerves": Psychological disorder in sensation fiction', in Marina Benjamin (ed.), *A Question of Identity: Women,*

Science, and Literature (New Brunswick, NJ: Rutgers University Press, 1993), pp. 192–222 (p. 193).
24 Jenny Bourne Taylor, *In the Secret Theatre of Home: Wilkie Collins, Sensation Narrative, and Nineteenth-Century Psychology* (London: Routledge, 1988), p. 8.
25 Lyn Pykett, *The Sensation Novel: From 'The Woman in White' to 'The Moonstone'* (Plymouth: Northcote House, 1994), p. 21.
26 Anne-Marie Beller, 'Detecting the self in the sensation fiction of Wilkie Collins and Mary Elizabeth Braddon', *Clues*, 26:1 (2007), 49–61 (p. 50).
27 Kylee-Anne Hingston, '"Skins to jump into": The slipperiness of identity and the body in Wilkie Collins's *No Name*', *Victorian Literature and Culture*, 40 (2012), 117–35 (p. 118); Lilian Nayder, 'Science and sensation', in Mangham, *The Cambridge Companion to Sensation Fiction*, pp. 154–67 (p. 155).
28 Maria K. Bachman, '"Furious passions of the Celtic race": Ireland, madness and Wilkie Collins's *Blind Love*', in Maunder and Moore, *Victorian Crime*, pp. 179–94 (p. 179).
29 Melynda Huskey, '*No Name*: Embodying the sensation heroine', *Victorian Newsletter*, 82 (1992), 5–13 (p. 6).
30 John R. Reed, *Victorian Will* (Athens: Ohio University Press, 1989); Goldie Morgentaler, *Dickens and Heredity: When Like Begets Like* (Basingstoke: Macmillan, 2000).
31 Thomas Henry Huxley, 'On the study of biology', in *Collected Essays*, 9 vols (London: Macmillan, 1895), Vol. III, pp. 262–93 (p. 273).
32 Rick Rylance, *Victorian Psychology and British Culture, 1850–1880* (Oxford: Oxford University Press, 2000), pp. 23–4. Rylance notes a mid-century 'terminological shift from "soul" to "mind"', but both were usually seen as non-physical.
33 St George Mivart, 'Darwin's *Descent of Man*', *Quarterly Review*, 131 (July 1871), 47–90 (pp. 88–9). For Mivart's persistent conflicts with Darwin and Darwinism, see Gowan Dawson, *Darwin, Literature and Victorian Respectability* (Cambridge: Cambridge University Press, 2007), esp. Chapters 2, 4 and 5.
34 J. N. Willan, 'Extremes', *Belgravia*, 2 (January 1874), 298–302 (p. 299).
35 William Benjamin Carpenter, *Principles of Mental Physiology: With Their Applications to the Training and Discipline of the Mind, and the Study of Its Morbid Conditions* (London: H. S. King, 1874), p. x.
36 Lorraine J. Daston, 'British responses to psycho-physiology, 1860–1900', *Isis*, 69:2 (1978), 192–208 (p. 194).
37 Martin J. Wiener, *Reconstructing the Criminal: Culture, Law, and Policy in England, 1830–1914* (Cambridge: Cambridge University Press, 1990), p. 42.
38 Lucy Hartley, *Physiognomy and the Meaning of Expression in Nineteenth-Century Culture* (Cambridge: Cambridge University Press, 2001), p. 165.

Introduction

39 William Benjamin Carpenter, *Principles of Human Physiology: With Their Chief Applications to Psychology, Pathology, Therapeutics, Hygiene and Forensic Medicine*, 5th edn (London: J. Churchill, 1855), p. 548.
40 Henry George Atkinson and Harriet Martineau, *Letters on the Laws of Man's Nature and Development* (London: John Chapman, 1851), p. 6.
41 Anon., 'Miss Martineau and her master', *British and Foreign Medico-Chirurgical Review*, 8 (1851), 538–40 (p. 539). Carpenter was editing the *Medico-Chirurgical Review* at this time. The article derides Atkinson and Martineau as arrogant, illogical and credulous, but tellingly refrains from offering extracts, assuming that 'the less that is said about the book, the sooner will its unwholesome influence subside' (p. 539).
42 Gillian Beer, *Darwin's Plots: Evolutionary Narrative in Darwin, George Eliot and Nineteenth-Century Fiction*, 2nd edn (Cambridge: Cambridge University Press, 2000), p. 220. Darwin speculates that in the future 'light will be thrown on the origin of man and his history', but he does not suggest his own work has done this (Charles Darwin, *The Origin of Species* (Oxford: Oxford University Press, 1998), p. 394).
43 Thomas Henry Huxley, 'Scientific education', in *Collected Essays*, Vol. III, pp. 111–33 (p. 114).
44 Ward Beecher, 'Self-control', *Bow Bells*, 9:230 (December 1868), 531. It was common for this type of magazine to include snippets taken from other sources; *Reynolds's Miscellany* in fact quoted from Bulwer-Lytton's 'On self-control', telling its readers that 'a hasty temper is not the only horse that runs away with the charioteer on the Road of Life' (Edward Bulwer-Lytton, 'Self-control', *Reynolds's Miscellany*, 32:835 (June 1864), 397).
45 John Barlow, *On Man's Power over Himself to Prevent or Control Insanity*, 2nd edn (London: W. Pickering, 1849 [1843]), p. 28.
46 James Cowles Prichard, *A Treatise on Insanity and Other Disorders Affecting the Mind* (London: Sherwood, Gilbert and Piper, 1835), p. 297.
47 Although, as Graeme Tytler notes, the intellectual interchange between French and British psychiatrists moved in both directions (Graeme Tytler, 'Heathcliff's monomania: An anachronism in *Wuthering Heights*', *Brontë Society Transactions*, 20:6 (1992), 331–43 (p. 332)). Still the best overview of monomania and the medical profession in France is Jan Goldstein, *Console and Classify: The French Psychiatric Profession in the Nineteenth Century* (Cambridge: Cambridge University Press, 1987), Chapter 5. Dermot Walsh provides a succinct overview of monomania in Britain and Ireland, but inaccurately claims that monomania only entered 'English scientific literature' in the 1850s (Dermot Walsh, 'The birth and death of a diagnosis: Monomania in France, Britain and in Ireland', *Irish Journal of Psychological Medicine*, 31 (2014), 39–45). David W. Jones's informative discussion of moral insanity encompasses monomania in Britain, and acknowledges the French and German influences on the work of British medical men (David

Introduction

W. Jones, 'Moral insanity and psychological disorder: The hybrid roots of psychiatry', *History of Psychiatry* (10 April 2017), 1–17, DOI 10.1177/ 0957154X17702316 (accessed 10 May 2017)).
48 Anon., 'Cases of monomania', *Chambers's Edinburgh Journal*, 2:63 (April 1833), 88.
49 See Jones, 'Moral insanity', pp. 9–15; Helena Ifill, 'Wilkie Collins's monomaniacs in *Basil*, *No Name* and *Man and Wife*', *Wilkie Collins Journal*, 12 (2013) http://wilkiecollinssociety.org/wilkie-collinss-monomaniacs-in-basil-no-name-and-man-and-wife/ (accessed 21 October 2016).
50 Lennard J. Davis, *Obsession: A History* (Chicago: University of Chicago Press, 2008), p. 70.
51 See, respectively, Tytler, 'Heathcliff's monomania'; Diane Mason, 'Latimer's complaint: Masturbation and monomania in George Eliot's *The Lifted Veil*', *Women's Writing*, 5:3 (1998), 393–403; Ellie Cope, 'Undoing a "symmetrical existence": Boldwood's monomania in *Far from the Madding Crowd*', *Thomas Hardy Journal*, 26 (2010), 35–42.
52 For example, Mason's (very convincing) reading of Latimer's condition as 'masturbatory insanity' in George Eliot's 'The lifted veil' gives a lot of space to medical opinions about onanism, but very little to what she means by 'the pathology of monomania' (Mason, 'Latimer's complaint', p. 393). Shuttleworth touches on monomania, but not in detail ('Preaching', pp. 201–4), and Taylor's references to the condition in *In the Secret Theatre of Home* are generally subsumed into wider discussions of moral management. Laurence Talairach-Vielmas devotes a chapter to 'Monomaniac obsessions' in Collins's writing, but her emphasis remains quite squarely on the Gothic elements in his work (Laurence Talairach-Vielmas, *Wilkie Collins, Medicine and the Gothic* (Cardiff: University of Wales Press, 2009), pp. 18–52). Marina van Zuylen has published an entire book on the subject, but states that the 'historical concept of monomania is central to' her work 'only as a point of departure'. Van Zuylen touches on some literary representations of monomania but does not discuss sensation fiction, and is generally more interested in real-life instances of men and women who adopt 'obsessive strategies' in order to 'keep the arbitrary out of their lives' (Marina van Zuylen, *Monomania: The Flight from Everyday Life in Literature and Art* (Ithaca, NY: Cornell University Press, 2005), pp. 3, 1).
53 Wilkie Collins, *The Woman in White* (Oxford: Oxford University Press, 1998), p. 80.
54 Mary Elizabeth Braddon, *Lady Audley's Secret* (Oxford: Oxford University Press, 1998), pp. 254, 287.
55 Henry Maudsley, *The Physiology and Pathology of Mind*, 2nd edn, rev. (London: Macmillan, 1868), pp. 169, 171.
56 Anon., 'Woman in her psychological relations', *Journal of Psychological Medicine and Mental Pathology*, 4 (1851), 18–50 (p. 23).

57 Francis Galton, 'Hereditary talent and character', *Macmillan's Magazine*, 12:68 (June 1865), 157–66; 12:70 (August 1865), 318–27.
58 See Diane B. Paul, *Controlling Human Heredity: 1865 to the Present* (New York: Humanity Books, 1998), Chapter 5.
59 Henry Maudsley, *Responsibility in Mental Disease*, 2nd edn (London: H. S. King, 1874), p. 22.
60 Daniel Pick, *Faces of Degeneration: A European Disorder, c. 1848–c. 1918* (Cambridge: Cambridge University Press, 1989), p. 106.
61 As degeneration is predominantly a *fin-de-siècle* phenomenon, the majority of critical works focus on later literary engagements with the subject. See, for example, Kelly Hurley, *The Gothic Body: Sexuality, Materialism, and Degeneration at the 'Fin-de-Siècle'* (Cambridge: Cambridge University Press, 1996); Andrew Smith, *Victorian Demons: Medicine, Masculinity and the Gothic at the 'Fin de Siècle'* (Manchester: Manchester University Press, 2004). Andrew Maunder has discussed female degeneracy in *East Lynne* (1861), but he treats it in terms of a general perceived moral deterioration of society and does not focus on the hereditary aspects of degeneration or specific theories (Andrew Maunder, '"Stepchildren of nature": *East Lynne* and the spectre of female degeneracy, 1860–1861', in Maunder and Moore, *Victorian Crime*, pp. 59–71).
62 William Greenslade, *Degeneration, Culture, and the Novel, 1880–1940* (Cambridge: Cambridge University Press, 1994), p. 2.
63 John Berwick Harwood, 'The servants' hall', *Belgravia*, 9 (January 1873), 331–9 (p. 332).
64 Anon., 'The management of servants', *Temple Bar*, 1 (March 1861), 545–57 (p. 545).
65 Thomas Henry Huxley, 'The school boards: What they can do, and what they may do', in *Collected Essays*, Vol. III, pp. 374–403 (p. 393).
66 Robert Lee Wolff briefly discusses this novel in relation to Braddon's satirising of cant (*Sensational Victorian: The Life and Fiction of Mary Elizabeth Braddon* (New York: Garland, 1979), pp. 244–7). Emma Liggins discusses Braddon's engagement with the Woman Question in some of her 1870s fiction but explores 'women's leisure and female attitudes to money', rather than education (Emma Liggins, 'Her mercenary spirit: Women, money and marriage in Mary Elizabeth Braddon's 1870s fiction', *Women's Writing*, 11:1 (2004), 73–87 (p. 74)).

Part I

Self-control, willpower and monomania

1

Basil and *No Name*

> I have not thought it either politic or necessary, while adhering to realities, to adhere to every-day realities only … Those extraordinary accidents and events which happen to few men, seemed to me to be as legitimate materials for fiction to work with … as the ordinary accidents and events which may, and do, happen to us all.[1]
>
> (Wilkie Collins, dedicatory letter, *Basil*, 1862 [1852])

A defensive tone is apparent in Collins's dedicatory letter to his second published novel, *Basil: A Story of Modern Life* (1852), as he goes to some lengths to assert that while he hopes to 'fix' his readers' interest by depicting events '*beyond*' his own experience', he is still 'adhering to realities' (p. 4, emphasis in original). However, Collins's critics were not convinced by his claims to veracity. While Charles Dickens tactfully suggested that 'the probabilities here and there require a little more respect than you are disposed to shew them', professional reviewers were more scathing, often provoked by what they perceived to be an immoral content in this novel of seduction and adultery.[2] The *Westminster Review*, for example, insisted that *Basil* offered 'scenes of fury and passion, such as, happily, real life seldom affords'.[3]

It is certainly true that many of the characters in *Basil* display behaviour that is rarely to be found in daily life. One of the most extreme characters is Robert Mannion, who blames the eponymous narrator for marrying Mannion's employer's daughter, Margaret, whom Mannion had previously intended to be 'my wife, my mistress, my servant, which I choose' (p. 189). Furthermore, Basil's father was the 'patron' of Mannion's father and allowed him to be hanged for forging his signature, an event Mannion believes initiated his own exclusion from respectable society (p. 182). In retaliation, Mannion first consummates his illicit relationship with Margaret (in Basil's hearing), and then vows to persecute Basil by following him to the ends of the earth, systematically destroying any social standing he may manage to achieve. In what reads as a near parodic reversal of Mary Shelley's *Frankenstein* (1818, a novel that Collins knew and enjoyed as a young man[4]) Mannion, already psychologically a "monster", and now hideously disfigured from a confrontation with Basil, chases his prey as far as the Cornish coast before shaking a threatening fist at Basil from the edge of a cliff, accidentally losing his balance, and plunging to his death.[5] From his thirst for revenge and impure intentions towards a young woman, to his final and fatal menacing gesture, Mannion seems a classic melodramatic villain.

To find elements of melodrama in an early sensation novel is not surprising; the mid-Victorian theatre was 'dominated by melodrama',[6] and, as Winifred Hughes has clearly demonstrated, sensation novelists 'shamelessly exploited the familiar stereotypes of popular melodrama', even though they abandoned the dramatic form's 'moral certainty'.[7] Collins, who himself took part in a number of amateur theatrical events alongside Dickens, and went on to write melodramatic adaptations of his own works, explicitly asserts in his dedication to *Basil* that 'the Novel and the Play are twin-sisters in the family of Fiction', which means that the 'Novel-writer is privileged to excite' the same 'strong and deep emotions' as the 'Play-writer' (p. 4). Yet acknowledging that *Basil* draws on a genre characterised by elements that include 'strong emotionalism', 'extreme states' and 'inflated and extravagant expression' does not encourage the sense that Collins has adhered to realities.[8] The *Westminster Review* clearly did not see Mannion as a realistic character, and dismissed him as a villain 'gifted with a fiend-like perseverance, which, happily for mankind, does not exist', and went on to explain that 'man becomes weary, after a time, of one passion, or one pursuit, and the less principle he has to bind him to a straight course, the more does he diverge into fresh paths' (anon., 'Progress of fiction', p. 373). However, Hughes also identifies an eagerness on the part of sensation authors to 'provide some justification for the erratic behaviour of their murderers, bigamists, and adulteresses' in order to be seen to represent some form of reality; this means they are

> driven to exploit the irrational elements of the psyche, the obscure and unreasonable motivations that in the twentieth century are associated with the subconscious ... Evil or antisocial action is no longer the direct result and expression of evil character, as in conventional melodrama, but derives from combinations of circumstance, weakness, insanity, impulse, "sensation" at its most basic.
>
> (Hughes, p. 58)

Basil *and* No Name

Mannion, importantly for this discussion, is diagnosed by a doctor as a 'dangerous monomaniac' (p. 223), and he is 'fiend-like' precisely because he is incapable of becoming 'weary' of the fixed idea that has taken over his consciousness – his desire for revenge against Basil.[9] This use of a medically and publicly recognised condition, as well as the inclusion of a letter that explains the unfortunate combination of events that causes it, is one of the ways in which Collins attempts to 'adhere to ... realities'.[10]

Basil is a repentant memoir supplemented with letters by other characters, which is an early example of Collins's use of multiple narrative forms and narrators, a format he would develop most fully in *The Woman in White* (1860). After being hospitalised by Basil, who discovers his affair with Margaret and crushes his face into a freshly macadamised road, Mannion sends Basil a letter that reveals his true identity and purpose, and reveals his monomania; this is the focus of the first part of this chapter. However, Basil himself is also depicted in terms of early-nineteenth-century medical theories that emphasised the detrimental results of unrestrained passions; psychological peculiarities are shown to be determined by social and biological influences, but also the characters' disinclination to attempt to exert self-control. *Basil* as a whole displays a more symbiotic relationship among Victorian medical theories, sensation fiction and melodrama than Hughes suggests: as well as drawing on the conventions of melodrama, Collins presents, through his depiction of monomania, new ways of creating the 'strong and deep emotions' that are associated with the genre. In this way Collins engineers a situation in which characters are at once more "realistic" *and* participate in their own self-perpetuating melodrama.

Basil is a novel of delusion and impeded perception, in which characters act imprudently under the dictates of their own unreliable emotions. In *No Name*, contrastingly, a number of sharp-eyed, clear-headed characters plot and counterplot in pursuit of the Vanstone fortune. Magdalen Vanstone is one of these competitors – clever, resourceful and perceptive. Like Mannion, Magdalen is invested with many of the attributes of a monomaniac that are the result of recognisable emotions: grief at the death of her parents, shock at the discovery that she and her sister are illegitimate, and anger at the fact that their fortune is passed on to the next legal relative. The novel follows her transformation from a charismatic, charming young lady, into a brooding, scheming villainess, and finally into a redeemed and rewarded heroine. In his preface, Collins claims that he intended to depict 'the struggle of a human creature, under those opposing influences of Good and Evil, which we have all felt, which we have all known'.[11] In sensational form the circumstances Magdalen finds herself in, and her responses to them, take her beyond the likely experience of *No Name*'s general readership, and we once again find Collins 'adhering to realities' that are not of the 'every-day' variety in his portrayal of monomaniacal drives. Nevertheless, he hoped to fulfil his desire of making Magdalen 'a pathetic character … by a resolute adherence, throughout, to the truth as it is in Nature' (p. xxvii), and as the following reading of Magdalen shows, he has taken pains to portray the psychological and environmental determining factors that influence her behaviour during the course of the novel.

Magdalen is presented to the reader by an omniscient narrator who often describes her thoughts and feelings with compassion; Collins obviously wanted to generate reader sympathy for her through understanding of her emotional state (even when she is most alienated from the world). This is in contrast to Mannion, whose explanatory letter may allow us to view him with sympathy (Heller, p. 75), but who is far too much of a stage villain really to feel for. Moreover, Mannion's desires, dominant idea and morality coincide: he hates Basil, desires revenge upon him and cares nothing about the moral consequences; in fact, his monomaniacal delusion leads him to believe that he is destined to destroy his enemy. Although Magdalen's fixed idea gives her unwavering drive and focus, she experiences inner conflict over her actions; she wants the fortune and is monomaniacally driven to win it, but despises the dishonest lengths she must go to in order to be victorious. Through this revelation of what Graham Law and Andrew Maunder call 'Magdalen's embattled psychology' Collins introduces two issues for speculation that receive more direct and exploratory attention than in *Basil*: the extent to which nurture and circumstance may influence the basic nature of an individual, and the difficulty of achieving self-control.[12] It is perhaps telling that Collins chose to revise *Basil* at much the same time as he was writing *No Name*; themes and mental states that are used for sensational effect in the earlier novel become issues for more sustained and nuanced consideration in the more mature and lengthy work.

While *Basil* is mainly informed by early Victorian theories about the sway of the passions, *No Name*, written a decade later, engages with mid-Victorian psycho-physiological theories of the relationship between the will and the emotions. This is not to say that there is a sudden change in the way that doctors, scientists and philosophers viewed character development; texts and ideas build on and feed into each other, often resulting in a change of tone or focus more than a brand-new theory. The mid-century theories discussed here in relation to *No Name* asserted (like much earlier thinking on the subject) that the cultivation of the willpower was the most important means of achieving self-determination, but they were also increasingly wary of the fact that achieving the necessary level of cultivation was dependent on a number of internal and external factors that the individual may be unable to control in the first place.

The second half of this chapter looks at how Collins's depiction of Magdalen does not just reflect, but reflects *upon*, these notions of character formation, and conveys his own belief that individuals have inbuilt capacities for good and evil. *No Name* is one of the sensation novels that has most often been read by scholars as revealing the constructed nature of gender and class identities, because of Magdalen's vacillating social status and adoption of disguises of figures occupying different social groups (including a governess and a servant). In discussing *No Name*'s 'engagement with the "Woman Question"', Law and Maunder argue that Magdalen 'negotiates and reacts against a set of ideologies that are simultaneously constructs and very real for her' (pp. 87–8). Jenny Bourne Taylor similarly observes that 'what *No Name* reveals above all is the impossibility of representing a coherent female subjectivity, a "true nature"' (p. 134). For this discussion, however, it is important to differentiate between Collins's portrayal of gender as a role, socially created and performed by individuals, and the assertion in his work that there are 'forces of inborn and inbred disposition' (*No Name*, p. 116) within people (regardless of gender) that may be enhanced or suppressed, but cannot be fundamentally modified, and that will work with circumstance to dictate behaviour.

Hughes accurately observes that Magdalen's moral struggle 'never seriously affects the realm of action', but her further assertion that the 'real challenge is not to the heroine's virtue, but to her intelligence and daring' does not sufficiently allow for the pages that Collins devotes to the inner conflict among different facets of Magdalen's personality (p. 145). In fact, as H. F. Chorley claimed in his (largely unfavourable) review of the novel, Magdalen is 'virtually, the book', and her story shows the ease with which potentially "good" people can fall victim, unawares, to both circumstance and their own lesser natures.[13]

The depiction of Magdalen's internal conflict may make the reader more inclined to pity her, but also raises questions about personal agency and responsibility; indeed, as we shall see, several Victorian reviewers were very *dis*inclined to feel anything but contempt for her. Medical and popular articles about insanity, criminality and deviant behaviour expressed ongoing concern about the difficulties of assigning responsibility and blame if the vulnerable and precarious status of self-control was acknowledged. *No Name* explores these issues by making Magdalen clearly aware of the impropriety and immorality of what she is doing, but by also making it unclear to what extent she is unable, or unwilling, to stop herself; this lack of clarity echoes some of the paradoxes of Victorian theories of willpower that will be explored in this chapter. By comparing these two novels, we can see how Collins becomes increasingly interested in concerns of character formation, and uses the condition of monomania to explore issues of self-control and the difficulties of deciding when, why and how we should feel sympathy for people who do "bad things".

'I cannot leave you if I would': (self-)delusion and unruly passions in *Basil*

In one of the key works that brought monomania to the English medical (and subsequently popular) imagination, J. E. D. Esquirol described monomania in the following way:

> the intellectual disorder is confined to a single object, or a limited number of objects. The patients seize upon a false principle, which they pursue without deviating from logical reasonings, and from which they deduce legitimate consequences, which modify their affections, and the acts of their will. Aside from this partial delirium, they think, reason and act, like other men. Illusions, hallucinations, vicious associations of ideas, false and strange convictions, are at the basis of this delirium.[14]

Although in the later nineteenth century monomania was mainly associated in the public mind with obsession, the presence of a particular delusion that influences subsequent behaviour was, as Esquirol's definition suggests, the key feature of early medical definitions. The presence of delusion is important in Collins's portrayal of Mannion because, despite having carefully plotted Basil's downfall for some time, it is only after his encounter with Basil and the newly surfaced road that Mannion categorically manifests a palpable 'false principle'. Mannion's letter is composed during his recovery after being assaulted by Basil. During the course of the letter, Mannion states his interpretation of events so far, and his intentions for the future:

> Lying in this place at night, in those hours of darkness and stillness when the surrounding atmosphere of human misery presses heavy on me in my heavy sleep, prophecies of dread things to come between us, trouble my

spirit in dreams. At those times, I know, and shudder in knowing, that there is something besides the motive of retaliation, something less earthly and apparent than that, which urges me horribly and supernaturally to link myself to you for life; which makes me feel as the bearer of a curse that shall follow you; as the instrument of a fatality pronounced against you long ere we met—a fatality beginning before our fathers were parted by the hangman; perpetuating itself in you and me; ending who shall say how, or when?

(pp. 200–1)

Mannion's letter reveals his belief that he is no longer entirely in control of his own behaviour and is imbued with a sense of compelling fatality: he feels forced to pursue Basil because of a supernatural 'something'; he perceives himself as a man who has gained special knowledge of his own role in a grand providential scheme. It is this conviction that makes him such a formidable opponent; Basil immediately feels this 'monstrous declaration of enmity' start 'to exercise its numbing influence [and] to cast its blighting shadow over [his] heart' (p. 210).

Mannion's delusion takes firmer hold as the story progresses, and he later tells Basil: 'Where you go, I have the limbs and the endurance to go too! I tell you again, we are linked together for life; I cannot leave you if I would. The horrible joy of hunting you through the world, leaps in my blood like fire!' (p. 257). Once again Mannion's compulsion is 'horrible', but whereas before he spoke of 'dread' at what may happen, now he enjoys executing the revenge he has been planning for so long, giving the impression that he can fully indulge his desires. Importantly however, when he was carefully plotting to seduce Margaret to shame Basil he (as far as we know) chose to act out his revenge; now he is compelled to do so. Along with the presence of delusion, insurmountable urges were one of the main indicators of monomania, as discussed presently.

Although Mannion does not have a palpable delusion until after Basil's attack, his mental state is certainly deteriorating prior to this. James Cowles Prichard brought the term "moral insanity" into popular use in England in the 1830s. Like monomania this was referred to as a form of partial insanity (Esquirol in fact used the term 'affective monomania', p. 320), and is a useful one in the analysis of Mannion's character formation. "Moral" had particular connotations within nineteenth-century medical discourse, as Janet Oppenheim summarises: by '*moral* Victorian alienists 'understood both the synonymous adjective *ethical*, but also the idea of emotional, mental, or nonphysical influences. Thus if they spoke of the moral causes of insanity, they referred to emotional trauma, such as overpowering grief, passion, disappointment, or fright.'[15] Moral insanity allowed for the fact that not all insanity was characterised by the presence of delusion, hallucination or illusion. It consisted of a 'morbid perversion of the feelings, affections and active powers' (Prichard, *Treatise*, p. 12). Although he drew the distinction (the presence of delusion) between monomania and moral insanity, Prichard acknowledged that there was often a connection between the two. A patient could suffer from moral insanity only to have his or her imagination become fixated on one 'particular illusion'; at this point moral insanity became monomania (Prichard, *Treatise* p. 28).

Collins is making use of the fact that both monomania and moral insanity were characterised as forms of "partial insanity", and this could make for a dangerous and unpredictable individual. As the *Lancet* observed in a series of articles on various forms of insanity: 'delusions in *monomania*, and in other states of insanity, may remain silent, till discovered by some accidental outbreak, when demonstrations of a painful character frequently and unexpectedly occur'.[16] One example of such an unexpected and 'painful' revelation of a delusion was reported in the same journal later in the year when 'a well-conducted servant girl, twenty-three years of age', who had 'never showed any signs of mental aberration' chopped off her left hand and thrust her arm into the fire. The *Lancet* concludes that the 'patient seems to be strictly *mono*-maniac, as she gives very apposite and satisfactory answers respecting her age, state of health, family, and various other circumstances' but, when questioned about her self-mutilation, 'she invariably answers that God told her to do it'.[17] This report emphasises both the 'false and strange convictions' that characterise monomania, and also the fact that as far as those around her were concerned, the woman's 'well-conducted' behaviour was not of a sort to arouse concern. Collins makes the most of the dramatic possibilities afforded by the monomaniac's ability to maintain a façade of normality that hides growing insanity; Mannion easily wins the trust of his employer and seems remarkably self-controlled, making him a particularly insidious enemy.

Whilst it is not conclusively stated that Mannion is insane, rather than just angry and immoral, in the years prior to his disfigurement, in the context of Victorian medical discourse he is certainly a candidate for a diagnosis of moral insanity developing into monomania. Mannion's mother was so traumatised by her husband's execution that she was 'deprived ... of reason' and 'died in a public mad-house' (*Basil*, p. 183). Insanity was not considered to be *necessarily* hereditary in the Victorian period, but it was generally understood that a 'constitutional predisposition' must exist, as not all people exposed to similar trying circumstances were in danger of going insane (Prichard, *Treatise*, p. 157). The circumstances of the death of Mannion's mother suggest that there is such a 'predisposition' in the maternal line, and not only that the shock of his father's death may have destabilised Mannion's mother, but also that Mannion's subsequent social ostracism could well have led to his own loss of sanity.

How much Mannion can be held responsible for his own deteriorating mental condition, and how much heredity and circumstance has determined his behaviour, is open to speculation. Taylor notes that while the doctor who treats Mannion insists that his insanity is inherited or due to brain damage, Mannion's letter 'sets up an alternative moral and social framework which challenges the one within which it is framed' by drawing attention to the difficult circumstances he finds himself in after his father is hanged (pp. 92–3).[18] Simon During observes that medical cases of monomania were often presented as 'motiveless' and apolitical, but suggests that 'the silence surrounding monomania often shadows resentment' towards an inequitable society.[19]

Certainly, whilst Collins appropriates an extreme mental state for his fiction, the emotions that motivate Mannion are entirely recognisable (anger, jealousy, bitterness, a sense of humiliation and exclusion) and it is the prejudices of society (as much as Basil's father's individual action) that have made Mannion what he is. Mannion describes the years after the death of his father, when 'the gallows still rose as the same immoveable obstacle between me and fortune, between me and station, between me and my fellow-men' (p. 184). In a pertinent 1843 article protesting against capital punishment, the doctor T. C. Morgan declared: 'We shall even find reason to believe, that it is the imputed sane who lead the acknowledged maniacs into their moonstruck mischiefs. The deluded wretch whose hallucination prompts him to strike at the life of a minister, does not invent the public distresses which give a specific direction to his insane impulse.'[20] Society's unwillingness to acknowledge Mannion as a blameless citizen (rather than the son of a felon) both drives him to insanity and, because it leaves him with no desire to respect conventional morality or laws, shapes the form that insanity takes.

However, Collins retains a sense of ambiguity in this letter; it is never entirely apparent to what extent the memory of the gallows is an obstacle perpetuated by Mannion, who admits that he is 'morbidly sensitive on this point' (p. 184) and distances himself from others because of it. Moreover, although Mannion's letter may help us understand his frustration and desire for revenge, he is predominantly viewed through the fearful and disapproving eyes of Basil and is not, on the whole, a character the reader relates to easily.

Whilst, therefore, the commonness of Mannion's feelings does invite a social critique, they serve more to suggest the fine line that was perceived to lie between sanity and insanity, particularly in the first half of the Victorian period, when an emphasis was placed on the unruly passions as a cause of mental disorders. John Barlow argued that anyone who doubted that the key to preventing insanity was to maintain strict control over one's thoughts should 'note for a short time the thoughts that pass through his mind, and the feelings that agitate him: and he will find that, were they all expressed and indulged, they would be as wild, and perhaps as frightful in their consequences as those of any madman' (p. 71). In order to describe monomania in recognisable terms, the doctor Henry Holland (in the same year *Basil* was published) also brought the possibility of insanity closer to home for his readers: 'Most persons have felt at one time or other … some dominant idea or feeling to possess the fancy; retaining its hold with a sort of malignant power, despite all efforts to shake it off; and by degrees distorting the subject, especially if it be a painful one, into a thousand false and alarming shapes.'[21] In accounts such as these, emotions that prompted excessive behaviour could literally be considered maddening.

Whilst Mannion is the only explicitly diagnosed monomaniac in *Basil*, other characters frequently find themselves possessed by a single idea, urge or desire that has its basis in a recognisable but exaggerated emotion and that leads to clouded judgement and (at best) improper behaviour: Margaret is obsessed with Mannion, as is Basil, who has previously been obsessed with Margaret; Mannion is obsessed with his desire to torment Basil, which develops into his assertion that he is compelled by forces beyond his control. The whole text has an obsessive intensity redolent of monomania; the *Athenaeum* described it as having a 'vicious atmosphere' that 'weighs on us like a nightmare' (Maddyn, p. 1323). In this way Collins draws on both the medical definition of monomania as a condition in which the sufferer was insane in relation to one 'particular illusion' but seemed otherwise sane (Prichard, *Treatise*, p. 28), and on the growing public tendency to associate monomania predominantly with obsession, those instances in which the consciousness became dominated by a single thought that takes on a 'malignant power'.

Whilst, on the one hand, the monomaniac was a frightening figure because his or her monomania could easily go undetected, descriptions

Basil *and* No Name

of insanity also often alluded to the fact that a monomaniac would be driven by his or her dominant idea to breach the bounds of social acceptability. For example, Prichard saw little difference between madness and eccentricity; the important question for him was the point at which an individual became 'unfit to be at large', unable to function competently and safely in society.[22] Similarly, Carpenter explained to his readers that if a 'dominant idea' holds sway over an individual, and if 'the conduct which it dictates should pass the bounds of enthusiasm or eccentricity, we say that the individual is the subject of Monomania' (*Human Physiology*, p. 611). Such descriptions can obviously be applied to Mannion, but the intensity of Basil's emotions also contributes to the overall obsessive tone of the novel. For example, when Basil first sees Margaret his 'ideas [are] in utter confusion' and he has 'no distinct impressions, except of the stranger beauty whom [he] had just seen' (*Basil*, p. 31). In a blatant breach of propriety, Basil tracks Margaret to her home and arranges a meeting with her. The inability to maintain self-possession (in relation to one object) is integral to the concept of monomania, but also of falling in love; an individual is mentally overtaken by whatever (or whoever) has influenced them, and is ruled by his or her fascination for it.

Collins also played with the fine line between love and obsessive insanity in a short story published just before *Basil*. In 'The twin sisters: A true story' (1851), the protagonist, Mr Streatfield, is 'seized with that amiable form of social monomania, called "love at first sight"'.[23] Mr Streatfield loses all self-control at the sight of a pretty face in a manner anticipatory of Basil's reaction to Margaret: 'he flung himself back in the carriage, and tried to examine his own feelings, to reason himself into self-possession; but it was all in vain' (p. 278). Neither love story has a positive outcome: in 'The twin sisters' Jane Langley is left a perpetual spinster after been rejected by Streatfield as the wrong twin, and Basil's obsession with Margaret blinds him to her real nature. *The Woman in White* provides a contrast, as Walter Hartright is certainly struck by the looks of Laura Fairlie, and freely admits that on the first day he saw her 'I let the charm of her presence lure me from the recollection of myself and my position' (p. 53). Yet Hartright overcomes these desires until he is in a situation to propose marriage within the bounds of convention and acceptability, which results in a happy ending.

The monomaniacal tone of much of *Basil*'s narrative is largely responsible for the melodramatic feeling of the story. This is because from the moment that Basil sees Margaret, to the moment he suffers his final breakdown after witnessing Mannion's death, he is unable to see the world through clear eyes. After overhearing Margaret's infidelity, Basil is overcome by 'ONE THOUGHT': that of murdering Mannion. He describes how 'before the fell poison of that Thought, all other thoughts – good or evil – died' (p. 130). Again, Collins's readers would have been reminded of the fixative, overwhelming quality of monomania. When he later sees Margaret, Basil's condition is intensified as his attention shifts from Mannion to her, and he is 'influenced' by the 'strange instinct of never losing hold of her' (p. 133). This desire is manifest in Basil's delusion that, long after Margaret has run away, '*her* track and *my* track were one; that I had just lost my hold of her, and that she was just starting on her flight' (p. 134, emphasis in original). Passers-by perceive Basil to be mad, and although this scares him, he continues to pursue the image of Margaret. This shift in focus is not actually at odds with some accounts of monomania; Prichard asserted, for example, that rather than being fixed, the 'dominant illusion … is ever liable to change as to its subject'.[24] Basil's dominant thought and subsequent delusion are expressive of a more general emotional disturbance.[25]

So, both Mannion and Basil are depicted as monomaniacs more and less explicitly (respectively) at points in the novel, driven by common emotions taken to extremes. Collins represents these two characters in accordance with early-nineteenth-century theories of insanity that proposed that "the passions" were at the basis of mental breakdown. Like many others, the physician John Conolly emphasised the fact that the same passions that inspired 'poetry, eloquence, invention, persevering labour' were also those that 'when unrestrained, have ruined the mind', and observed:

> It has been said that anger is a short madness; and it has been said, as truly, that no man can at once be in love and be wise: and, in like manner, we may observe each passion and emotion in excess disturbing the mind by a direct impairment of the comparing power, and, consequently, the judgement. Until the tyranny of the passion is past, the attention is forcibly withheld from all objects which would correct the false decision.[26]

In *Basil*, anything that would restore the influence of 'the comparing power' is given little or no attention in favour of anything that will intensify the wayward passions that have taken over the text. Hence, Basil fails to be swayed by his sister Clara's calming influence and is instead enraptured by Margaret's intoxicating sensuality, as symbolised in his intense, erotic dream about two women, one innocent and pure whose pleading is ineffectual, one sensual and seductive who draws him away into a 'dark wood' (p. 41). Conolly was a leading advocate of the non-restraint system in lunatic asylums, which worked on the assumption that restoring the patient's mental balance was a case of nurturing his or her own power of self-control. Conolly particularly advocated aiming for mental tranquillity: 'all excitement of mind, and all bodily irritation, all foolish indulgence, and all exciting topics of discussion' should be 'carefully avoided'.[27] Such a state is the antithesis of the atmosphere cultivated in *Basil*.

A lack of self-possession did not always result in insanity, but it was rarely described as a good thing. Edward Bulwer-Lytton's 'On self-control', an extract from which opened *Creating Character*, asserts that

> Self, left to itself, only crystallises atoms homogeneous to its original monad. A nature constitutionally proud and pitiless, intuitively seeks, in all the culture it derives from intellectual labour, to find reasons to continue proud and pitiless—to extract from the lessons of knowledge arguments by which to justify its impulse, and rules by which the impulse can be drilled into method and refined into policy.
>
> (p. 208)

Bulwer-Lytton's assessment of the self describes for a popular readership the unconscious and detrimental influence of personality traits left unchecked. Neither Basil nor Mannion struggles particularly hard against his natural impulses; instead they find themselves in situations that intensify the obsessive elements of their personalities. As retrospective narrator, for example, Basil explains that when he followed Margaret from the omnibus he allowed himself to believe that he was 'only animated by a capricious curiosity to know the girl's name, which once satisfied, would leave me at rest on the matter, and free to laugh at my own idleness and folly' (p. 32). Instead, this is the means of consolidating his new obsession.

The characters' actions create a self-sustaining, emotionally intense atmosphere. After he has the dream about the two women Basil wonders whether it was 'a warning', but dismisses this possibility as 'ridiculous'; he cannot, however 'also dismiss from [his] heart the love-images which that dream had set up there for the worship of the senses', which continue, 'growing and strengthening with every minute', until 'the love-thoughts of Margaret alone remained, and now remained unquestioned and unopposed' (pp. 42–3). Later in the novel, Basil (like Mannion) professes to feeling like the victim of some fatal influence: 'a superstitious conviction that [his] actions were governed by a fatality which no human foresight could alter or avoid' leads him to await 'events with the uninquiring patience, the helpless resignation of despair' (p. 220). This on the one hand allows for the reader to entertain the possibility that there are supernatural forces at work (an option that Collins always likes to keep open in his novels), but also shows how easily these characters resign themselves to their dominant emotions and desires.

Tim Dolin and Lucy Dougan have astutely observed that Basil's older brother, Ralph, is a potential antidote to the escalating emotional intensity of Basil's narrative:

> With his buffoonish ways and superficial ideas, Ralph ought to be a rather silly character, but, surprisingly, his appearance breaks a spell in which both Basil and the reader have for pages been held, claustrophobic and paranoid. Suddenly the air is cleared, the diabolical Mannion seems more like a schoolyard bully, and we feel that we, too, have let things get somewhat out of proportion.[28]

As Basil explains at the beginning of the novel, Ralph is sent to live abroad by his father after an 'awkward love adventure' with a tenant's daughter (p. 16). His first visit home to England conveys something of his infectiously revitalising manner: 'It was as if the fiery, effervescent atmosphere of the Boulevards of Paris had insolently penetrated into the old English mansion, and ruffled and infected its quiet native air' (p. 17).[29] When Ralph later tries to assist Basil through a combination of blackmail, threat and hush money, it is increasingly apparent that he, who is 'gay, hearty', 'reckless, boisterous' and 'determined to be his own master' (p. 15) is out of place in the world of Basil's narrative, and functions precisely as a contrast to the highly strung, obsessive central characters.[30]

Ralph's resistant and subversive presence is short-lived. When he arrives soon after Basil has received the letter from Mannion, the influence of that communication is too compelling to be dismissed by Ralph's optimism: Ralph laughs at the news that Basil has placed Mannion in hospital, but Basil 'remembered Mannion's letter, and shuddered' (p. 207). Readers may, for a moment, realise that things have got 'somewhat out of proportion', but they are swiftly plunged back into Basil's neurotically intense narrative, which is retrospective for the majority of the book, supposedly with the benefit of hindsight, but is actually written while Basil is in hiding in Cornwall, still very much under the influence of Mannion.

It is only in the final few pages that Basil is free from fear and obsession. Having experienced a mental and physical breakdown after the death of Mannion, Basil is reunited with his family and nursed back to health. The deaths of Mannion and Margaret, whose names he says he 'shall never pronounce again' (p. 270), and his complete removal from his former emotionally intense environment have apparently worked in much the same way as Conolly's non-restraint system, providing the calm surroundings necessary for recovery. If, however, as Taylor suggests, the aim of moral management was to encourage patients to 'reshape themselves by taking up fitting accomplishments for their gender and station' (p. 35), then Basil's position at the end of the story is particularly telling. He ends up living quietly with his sister Clara (on her estate, passed down the maternal line) 'in obscurity, in retirement, in peace' (p. 271). Whereas Conolly envisaged that with treatment 'customary occupations long interrupted, exercise long neglected, social conversation long shunned or almost forgotten for want of opportunities, and a lively interest in persons and things around [the patient] gradually form a part of their daily asylum life' as they move towards reintegration into wider society (*Treatment*, p. 154), Basil displays no 'longing to return to the busy world' (p. 271). Basil assures his correspondent (the doctor who nursed him back to health) that his is 'not a repose that owns no duty', and that he serves 'the poor and the ignorant, in the little sphere which now surrounds' him (p. 271). It appears that Basil spends his time visiting the needy, a standard sign of female virtue (as discussed in Chapter 2), and his 'little sphere' resembles that of the unmarried lady who could devote herself to her family and the disadvantaged people in her parish.

It could be seen as liberating that Basil no longer feels the need to conform to conventions of masculinity to which he is not suited – he is after all content. However, Basil's situation also reflects Conolly's description of the life of a patient in whom a 'cure' proves 'impossible' but in whom, under moral management, 'the worst features of the malady disappear': 'Nothing occurring, from day to day, to exasperate the patient; no unkind thing being ever done; no unkind expression ever addressed to him; no ungentle emotion ever roused; the patient's hours and days glide on in peace and content' (*Treatment*, p. 155). Whereas Valerie Pedlar suggests that the 'fact that his letter is written to a doctor makes it a sort of post-recovery check-up, a confirmation that healing has taken place' (Pedlar, p. 69), I would suggest that this same letter makes it seem that Basil must always remain under moral management; he cannot look again upon the 'glory and the glitter' of the "outside" world because it 'would dazzle and destroy' him (p. 271).

Viewed as a novel that engages with notions of character formation, *Basil* is informed by medical and psychological theories of the period that warned that the indulgence in passions and pursuit of desires without restraint lead to ruin. Both Mannion and Basil are too willing to bow to the dictates of a fatality of their own imagining and to succumb to situations that are the creation of their own uncontrolled emotions and urges. The cultivation and assertion of willpower was thought essential to the control of the emotions and the behaviour, but it is something the characters of *Basil* do not exercise. Little space is given, in this novel, to the extent to which the characters could have resisted their urges if they had wanted to. In *No Name*, however, the struggle between the will and a monomaniacal drive is given centre stage.

'Like a possession of the devil': willpower and internal conflict in *No Name*

Like Mannion, Magdalen Vanstone's fixation originates in a desire to retaliate against a perceived wrong: the death of her parents leaves Magdalen and her sister without the fortune they believe to be rightly theirs. Collins draws on the medical discourse of monomania to describe Magdalen's behaviour as she attempts to win back her inheritance: she becomes 'haunted day and night by the *one dominant idea* that now possessed her' (p. 544, my emphasis). When Magdalen goes to visit Noel Vanstone, the inheritor of the fortune (whom Magdalen eventually marries under an assumed name), she presents herself to him disguised as her ex-governess Miss Garth, concerned about what her former pupil may do. As well as allowing her to assess her enemy, this visit permits Magdalen to express her feelings and her intentions to him, albeit in the third person. Magdalen's tone reveals the extent to which her dominant idea (that of restoring her fortune to herself and her sister) has taken over her every action. She begins by admitting that 'she clings to the hope of hastening her marriage [to her fiancé, Frank], and to the hope of rescuing her sister from a life of dependence', but goes on to assert that 'if both those objects were accomplished by other means, nothing would induce her to leave [Noel] in possession of the inheritance which her father meant his children to have' (p. 236). All other considerations have become secondary to the achieving of her goal. Magdalen speaks with self-awareness of the power her desire has over her as she denounces the law that has rendered her illegitimate: 'It is your law – not hers. She only knows it as the instrument of a vile oppression, an insufferable wrong. The sense of that wrong haunts her, like a possession of the devil. The resolution to right that wrong burns in her like fire' (p. 236). In these few sentences, which closely echo the tone and imagery of parts of Mannion's confessional letter, the obsessive, compelling quality of monomania is clearly conveyed.

In addition to these rather melodramatic declarations, Collins includes a number of more analytical passages that reveal the effect that Magdalen's monomania is having on her. Shortly before her marriage to Noel Vanstone, Magdalen, disturbed by a dream, steps outside in order to contemplate her situation:

> By slow degrees, her mind recovered its balance, and she looked her position unflinchingly in the face. The vain hope that accident might defeat the very end for which, of her own free will, she had ceaselessly plotted and toiled, vanished and left her; self-dissipated in its own weakness. She knew the true alternative, and faced it. On one side, was the revolting ordeal of the marriage – on the other, the abandonment of her purpose. Was it too late to choose between the sacrifice of the purpose, and the sacrifice of herself? Yes! too late. The backward path had closed behind her. Time that no wish could change, Time that no prayers could recall, had made her purpose a part of herself: once she had governed it; now it governed her. The more she shrank, the harder she struggled, the more mercilessly it drove her on. No other feeling in her was strong enough to master it – not even the horror that was maddening her; the horror of her marriage.
> (p. 396)

Lennard J. Davis writes of 'obsession' as 'a battle of selves in which a compulsive self struggles with an observing self', and the ineffectuality of the latter is evident here (p. 31). Magdalen is reflecting clearly (and discontentedly) upon her behaviour, yet nothing is strong enough to dislodge her dominant idea or to stop it from governing her actions; importantly, she never learns to enjoy abandoning herself to her 'purpose' as Mannion does, which is one way that Collins hopes to retain our sympathy for her. By distinguishing between her dominant idea, which pushes her 'mercilessly' and without deviation on towards her marriage, and Magdalen's emotional response to it, which maddens her, Collins ironically portrays monomania as a cool-headed, merciless controller that overcomes the "madness" of emotional disruption. Shortly after this moment, Magdalen stumbles on her dress as she goes up the stairs 'from sheer inattention to the common precaution of holding it up'; this is a sign that her obsession is so all-consuming that the 'trivial daily interests of life had lost their hold on her already' (p. 402). It is not long after this that Magdalen considers suicide (pp. 401–9); she is living in a world of exaggeration in which only that most drastic of measures is a possible alternative to achieving her goal.

Mid-Victorian theories of insanity asserted that it was important to identify whether the emotions or the intellect were at fault. Monomania could be associated with both. For example, the psychiatrist John Charles Bucknill (writing about moral insanity) emphasised disrupted emotion over intellect as a cause of insanity and suggested that those who felt otherwise (particularly in the legal world) were adversely influenced by a utilitarian philosophy that 'developes [sic] all the natural and healthy emotions of the human mind from the operation of the reasoning faculties'. Such a philosophy necessarily disallowed 'the possibility of the secondary and dependent faculties [i.e. the emotions] becoming perverted and diseased, while their origin and cause remained healthy', and therefore seemed 'imperatively to forbid the supposition that moral insanity can exist without previous intellectual disease'.[31] Bucknill dismissed such theories, claiming that it was emotion, not intellect, that prompts an individual to action and concluding that '*insanity is always in the first instance emotional*' because 'in the varied play of the emotive faculties, is to be found the true key of human action' (pp. 85–6, emphasis in original). Although Collins does not necessarily endorse Bucknill's emphatic '*always*', Magdalen's behaviour certainly has its source in a disrupted emotional state, and in the above extract, the two things suggested as possible combatants of her monomania are both emotions: horror and hope. Magdalen's intellectual and reasoning faculties can monitor her situation, but they are not otherwise brought into the struggle.

Doctors observed that the change in an insane person's emotional state led to alterations in their relationship with those around them, as Esquirol explained in his description of a lunatic asylum: 'social bonds are broken; habits are changed; friendships cease; confidence is destroyed … With no community of thoughts, each lives alone and for himself. Egotism isolates all' (p. 20). Esquirol emphasises the emotional isolation of the lunatic in relation to family and friends: 'the insane often entertain an aversion towards persons who were previously dear to them. They insult, misuse, and fly from them. It is a result, however, of their distrust, jealousy and fear. Opposed to all, they fear all.' Esquirol adds that feelings of affection for friends and relations may remain, but that 'this tenderness, which is sometimes excessive, exists without confidence, and without intimacy' (pp. 26–7). Magdalen's behaviour towards her friends and family is in keeping with Esquirol's descriptions. At the news of her father's death, she is curiously unresponsive, telling others: 'Don't speak to me; don't touch me. Let me bear it by myself' (p. 83). Once Frank has abandoned her after the loss of her fortune, Magdalen refuses to see any of her old acquaintances. She tells her sister Norah, in a letter, that she will see her eventually, and assures her 'My heart is true to you, Norah – but I dare not see you yet' (p. 259). Her letter to Miss Garth shows a further distancing as she concludes that the 'best thing you can do for both of us, is to forget me' (p. 260). This condition of emotional withdrawal was known as "moral alienation", a doubly pertinent phrase here, as Magdalen is both emotionally and ethically isolated from her previous life (Esquirol, p. 27). Read in this light the 'unscrupulous selfishness' that provoked Chorley's disdain of Magdalen may be viewed as a symptom of her monomania (p. 10).

For many medical theorists, the key to controlling wayward emotions (and therefore to fending off potential insanity) was the assertion of willpower. This was because 'virtually all Victorian and Edwardian attitudes toward adult mental health and illness were constructed' on the 'concept of the will', and the 'ability to reason, to exercise judgement, to fulfil one's role in life were all contingent on the operations of the will, for if that became inadequate to its directing task, the personality disintegrated' (Oppenheim, p. 43). The will was a guiding force that directed, suppressed or enhanced the multitude of thoughts and emotions that arose either from within the mind through mental association or as a response to external stimulus; it chose which impulses to respond to, and what form those responses should take.

The most frequent exponent and explicator of willpower in the mid-Victorian period was William Benjamin Carpenter. His theories are worth looking at in some detail as they align closely with Collins's depiction of Magdalen. Carpenter described the will as carrying 'into action the determination of the intellect'[32] by way of the cerebrum, 'the instrument of all psychical activity', which conveys psychical desires and impulses to the physical body, prompting the actions which result in their achievement (*Human Physiology*, p. 653). Carpenter's theory of will was directly linked to his conception of character formation:

> Our characters are in the first instance formed *for* us by our original constitution and the conditions of its early development. But in proportion as the Will acquires domination over the Automatic tendencies, our characters are shaped *by* ourselves; the succession of our ideas and the play of our emotions are brought under its regulation; and our conduct in life comes to be the expression of our best energies, directed by the motives which we elect as our guiding principles of action.
>
> ('Physiology', p. 199)

Although this reads as a rather positive image of self-cultivation through the exertion of the will, there were limitations because the will did not create thoughts or emotions, its power was purely directional. 'Automatic tendencies' in the mind were the non-physical equivalent of bodily automatic actions such as the heartbeat or breathing, over which the individual had little or no control: a person could not help the thoughts and emotions that were prompted by mental association with a previous thought or external stimuli. These mental processes were, however, subject to volitional control, and a 'duly cultivated' will could 'regulate the course of Thought and the degree of Emotional excitement; intensifying some of these actions, and repressing others, by determinant efforts directed with that special purpose' (Carpenter, *Human Physiology*, p. 652).

Moreover, the 'original constitution' and 'early development' may not be conducive to cultivating willpower. If the will failed to control the thoughts and emotions, the 'reflex power' of the cerebrum was allowed 'too great a predominance, so that trains of ideas and states of feeling succeed each other automatically, and all the actions of the individual are simply the expressions of these' (Carpenter, *Human Physiology*, p. 653). Whilst the will was 'guided by the Intelligence' it was also 'acted-on by the desires and emotions' (p. 12). The strength of a person's willpower was measured by the extent to which the will could perform its controlling function, only allowing action as a response to constructive and desirable emotions. The degree of self-determinism a person possessed was therefore reliant on the strength and cultivation of the willpower: 'in proportion as [a person] acquires the power of *self-control*, does he become capable of emancipating himself from the domination of his automatic tendencies, and of turning his faculties to the most advantageous use' (Carpenter, 'Physiology', pp. 207–8).

Whilst the key to personal development was self-control, Carpenter saw insanity as characterised by 'a partial or complete deficiency in the Volitional control over the current of thought, and consequently over the actions which are the expressions of it' (*Human Physiology*, p. 656). In the case of monomania:

> some one particular tendency acquires a dominance over the rest; and this may happen, it would seem, either from an extraordinary exaggeration of the tendency, whereby it comes to overmaster even a strongly-exercised Volitional control; or, on the other hand, from a primary weakening of the Volitional control, which leaves the predominant bias of the individual free to exercise itself.
>
> (*Human Physiology*, p. 659)

Carpenter gives an impression of internal conflict; the volition is in combat with a persistent 'tendency' that singles itself out from the other automatic thoughts and emotions that the will directs. Collins is similarly building up a multi-layered image of the human psyche in which the will and the emotions fight for control. Magdalen's dominant idea is an automatic response to the loss of her parents, her lover and her fortune, which has taken control of her cerebral functions, overwhelming all other emotional impulses and subjugating her will.

At the root of Collins's depiction of Magdalen, however, is the conviction that each person has what Carpenter calls an 'original constitution', that which we have within us at birth and which will be improved or marred by the external influences to which we are exposed ('Physiology', p. 199). After Mr and Mrs Vanstone are killed, Miss Garth is shocked when Magdalen eavesdrops outside a window to learn the truth about her and her sister's illegitimate status and disinheritance. Musing on the responses of the sisters to their parents' deaths, Miss Garth wonders if she has misunderstood the apparently open and exuberant Magdalen, and her reserved, sombre sister Norah, who 'patiently accept[s] her hard lot' (p. 598). Miss Garth begins to have thoughts which, the narrator is certain, 'have startled and saddened us all' (p. 115). This passage is worth quoting at length because, although written as speculation, it reveals basic beliefs and uncertainties upon which Collins draws, and that he depicts throughout his fiction:

> Does there exist in every human being, beneath that outward and visible character which is shaped into form by the social influences surrounding us, an inward, invisible disposition, which is part of ourselves; which education may indirectly modify, but can never hope to change? Is the philosophy which denies this, and asserts that we are born with dispositions like blank sheets of paper, a philosophy which has failed to remark that we are not born with blank faces – a philosophy which has never compared together two infants of a few days old, and has never observed that those infants are not born with blank tempers for mothers and nurses to fill up at will? Are there, infinitely varying with each individual, inbred forces of Good and Evil in all of us, deep down below the reach of mortal encouragement and mortal repression – hidden Good and hidden Evil, both alike at the mercy of the liberating opportunity and the sufficient temptation? Within these earthly limits, is earthly Circumstance ever the key; and can no human vigilance warn us beforehand of the forces imprisoned in ourselves which that key *may* unlock?
>
> (p. 116)

Here Collins reacts to a Lockean *tabula rasa* philosophy that developed into nineteenth-century associationism and theorised that 'the mind was primarily created in experience and the role of innate ideas was negligible', and 'that mental life is derived from sensory and perceptual stimulation. In childhood, these stimuli establish the fundamental structures of mind, which is empty without them' (Rylance, pp. 40, 57). It assumed, in other words, that babies are 'born with blank tempers'. Collins does not deny that the association of ideas had an influence on character formation, but he objects, in the above passage, to the idea that the mind is 'empty' to begin with.[33] The alternative that Collins offers is delivered in sensational terms: the references to hidden, indelible 'forces of Good and Evil' not only depict humans as unable to suppress or develop fundamental aspects of their nature, but show them to be at the mercy of circumstance. The repeated reference to 'ourselves' implicates the reader in this powerlessness and negates the possibility of self-improvement at the most fundamental level.

However, it is significant that Collins refers to Good *and* Evil. Magdalen (unlike *Basil*'s Margaret, who has 'most of the bad instincts of an animal; none of the good' (p. 191)) is not an evil woman who has been educated for a time into acting in an acceptable manner until she is exposed to 'the sufficient temptation'; she contains potential for development in both directions. Collins aimed to make Magdalen's 'a pathetic character even in its perversity and its error' (p. xxvii); one means of achieving this is by regularly reminding the reader that there are inherently admirable qualities in Magdalen. For example, when she visits Noel Vanstone, Magdalen may be disguised as Miss Garth but her words are honest: 'If that miserable girl was married and rich with millions tomorrow, do you think she would move an inch from her purpose? I tell you she would resist, to the last breath in her body, the vile injustice which has struck at the helpless children, through the calamity of their father's death!' (p. 236). Even though she adopts some distinctly improper means of achieving her goal, Magdalen acts out of a sense of 'injustice', not for mercenary purposes.

Furthermore, by the end of this speech Magdalen inadvertently speaks in her own undisguised voice, a mistake that Collins attributes to her internal moral struggle: 'once more, her own indomitable earnestness had betrayed her. Once more, the inborn nobility of that perverted nature had risen superior to the deception which it had stooped to practise' (p. 236). The implication is that there is something intrinsically honourable within Magdalen that sabotages her own dishonesty, and Collins emphasises the inherence of her admirable features; 'perverted' suggests that circumstances have driven Magdalen's nature in an "unnatural" direction that it would not have pursued otherwise. By championing Magdalen's inherent goodness in this way, Collins implies that Magdalen's original constitution is basically virtuous, although capable of immoral and improper behaviour.

Despite claims of Magdalen's 'inborn nobility', and although Collins 'positions her so that we feel sympathy for her' (Law and Maunder, p. 87), some Victorian reviewers refused to be won over. In his review Chorley was insensitive to the fact that Magdalen was following a 'strong desire to right a cruel injustice' (*No Name*, p. 10). Whereas Collins suggests there must be 'nobility' within Magdalen because she is able to do the right thing in the end, Chorley reverses this and asserts that there must be 'coarseness, as well as meanness, in one capable of such actions and expedients as these ... her persistence in her evil purpose can only be explained by admitting that there existed in the heroine's character hard and (we repeat) coarse elements, which deprive her of our sympathy' (*No Name*, p. 11). Chorley's insistence that there must be something fundamentally disagreeable in Magdalen's 'character' that allows her to act as she does, and by default renders her unsympathetic, is an attitude that we will see, more implicitly, at work in the narrative drive of *The Lady Lisle* in Chapter 3.

In contemporaneous debates regarding insanity, criminality and personal responsibility, it was widely acknowledged that the situation was not so simple: doctors spent much time and effort attempting to pinpoint the root and causes of an individual's moral perversion; only after considering these options could one decide (and then not necessarily easily) how much 'sympathy' an individual deserved. Personal responsibility was not only dictated by whether or not a person could control his or her own behaviour, but by which aspects of his or her physical and mental constitution were dictating that behaviour. It was also important to consider why such people had begun to suffer from whatever condition was afflicting them, and what role their wills had played in the course of events. For example, John Barlow claimed of monomania that it 'is more often owing to a want of moral control over the mind than to any unsoundness of the intellectual faculties' (p. 73).

Carpenter's theories of insanity show a similar endorsement of moral management and the assertion of self-discipline. In the case of moral insanity, for example, he argued that 'nothing else is requisite, than that [the patient] should exercise an adequate amount of self-control' (*Human

Physiology, p. 659). Carpenter separated actions into three 'modes': the previously discussed automatic, which the will did not control; voluntary, which were guided and permitted by the will; and volitional, in which an assertion of willpower was required to perform acts ('Physiology', p. 195). So while the will could not prevent the occurrence of inappropriate or undesirable thoughts and feelings, Carpenter insisted that 'it is the *acceptance* of them by the *permission* of the will, that makes them Voluntary, and brings them within the sphere of moral action; whilst it is the *intentional direction* of the attention to them, which gives them their Volitional character, and makes the *ego* fully responsible for them' ('Physiology', p. 214, emphasis in original). If people did not exercise their wills to the best of their ability then they became proportionally responsible for their behaviour.

Although Magdalen eventually fights her fixed idea, she is described as having initially pursued her goal 'of her own free will'; her purpose had initially been 'governed' by her, rather than vice versa (p. 396). Magdalen has, it would appear, brought this situation upon herself, abandoning herself to the emotions that subsequently overtake her. Collins therefore intimates that her behaviour would, at least for a moment, have fallen into what Carpenter would deem the category of voluntary (if not volitional) actions, allowing the desire to regain her fortune to take control and thus making her at least partially morally responsible. However, Collins's insistence in his preface that we have all encountered internal struggles like Magdalen, implies that the people whom Collins liked to call 'readers in general' (as opposed to 'readers in particular', i.e. not reviewers, specialists or people who may take offence at particular aspects of his story) may be somewhat more forgiving than Carpenter and realise that to 'exercise an adequate amount of self-control' is not always easy.[34]

Collins's portrayal of Magdalen shares some of the ambiguities and difficulties of mid-Victorian psycho-physiological theories such as Carpenter's. As we have seen, both Collins and Carpenter subscribe to the idea that people possess inherent personality traits or tendencies that may be altered by later life experiences. It therefore follows that some individuals will naturally possess more or less willpower and/or powerful emotions than others; some will have more chance of successful self-cultivation than others. There is much in the descriptions of Magdalen to suggest that her emotions are inherently intense and not easily restrained. She is good-natured but wild and excitable: she has 'large, electric, light-grey eyes' that 'were hardly ever in repose; all varieties of expression followed each other over the plastic, ever-changing face, with a giddy rapidity which left sober analysis far behind in the race' (p. 8). The narrator maintains that this is a sign of 'overflowing physical health' (p. 9), but such incessant movement also suggests emotional or mental instability.

Magdalen hungers after any event that will thrill her nerves: 'I want to go to another concert – or a play, if you like – or a ball, if you prefer it – or, anything else in the way of amusement that puts me into a new dress, and plunges me into a crowd of people, and illuminates me with plenty of light, and sets me in a tingle of excitement all over, from head to foot' (p. 10). Merely expressing her craving for physical and emotional stimuli generates great excitement, and such a 'capacity for pleasure is somewhat alarming in a young woman' (Huskey, p. 10), implying 'overabundant sexual energies' that are 'accompanied by more menacing ideas of excess' (Mangham, p. 184). Similar signs of 'excess' are apparent when the narrator describes how Magdalen has a 'curious fancy for having her hair combed at all times and seasons' (p. 39):

> The girl's fervid temperament intensified the essentially feminine pleasure that most women feel in the passage of the comb through their hair, to a luxury of sensation which absorbed her in enjoyment, so serenely self-demonstrative, so drowsily deep, that it did irresistibly suggest a pet cat's enjoyment under a caressing hand.
>
> (p. 40)

This suggests an ardent nature that feels emotional and sensual pleasures intently, far more than 'most women feel', and is inclined to indulge and become 'absorbed' in them.

Such an excitable, powerful capacity for emotion would require the restraining influence of a strong and disciplined will. Barlow stated that to 'educate a man, in the full and proper sense of the word, is to supply him with the power of controlling his feelings, and his thoughts, and his actions' (p. 59). Carpenter believed that the willpower should be trained from infancy because 'those early habits of thought and feeling, which exert an enormous influence over our whole subsequent mental life, are formed *for* us rather than *by* us' ('Physiology', p. 205). For this reason, Carpenter was a great advocate of education that helped 'the development of the self-directing power' (*Human Physiology*, p. 551) and speculated that a person who had not been sufficiently educated in this way may be capable of exercising volition under normal circumstances, but may not have made a habit of doing so. Carpenter argued that if a girl drowned herself after a lovers' quarrel, or a maid killed a child in a temper, she may be temporarily insane, but would be 'morally responsible for that crime, in so far as she has habitually neglected to control the wayward feelings whose strong excitement has compelled her to its commission' ('Physiology', p. 216). There is much in Collins's depiction of Magdalen to suggest that she is not an individual who is used to exerting (and so developing) the controlling power of her will, leaving it defenceless when she is influenced by her own wayward emotions. Lyn Pykett argues that Collins shows how 'the disaster which befalls the Vanstone sisters is the result of an unjust law' but that 'the novel's focusing on Magdalen's excessive emotions and her scheming also has the effect of transferring the reader's attention, and perhaps also the blame ... onto her perverse femininity and her obsessive desire for revenge and restitution' (*Sensation Novel*, pp. 23–4). Certainly the blame of critics such as Chorley fell heavily on Magdalen, and Carpenter's theories above also suggest that Magdalen is to an extent 'morally responsible'. However, as I have argued, Collins still tries to elicit reader sympathy, and it may also be asked why Magdalen's willpower is so uncultivated.

Prichard also placed great emphasis on a lack of early discipline in pinpointing reasons for insanity: 'by too great indulgence and a want of moral discipline, the passions acquire greater power, and a character is formed subject to caprice and to violent emotions: a predisposition to insanity is thus laid in the temper and moral affections of the individual' (*Treatise*, p. 172). This is particularly relevant to Magdalen's situation. Collins takes care in describing Magdalen's home life and behaviour before the death of her parents, revealing a loving but overly indulgent environment with little discipline. For example, at one point Magdalen wants to perform in a play and finds it easy to convince her father:

> 'Say yes', she pleaded, nestling softly up to her father, and pressing her lips with a fond gentleness to his ear, as she whispered the next words. 'Say Yes—and I'll be a good girl for the rest of my life.'
> 'A good girl?' repeated Mr Vanstone—'A mad girl, I think you must mean.'
> (p. 33)

Mr Vanstone's constant lenience allows Magdalen to follow her every whim without forethought or deliberation, and fails to prepare her mentally or morally for the disaster to come, making his words both prophetic and causal. Despite the remonstrations of Miss Garth and Mrs Vanstone, Magdalen's father is unconcerned about his daughter's high spirits: 'she's an unbroken filly. Let her caper and kick in the paddock to her heart's content. Time enough to break her to harness, when she gets a little older'

(p. 11). Obviously these words are ill-fated, as the death of her parents means that Magdalen has no opportunity to be '[broken] to harness'.

Later in the novel, Magdalen's erratic energies become focused on the achievement of her dominant idea, resulting in a distinct physical change: 'there was a settled composure on her face which, except when she spoke, made it look as still and cold as marble. Her voice was softer and more equable, her eyes were steadier, her step was slower than of old' (p. 267). This is reminiscent of Mannion's 'extraordinary regularity of feature' (*Basil*, p. 90), yet Magdalen never quite achieves the same level of physical restraint, as she has developed 'a little nervous contraction on one side of her mouth, never visible there before', which is a telling sign of inner strife (p. 267).[35] Although Magdalen is driven to pursue her purpose as forcefully as Mannion, she has several emotional outbreaks that are representative of her disgust at her own actions. For example, as the wedding approaches, Magdalen demands that she be allowed two days away from Vanstone, as she has been 'tortured enough'; she has a passionate outbreak and then asks Captain Wragge for forgiveness on the grounds that she is 'only a girl' (p. 358). Yet even as she voices her disgust of Vanstone, she declares 'I'll go through with it to the end' (p. 358), and she most certainly does; it takes Noel's discovery of her real identity, and then his death to end the relationship. Whilst Magdalen apologises for being 'only a girl' because it stops her from being able to endure Vanstone's company any longer, it is also a reminder of her youth and inexperience, and the fact that she is psychologically unprepared to resist her monomaniacal imperative. Carpenter asserted that 'a great deal of what is commonly termed *wilfulness* is in reality just the contrary of willfullness; being the direct result of the *want* of volitional control over the automatic operation of the brain' ('Physiology', p. 206); this seems particularly pertinent here.

Magdalen's recovery and redemption are equally enmeshed with notions of character formation. Sally Shuttleworth observes a tendency in Victorian sensation fiction for women to suffer from insurmountable hereditary insanity, a situation that reflects their 'negative economic placement' in society. Conversely, men tend to be 'placed in positions of economic possibility', and in a corresponding manner 'the threat of insanity that hangs over them is rarely an inescapable physiological destiny, but rather a partial, temporary form, which can be shaken off through self-discipline and a transformation of lifestyle' ('Preaching', pp. 205–6). Collins does not stick to this formula. Magdalen (despite her 'negative economic placement') appears to suffer from a "masculine" form

Self-control, willpower and monomania

of insanity: by an effort of willpower she finally overcomes her revengeful desires and seems ready to regain the ranks of respectability (unlike Basil, who is never quite fit to re-enter the 'busy world'). Thus, when Magdalen discovers that Norah, through marriage, has come into possession of the fortune that she has been pursuing throughout the novel, 'Good and Evil struggled once more which should win her':

> All the higher impulses of her nature, which had never, from first to last, let her err with impunity – which had tortured her, before her marriage and after it, with the remorse that no woman inherently heartless and inherently wicked can feel – all the nobler elements in her character gathered their forces for the crowning struggle, and strengthened her to meet, with no unworthy shrinking, the revelation that had opened on her view ... she had victoriously trampled down all little jealousies and all mean regrets; she could say in her heart of hearts, 'Norah has deserved it!'
>
> (p. 598)

So it comes down to a battle between the 'inbred forces of Good and Evil' that Miss Garth worried about earlier in the novel. A physiologist such as Carpenter would describe the process as Magdalen's volition having finally found the strength it needs to overcome her monomaniacal drive, but Collins frames the struggle in affective terms in order once again to insist that Magdalen is not 'inherently heartless and inherently wicked'. While her 'nobler elements' (fortified by the 'growth of her gratitude' to Captain Kirke, the man who saves her from poverty and death, and whom she will go on to marry (p. 598)) are described as *un*shrinking, the purpose that has governed her so powerfully has shrunk to a combination of 'little jealousies' and 'mean regrets', becoming manageable and suppressible. This belief in innate goodness that can overcome evil tendencies or temptations continues throughout Collins's fiction and will be revisited in the discussion of Anne Silvester in Chapter 5. Amanda Mordavsky Caleb has also shown that Collins's last finished novel, *The Legacy of Cain* (1889), makes a similar implication that humans have 'an inherently good nature', even though 'they may also possess many vices'.[36]

However, while the narrator speaks of Magdalen's 'dead passions' and the 'grave of her buried hopes', and while Magdalen's moral struggle is represented as her coming to terms with the realisation that 'the recovery of the lost fortune was her sister's triumph, not hers', it is also important that 'Magdalen's own scheme to recover' the fortune 'had opened the way' to Norah's marriage to the inheritor of the fortune and 'brought husband and wife together' (p. 598). Moreover, as Hughes points out, 'Magdalen gets exactly what she wants' (p. 152); the fortune has been returned to the family. Magdalen, furthermore, is temporarily the recipient of half the fortune bestowed by the Secret Trust; she chooses to destroy it and this is described as the 'last sacrifice of the old perversity and the old pride' (p. 607), but it is also something of an empty gesture, as her aim was to have the fortune restored regardless of how it was done. Magdalen's dishonest plans are therefore only partially thwarted, and her monomaniacal purpose, her dominant idea, has been satisfied. This is one reason why Collins was not entirely successful in making Magdalen a 'pathetic' character as far as some critics were concerned. In her negative review of *No Name*, Margaret Oliphant was clearly unconvinced by Magdalen's recovery at the end of the novel. Oliphant complained that Magdalen was allowed to emerge, 'at the cheap cost of a fever, as pure, as high-minded, and as spotless as the most dazzling white of heroines'.[37]

The critical dislike of Magdalen, and the unwillingness to allow her moral leeway, reflects the fears articulated by those concerned with the relationship among personal responsibility, crime and insanity. In 1864, for example, the *Cornhill Magazine* introduced partial insanity to its readers: whereas in the "classic" form of insanity a man's 'hostile demeanour and murderous designs would be natural and legitimate, if his impression as to the facts were correct', in the other type, 'a man may feel that he is on the verge of committing murder or suicide' and be compelled to act because 'he is the sport of an irresistible impulse'.[38] Whilst many felt that if an individual was truly incapable of controlling his or her own behaviour on account of insanity they were entitled to sympathy and help, rather than punishment, it was also widely recognised that there was a danger of criminals being either unfairly incarcerated, or given the means to evade execution by being declared insane; the fear was, as Maudsley observed, that people would start 'making out all sorts of vice and crime to be insanity'.[39]

In 1850 the *New Monthly Magazine* ran an article that began by citing the case of Robert Pate, who suffered from 'imaginary persecutions', made 'an assault upon the person of her Majesty' and was subsequently transported for seven years.[40] The article asserts that insane criminals should not go unpunished, but suggests that conventional punishment is inappropriate. It adopts the view-point not only that insanity is difficult to measure, but that to speak of sanity itself as a normal mental state is rarely appropriate. The article advises its readers that the question for consideration 'in estimating the qualities of our fellow-creatures, is not whether anyone exists whose mind and body are thus perfectly sane, but what is the relative degree of his or her divergence from the perfect type' (p. 405). It goes on to assert that 'few crimes are committed in a state of sanity': theft is therefore a 'mere manifestation of uncontrolled or diseased acquisitiveness'; violent and murderous acts are often 'the result of passions aroused to a maddened and uncontrollable degree' (p. 406). In this manner, the article separates a diagnosis of insanity from a right to leniency, observing that 'if insanity was to be a shield to either punishment or prevention, the plea might be advanced in almost every instance of evil done' (p. 407). The article solves the dilemma of how to treat a criminal who was not in their right senses at the time of committing the crime by classing 'confinement in an asylum and medical treatment' as a form of punishment (p. 404). A consideration of the extent to which a criminal has departed from a sane state at the point of committing the crime, as well as his or her current mental state, should dictate whether a "medical" or "criminal" punishment is more appropriate.

Only three weeks before *No Name* was serialised in *All the Year Round* (it ran from March 1862 to January 1863) the journal ran an article that would not have favourably predisposed readers towards Magdalen and her behaviour. It argued that "mad-doctors" were far too quick to condemn people as lunatics who exhibited antisocial or otherwise inappropriate behaviour. As in the *New Monthly Magazine*, this article suggests that perfect sanity is a rare condition. It draws a comparison between mental and physical health in order to suggest that unsoundness of mind, unless very severe, should not be considered unnatural:

> There is no clear dividing line between sickness and health of mind; unsoundness of mind is, no doubt, as various and common as unsoundness of body ... But we do not condemn our bodies as unfit for use when there are corns on our toes ... [we] do our duty in the world as far as our infirmity permits. So it is with the mind. Every man has his weak place; his twist, his hobby.[41]

By essentially asserting that no one is entirely mentally stable, this article gives the impression that everyone is in the same boat, and must therefore do the best they can. The writer goes on to argue that 'in honest truth, every criminal is a lunatic; but he is a lunatic who would admit, except under the most obviously exceptional conditions, any such plea as a bar to responsibility' (p. 511). Whilst the opinion that crime is a sign of lunacy is in keeping with the *New Monthly*'s claim that to break the law is not to be 'in a state of sanity', the tones of the articles are very different. Rather than advocating medical treatment for lunatic criminals, this article explicitly prioritises social order over any concept of absolute justice. *All the Year Round* insists that an individual may inherit 'characters or forms of mind as well as forms of body, and a neglected untaught man may be no more able to control this or that evil turn of character, than he may be able to control the shape of his nose' (p. 511). Yet this acknowledgement does not prompt a sympathetic response when considered in the light of criminality, as judges 'must give up society to anarchy, or shut their eyes to such metaphysical distinctions' (p. 511). Emphasis is moved from the diagnosing of lunacy to the crime itself. Such opinions resemble those adopted by critics such as Chorley in relation to Magdalen. Whilst they generally observe that she has a valid grievance, it is the means she adopts to overcome that grievance that are reprehensible, whether or not she is able to help herself.

Collins tried to make Magdalen both sensational and sympathetic, but by engaging with theories of character formation that emphasised the need for willpower and self-control, he raised the same ethical and social dilemmas concerning personal responsibility and the assignment of blame as those debated in medical and popular works on the subject. Such theories placed their faith in the power of the will, at the same time as they emphasised its vulnerability to fierce passions, poor cultivation and abuse. Whilst *Basil* is about what happens when the passions are not kept in check, *No Name* is about the difficulty of keeping them in check without conducive circumstances or correct training. Mary Elizabeth Braddon's *John Marchmont's Legacy*, discussed in the next chapter, also depicts a character's internal struggle with self-control, but rather than showing the response to an unfortunate experience, Braddon explores what happens when a person's 'original constitution' is fundamentally at odds with the role they are expected to play in the world.

Notes

1 Wilkie Collins, *Basil* (Oxford: Oxford University Press, 2005), p. 4. Although this is the revised 1862 text, all the relevant themes and characterisation for this discussion were in place in the original 1852 version.
2 Charles Dickens, letter to Wilkie Collins, 20 December 1852, in *The Letters of Charles Dickens*, ed. Graham Storey *et al.*, 11 vols (Oxford: Clarendon Press, 1965–99), Vol. VI (1850–2), pp. 823–4.
3 Anon., 'The progress of fiction as an art', *Westminster Review*, 60:118 (October 1853), 342–74 (p. 372).

4 Andrew Lycett, *Wilkie Collins: A Life of Sensation* (London: Random House, 2013), pp. 54–5.
5 As Tamar Heller observes, 'the intellectual, Basil, creates monsters he is not able to control' (Tamar Heller, *Dead Secrets: Wilkie Collins and the Female Gothic* (New Haven: Yale University Press, 1992), p. 62), but in the final pursuit it is the creature, Mannion, who hunts his creator.
6 George Rowell, *Nineteenth-Century Plays* (London: Oxford University Press, 1953), p. v.
7 Winifred Hughes, *The Maniac in the Cellar: Sensation Novels of the 1860s* (Princeton: Princeton University Press, 1980), p. ix.
8 Peter Brooks, *The Melodramatic Imagination: Balzac, Henry James, Melodrama, and the Mode of Excess* (New Haven: Yale University Press, 1976), pp. 11–12.
9 This is not to say that Collins places unequivocal faith in the word of medical men; several of his novels portray unskilled and/or unethical practitioners, such as *Armadale*'s abortionist, Dr Downward, and *Heart and Science*'s (1883) vivisector, Dr Benjulia.
10 Collins often researched specific medical conditions for his fiction. For example, in *Poor Miss Finch* (1872), which features several far-fetched coincidences, the anti-epilepsy treatment that turns Oscar Dubourg blue, the operation that temporarily restores Lucilla Finch's eyesight, her phobia of dark colours and her disillusionment with the visible world are all based on recorded cases. See Catherine Peters's introduction and notes to Wilkie Collins, *Poor Miss Finch*, ed. Catherine Peters (Oxford: Oxford University Press, 2000), pp. x–xiii, p. 428.
11 Wilkie Collins, *No Name* (London: Penguin, 2004), p. xxvii.
12 Graham Law and Andrew Maunder, *Wilkie Collins: A Literary Life* (Basingstoke: Palgrave Macmillan, 2008), p. 87.
13 H. F. Chorley, 'No Name', *Athenaeum*, 1836 (January 1863), 10–11 (p. 10).
14 J. E. D. Esquirol, *Mental Maladies: A Treatise on Insanity*, trans. E. K. Hunt (Philadelphia: Lea and Blanchard, 1845), p. 320.
15 Janet Oppenheim, *Shattered Nerves: Doctors, Patients and Depression in Victorian England* (New York: Oxford University Press, 1991), p. 41.
16 Joshua Burgess, 'The policy and pathology of insanity', *Lancet*, 58:1463 (13 September 1851), 246–7 (p. 246), emphasis in original.
17 Anon., 'Religious monomania; self-mutilation', *Lancet*, 58:1472 (15 November 1851), 456.
18 Jenny Bourne Taylor, *In the Secret Theatre of Home: Wilkie Collins, Sensation Narrative, and Nineteenth-Century Psychology* (London: Routledge, 1988), p. 92–3.
19 Simon During, 'The strange case of monomania: Patriarchy in literature, murder in *Middlemarch*, drowning in *Daniel Deronda*', *Representations*, 23 (1988), 86–104 (pp. 87, 90). During's reading is useful, but I differ with his claim that once a motive can be assigned to monomania it ceases to be monomania (p. 87), as detrimental external factors could lead to a loss of sanity. Also, this presents what Esquirol called 'instinctive monomania' (just one of a plethora of monomanias) as monomania in its entirety (e.g. Esquirol, p. 320).

20 T. C. Morgan ['μ'], 'Monomaniacs and monomania', *New Monthly Magazine and Humorist*, 68:269 (May 1843), 43–51 (p. 47). Morgan plays with perceptions of boundaries here: it is of course the 'imputed' sane who attribute sanity to themselves and insanity to the supposed 'maniacs'.

21 Henry Holland, *Chapters on Mental Physiology* (London: Longman, Brown, Green and Longman, 1852), p. 140.

22 James Cowles Prichard, *On the Different Forms of Insanity in Relation to Jurisprudence* (London: Hippolyte Ballière, 1842), p. 66.

23 Wilkie Collins, 'The twin sisters: A true story', *Bentley's Miscellany*, 29 (March 1851), 278–91 (p. 278).

24 Prichard, *On the Different Forms of Insanity*, p. 169. Prichard argued that there was no such thing as actual "partial insanity": a monomaniac may seem sane in all but one delusion, but 'on careful inquiry it will be found that his mind is in many respects in a different condition from that of perfect health' (*Treatise*, p. 28). This was a point of contention for doctors in France as well as Britain (see W. L. Duffy, 'Monomania and perpetual motion: Insanity and amateur scientific enthusiasm in nineteenth-century medical, scientific and literary discourse', *French Cultural Studies*, 21 (2010), 155–66 (pp. 156–7).

25 For a more sustained reading of this scene, Basil's other breakdown and his recovery, see Valerie Pedlar, *'The Most Dreadful Visitation': Male Madness in Victorian Fiction* (Liverpool: Liverpool University Press, 2006), pp. 62–9.

26 John Conolly, *An Inquiry Concerning the Indications of Insanity, with Suggestions for the Better Protection and Care of the Insane* (London: John Taylor, 1830), p. 225.

27 John Conolly, *The Treatment of the Insane without Mechanical Restraints* (London: Smith, Elder, 1856), p. 151.

28 Tim Dolin and Lucy Dougan, 'Fatal newness: *Basil*, art, and the origins of sensation fiction', in Maria K. Bachman and Don Richard Cox (eds), *Reality's Dark Light: The Sensational Wilkie Collins* (Knoxville: University of Tennessee Press, 2003), pp. 1–33 (p. 19).

29 French literature and culture carried morally dubious connotations in the eyes of Victorian England, and in fact the *Athenaeum* took *Basil's* focus on the unpleasant details of its subject matter as a sign that Collins had 'enrolled' in 'the unwholesome [French] literary school' (Maddyn, p. 1323). Collins's fondness for Parisian living is apparent in his letters. In the years preceding the writing of *Basil* he frequently visited France as an escape from his responsibilities. See Wilkie Collins, *The Letters of Wilkie Collins*, ed. William Baker and William M. Clarke, 2 vols (London: Macmillan, 1999), Vol. I, pp. xxiii, xxvii.

30 Ralph ends up in peaceful retirement with an older mistress. In later years, Collins's antagonism towards the institutions and conventions of his society would be more explicitly revealed (such as in *Man and Wife*'s attack on British marriage laws), but Collins does not tacitly promote living in sin as an appealing alternative as he does in *Basil*.

31 John Charles Bucknill, 'The law and the theory of insanity', *British and Foreign Medico-Chirurgical Review*, 13 (January 1854) 76–93 (pp. 79–80).
32 William Benjamin Carpenter, 'The physiology of the will', *Contemporary Review*, 17 (April 1871), 192–217 (p. 198).
33 Collins often employed 'unconscious cerebration' (coined by Carpenter), which relied on the idea of the reflex association of thoughts proceeding 'without our knowledge' (Carpenter, *Human Physiology*, p. 609). Most famously, in *The Moonstone* (1868), a discussion about the jewel leads to the unconscious stealing of it (Wilkie Collins, *The Moonstone* (London: Pan, 1967), pp. 477–8). In *No Name*, Mrs Lecount realises who Magdalen is through an unconscious train of thought (p. 308).
34 See, for example, Wilkie Collins, *Armadale* (Oxford: Oxford University Press, 1999), p. 4.
35 Mannion's impervious face only slips once, when a flash of lightning shows a 'spectral look of ghastliness and distortion' in his features, and he seems to be 'glaring and grinning on [Basil] like a fiend' (*Basil*, p. 106).
36 Amanda Mordavsky Caleb, 'Questioning moral inheritance in *The Legacy of Cain*', in Andrew Mangham (ed.), *Wilkie Collins: Interdisciplinary Essays* (Newcastle: Cambridge Scholars Publishing, 2007), pp. 122–35 (pp. 132–3).
37 Margaret Oliphant, 'Novels', *Blackwood's Edinburgh Magazine*, 102:623 (August 1863), 168–83 (p. 170).
38 Coke Richardson, 'Extenuating circumstances', *Cornhill Magazine*, 9:50 (February 1864), 210–18 (p. 211). Other popular periodical accounts concerning the difficulty of defining and treating lunacy in relation to criminal cases include 'Criminal Lunatics', by Charles Thomas Browne (*Temple Bar*, 1 (December 1860), 135–43), which suggests that ordinary juries should not be used in criminal cases involving claims of lunacy.
39 Henry Maudsley, 'Practical observations on insanity of feeling and of action', *Lancet*, 87:2234 (23 June 1866), 679–80 (p. 679).
40 Anon., 'Responsibility of monomaniacs', *New Monthly Magazine and Humorist*, 89:356 (August 1850), 404–8 (p. 404).
41 Anon., 'M.D. and M.A.D.', *All the Year Round*, 6:148 (22 February 1862), 510–13 (p. 511). For another example of opposition to supposedly weak and indulgent attitudes towards crime and insanity, see anon., 'Insanity and its treatment', *Belgravia*, 10 (February 1870), 467–78, which protested against 'mischievous and indiscriminate kindness' being shown to the insane (p. 467).

2

John Marchmont's Legacy

The tenderness which is the common attribute of a woman's nature had not been given to her. She ought to have been a great man. Nature makes these mistakes now and then, and the victim expiates the error.[1]
(Mary Elizabeth Braddon, *John Marchmont's Legacy* [1863])

The previous chapter showed how Wilkie Collins's *Basil* and *No Name* draw on the condition of monomania in order to explore issues of self-control, willpower and agency. In *No Name* especially, Collins asserts that human beings have inherent character traits that will dictate their behaviour: circumstances may allow for the unlocking of some traits rather than others (for better or worse), but each person has 'inbred forces of Good and Evil' within them that cannot be fundamentally altered (*No Name*, p. 116).

Mary Elizabeth Braddon's *John Marchmont's Legacy* (1863) also engages with themes of self-control and the potential for self-development. Like Collins, Braddon explicitly depicts people as having fundamental personality traits that may work with or against the circumstances in which individuals find themselves, but there are a few clear differences in the two novelists' treatment of the topic. Whereas in *Basil* and *No Name* there is a triggering event that brings out the worst in people (Basil's encounter with Margaret, Mannion's encounter with Basil, the death of Magdalen's parents), *John Marchmont's Legacy* depicts individual character and external circumstances clashing destructively on a day-to-day basis. Also, whilst Collins's characters certainly do not always live up to society's expectations of their class and gender (Magdalen's unladylike behaviour, for example), in *John Marchmont's Legacy* Braddon more explicitly, and more sustainedly, explores Victorian assumptions about the nature of women, and asks what happens when a woman fails to accord with them.

Self-control, willpower and monomania

Braddon uses a narrative voice that is sometimes pitying, but also uncompromising, and that asserts that women naturally possess certain defining qualities, without which they become unwomanly 'mistakes' of 'Nature', victims in a social environment that is unable to sustain them. As the novel progresses, however, there is a growing counter-current that challenges this essentialist perspective of gender whilst maintaining a firm belief in the essential qualities of individuals.

Nature's primary 'victim' in *John Marchmont's Legacy*, and the focus of this chapter, is the poor rector's daughter, Olivia Marchmont, who lives her life according to rigorous, self-imposed ethical standards based on Victorian ideals of religion, class and gender. Olivia Marchmont possesses numerous personal qualities that could be perceived as positive, in fact she has 'all the elements of greatness ... genius, resolution, an indomitable courage, an iron will, perseverance, self-denial, temperance, [and] chastity' (p. 117). But unfortunately for Olivia, we are also told that it is 'not natural to her to be gentle and tender, to be beneficent, compassionate, and kind' (p. 69). Olivia's personality is at odds with her pious lifestyle, making her unpopular, unfulfilled and unhappy; this proves unsustainable, and during the course of the story Olivia succumbs to jealousy and hatred, is exploited by the novel's villain, and eventually loses her grip on sanity. Like Collins, Braddon draws on the prevalent discourse of monomania in her depiction of Olivia's mental deterioration, but significantly, whereas Magdalen experiences inner conflict because of her monomaniacal drive to win the Vanstone fortune, Olivia becomes associated with monomania as a result of the daily struggle she has been suffering as she tries to fulfil the role of a good woman.

Braddon told Bulwer-Lytton that she wanted to write a character (who it may be surmised is Olivia) 'more original' than previous ones (Wolff, 'Devoted Disciple', May 1863, p. 14). Whilst some modern critics have acknowledged Olivia to be a 'powerfully drawn and psychologically complex' character, at the time Braddon's efforts resulted in some scathing critical responses.[2] In his assertion (noted in the introduction, p. 7) that Olivia is 'as unreal as a hobgoblin', W. F. Rae picked out some of the most hyperbolic descriptions for mockery, such as a scene in which she is so enraged by jealousy that 'two streams of lurid light seemed to emanate from [her] dilated grey eyes' (p. 195). Such narrative exaggeration can hide the fact that Braddon clearly wants to explain why Olivia acts as she does.

Victorian stereotypes of womanhood

In order to explore the character of Olivia this chapter draws on two dominant Victorian conceptions of femininity (one social, one biological, both harnessed to the same patriarchal ideology) and builds on the well-established body of criticism that relates to them.[3] The first is the image of the Victorian ideal woman. Questions that were raised about women's social and domestic roles during the nineteenth century generated much literature about the nature of women. Notions of womanliness often blurred the boundaries between what was considered desirable and what was understood to be essential to womanhood; femininity was seen to be innate, not performative. For example, the *Welcome Guest* asserted that women inherently possess a 'softer character', 'easier faith', 'graceful flexibility' and a 'readier acknowledgement of authority'.[4] The ideal woman's character, occupations and mission were frequently referred to in works that addressed the nature and function of women, with little, if any, acknowledgement that she was an aspiration, not a reality. One of the most famous, and particularly demanding, set of criteria was offered in John Ruskin's 1864 lecture 'Of queens' gardens', which asserted that a woman should be 'incapable of error ... enduringly, incorruptibly good; instinctively, infallibly wise'.[5]

As modern critics have noted, the Victorians, influenced by these idealisations, faced difficulties in defining the nature of women. Jeni Curtis observes that

> the ideas of what constitutes a "natural" woman, the middle-class ideal of true womanhood, embodied in the literatures of surveillance, from conduct books to novels, are based on a fundamental paradox. If the books were written on the assumption that woman's nature is fixed and given, what then could be the need for books that also assume that women (and men) can be produced, shaped, and trained?[6]

Curtis therefore suggests that there is a 'repressed counter-assumption' in such literature that 'the nature of woman is suspect' (p. 79). June Sturrock similarly points out that newspaper narratives and fiction show 'the unease arising from a clash between the ideal and the reality of the domestic woman' (pp. 73–4).

This is not to say that ideal and real women were always unthinkingly conflated; several Victorians (and not only those that we would now think of as feminists) also acknowledged a disconnection between the two. In 1851, although claiming that 'a perfect woman is indeed the most exalted of terrestrial creatures – physically, mentally, morally', the *Journal of Psychological Medicine and Mental Pathology* also recognised that 'ideal perfection' is 'rarely, if ever' achieved (anon., 'Woman in her psychological relations', pp. 18, 21). Writing for the *Fortnightly Review* in 1865 Anthony Trollope commented that Ruskin's descriptions of womanhood were written with 'such a charm of exquisite verbal music that the reader ... is often tempted to forget that they have no definite tendency, and that nothing is to be learned from them by any woman living or about to live'.[7] In 1874 *Blackwood's Edinburgh Magazine* called for some level-headedness regarding the role of women in society: 'It is only when the imagination breaks loose, and people begin to discuss ideal woman as she ought to be, and actual woman as she is fancied to be, that the rein is given to considerable bitterness of feeling, and a good deal of sentimental foolishness on both sides.'[8]

John Marchmont's Legacy, published in the midst of these debates, tackles ideas of the ideal and natural woman. Braddon's novel asserts that Olivia's nature is almost entirely 'fixed and given' (Curtis, p. 79), but this nature is the antithesis of the ideal woman. The narrator repeatedly speaks in conservative terms about 'womanhood' and what attributes make 'womanhood beautiful' (p. 69). The thing itself becomes merged with the things that make it beautiful, and both are praised as desirable, but they are precisely what is lacking in Olivia's nature. Moreover, Olivia's supposed unwomanliness is directly connected to her inability to sustain an ethical lifestyle. As Ruskin's comments imply, the ideal woman's goodness was inextricable from her femininity. In order to perform her philanthropic duties, Olivia must suppress her natural inclinations and perform a function she is intrinsically unsuited for. Unable to fulfil her designated social role, her fall into sin comes to seem inevitable. The result of this, however, is not an implication that 'the nature of *woman* is suspect' (Curtis, p. 79, my emphasis), but that the natures of some women do not naturally conform to the Victorian ideal of womanhood. Gilbert distinguishes between the 'body as it has been represented', which is 'generalized ... almost never individual', and the subjective 'lived' bodies of 'real people who differ dramatically from "the" body which represents them' (*Disease*, pp. 15–16). Braddon's novel makes a similar differentiation between concepts of 'womanhood' that are posited as ideal, and individual women who may or may not correspond to these notions. Braddon's distinction rests on the assumption (which she shares with Collins) that each individual is born with an inherent character that may be influenced by environment, but never fundamentally altered. Mary

John Marchmont's Legacy

Poovey demonstrates that the Victorian 'notion' that '"instincts" and a "natural" difference between the sexes delineate social roles' is a historically specific 'concept of nature' that had 'material effects' on the everyday lives of Victorians.[9] By presenting a female character who naturally lacks many feminine qualities, Braddon implicitly acknowledges the 'historical specificity' of the concept of womanhood extolled in Victorian society and literature, and through the story of Olivia she shows the detrimental 'material effects' of trying to live up to such concepts. Even as Braddon's narrator tells us, in highly conservative terms, what it means to be womanly, Braddon is revealing that such qualities do not correlate with all women. It is therefore implied that not every woman (in fact, hardly any women) can fit the mould of the ideal woman, and that inextricably to attach notions of goodness and morality to it is both limiting and dangerous.

The second type of femininity with which this chapter is concerned is based on prevailing Victorian medical discourses that claimed the influence of women's reproductive systems on their behaviour could make them physically, mentally and emotionally volatile. Many doctors asserted that changes in the ovaries could lead to changes of personality including 'morbid appetites', 'hysterical' and 'monomaniacal cunning', 'numerous instances of strange and motiveless deceptions, thefts, and crimes', and 'moral insanity' (anon., 'Woman in her psychological relations', pp. 30–4). Henry Maudsley similarly claimed that some women were driven to commit violent acts 'under the influence of their special bodily functions' (*Responsibility*, p. 163). Olivia's malicious actions (mainly directed towards her stepdaughter, Mary), inspired by passionate unrequited love for her cousin Edward Arundel (who is in love with Mary), seem to confirm a connection between female sexuality and pathological behaviour. In biological terms Olivia could be described as *too* womanly, too much at the mercy of her female physiology. And yet, as Shuttleworth has established, when sensation fiction may appear 'to support the psychiatric framing of the female body', this often covers a conflicting questioning of medical authority and dominant assumptions about gender ('Preaching', p. 193). Braddon's depiction of Olivia is coupled with a critique of the limitations Victorian society placed on women's lives and, while her characterisation 'seems to agree with the alleged sexual-biological foundations of female violence', it also shows 'a direct connection between the narrow existences of nineteenth-century women and the incubation of insane violence' (Mangham, pp. 100, 102).

Braddon appropriates both the prevalent social construction of the ideal woman, and the equally popular physiological understanding of woman as dangerously under the sway of her special biology in her depiction of women in the novel. This leads to undoubted difficulties and apparent contradictions in the characterisation of Olivia, who is at once excessively womanly, and not womanly enough. The close readings in this chapter draw attention to the inconsistencies that are central to the depiction of Olivia, revealing an increasing confusion of cause and effect concerning the order of events shown to instigate her mental deterioration, and the process of deterioration itself. This may be a symptom of the high-pressured environment in which Braddon was working. In the month *John Marchmont's Legacy* commenced in *Temple Bar*, she complained to Bulwer-Lytton that 'the curse of serial writing & hand to mouth composition has set its seal upon me, & I have had to write a lot of things together' (Wolff, 'Devoted Disciple', December 1862, p. 10). Nevertheless, these inconsistencies reveal the incongruity of Victorian conceptions of gender, whilst simultaneously allowing for speculation about what it means to be womanly.

Hughes has argued that Braddon portrays the 'feminine ideal' as 'potentially treacherous, for both the women who conform and the men who worship them; the standard feminine qualities – childishness, self-suppression, the talent for pleasing – inherently contain the seeds of their own destruction' (p. 124). However, it is important to note that Braddon is also often commendatory of the ideal woman, and speculates about what conditions may cultivate her or prevent her development. This is shown by Braddon's employment of two other female characters, Mary Marchmont (Edward's first wife, and Olivia's stepdaughter) and Belinda Lawford (Edward's second wife), who are discussed at the end of this chapter. Critics are often dismissive of Mary and, especially, Belinda. In their introduction to the novel, Tōru Sasaki and Norman Page call Belinda and Mary 'no more than conventional heroines, well qualified to become, successively, the wives of the upright, manly, and fairly conventional hero' (p. xv). Yet it is crucial to recognise not only that Mary and Belinda differ significantly from one another, as well as from Olivia, but that the latter character is a key figure in this novel's engagement with conflicting forms of womanliness. By assessing what makes other characters so 'well qualified', we can discover what it is that makes Olivia so *unqualified* for Edward, and for her lifestyle. Moreover, we can ascertain what combination of determining factors will result in the prized ideal woman.

Olivia and the ideal woman

Olivia may seem like a strange focus for a book about character formation because, although her exceptional personality dominates this novel, Braddon does not explain how she has come by it. In a bitter moment, Olivia comments that the 'blood of the Dangerfield Arundels must have had some drop of poison intermingled with it ... before it could produce so vile a creature as myself' (p. 244). Here Olivia shares the readiness increasingly embraced (as demonstrated in later chapters) by many Victorians to attribute moral flaws to hereditary transmission. Tellingly, the mother is indicated as a possible source of corruption; not only was it the woman who married "into" a family, thus importing outside influences, but 'it was widely understood that mothers were more likely to bequeath insanity' (Mangham, p. 35). However, Olivia immediately counters this possibility by adding 'yet I have heard people say that my mother was a good woman' (p. 244). On the other side, Olivia shares her father's pride and energy, but the description of his 'wild' days at 'college' suggests a sociable and unrestrained personality unlike his daughter's (pp. 6–7). Heredity, therefore, does not clearly account for Olivia's character, nor are we given much useful information about her childhood. She consequently enters the novel as a grown woman with a developed, but unaccounted for, personality; she is fittingly likened to Pallas Athenë, who sprang fully formed from the forehead of Zeus (p. 78).

Nevertheless, Olivia's inherent qualities are paramount to her characterisation and she is immediately described as the possessor of 'dangerous gifts', a 'fatal dowry of beauty and intellect and pride' (p. 8). Yet, as her concerned father tells himself, she also possesses strict 'religious principles' and a 'sense of duty' that 'are strong enough to keep her right under any circumstances, in spite of any temptation' (p. 8). The implication is that as a beautiful, young, near-penniless woman, Olivia may be vulnerable to inappropriate propositions. Hubert Arundel's fears manifest in an ironic fashion as Olivia twice accepts inappropriate propositions, but neither man is swayed by Olivia's youth or beauty and she has little interest in their fortunes: first, John Marchmont asks to marry Olivia in order to secure a stepmother for his daughter, Mary; second, the villain Paul Marchmont makes a more sinister proposition concerning Mary. Most importantly, even before these key moments, it is Olivia's 'sense of duty' that initiates her downfall.

Olivia's life, the narrator informs us, may be 'told in these few words: she did her duty ... uncomplainingly, unswervingly' (p. 66). As a rector's daughter Olivia's duties would comprise of charitable works similar to those carried out by ladies of the landed gentry on their estates.[10] Olivia is a 'young saint' in 'shabby gowns' who earns the commendation of the local 'dowagers' and of the 'bishop of the diocese' for her displays of 'active devotion' (p. 66). She visits the homes of the sick whilst remaining 'sublimely indifferent to the foul weather without, to the stifling atmosphere within, to dirt, discomfort, poverty, inconvenience' (p. 67). To this extent Olivia's behaviour is in keeping with that of the ideal woman, who, as *Temple Bar* asserted in an article appearing the year before it serialised *John Marchmont's Legacy*, should be 'generally active and helpful, and charitable in thought and word and deed'.[11]

However, despite the approbation she earns, there is something disconcerting about Olivia that causes Mary to recoil involuntarily when they meet, prompting the narrator to ask: 'what was it in Olivia Arundel's handsome face from which those who looked at her so often shrank, repelled and disappointed?' (p. 63). The response takes the form of a lengthy physiognomic description of Olivia, a sample of which reads: 'The handsome mouth was rigid; the dark grey eyes had a cold light in them. The thick bands of raven-black hair were drawn tightly off a square forehead, which was the brow of an intellectual and determined man rather than of a woman' (p. 63). This analysis leads the narrator to a comprehension of what is so off-putting in Olivia's appearance: 'Yes; womanhood was the something wanted in Olivia Arundel's face. Intellect, resolution, courage, are rare gifts; but they are not the gifts whose tokens we look for most anxiously in a woman's face' (p. 63). The gifts 'we look for' are named explicitly in the following lines, as the narrator suggests that Olivia 'might have been a very great queen', but one who would show neither 'mercy' nor 'compassion' (p. 63). The guileless Mary is unaware of the reasons for her response (p. 64), but the narrator's use of the inclusive 'we' suggests that whether they know it or not, everyone looks for certain traits in women. This revelation of an incongruity between Olivia's outward performance of her duty, her inward personality and the attributes seen to befit her gender is corroborated throughout the novel and is the reason why each of Olivia's 'perfectly-modelled features' is 'beautiful to look at; but, as a whole, the face was not beautiful' (p. 63).

'Beautiful' becomes a key word in the descriptions of women in this novel and, in keeping with the established links between internal nature and external appearance, refers to both physical and moral attractiveness. The narrator emphasises the difficulties of interpretation posed by the dichotomy between Olivia's innate personality and the woman she is trying to be:

> How shall I anatomise this woman, who, gifted with no womanly tenderness of nature, unendowed with that pitiful and unreasoning affection which makes womanhood beautiful, yet tried, and tried unceasingly, to do her duty, and to be good; clinging, in the very blindness of her soul, to the rigid formulas of her faith, but unable to seize upon its spirit?
>
> (p. 69)

In this restatement that Olivia has been denied natural womanly gifts there is a slight modification, as here we told that Olivia lacks what 'makes womanhood beautiful', not womanhood itself. And in fact there are moments when Olivia is characterised in relation to other stereotypically feminine traits. For example, Olivia shuns fine clothes and 'there was no natural womanly vanity, no simple girlish fancy, which this woman had not trodden under foot, and trampled out in the hard pathway she had chosen for herself' (p. 67), implying that at least some vanity and fancy were within her initially. Moreover, although Olivia is 'unblest with many of the charms of womanhood' she is 'not entirely without its weaknesses' (p. 85); these weaknesses induce her to accept John Marchmont's hand in marriage as revenge against Edward (who has chosen Mary over her). So Olivia is not entirely unwomanly, she is the wrong *type* of woman; she is not the Victorian ideal of womanhood. Nevertheless, the overall drive of this early part of the novel works to conflate, rather than to distinguish between, the 'charms of womanhood' and womanhood itself; the things that are distinctively womanly (tenderness, mercy and so on) are also the things that make women beautiful. And, from this point onwards, the things that make women beautiful are also asserted to be the things that make them good (and vice versa). Similar claims are frequently repeated in the surrounding pages, aligning a woman's moral worth and beauty with her ability to act in a manner befitting her gender.

Two conflicting conceptions of "nature" emerge here – the traits that are inbuilt into Olivia's constitution, and those that are natural to womanhood (and make it lovely and good): 'it was not natural to [Olivia] to be gentle and tender, to be beneficent, compassionate, and kind ... That divine and universal pity, that spontaneous and boundless affection, which is the chief loveliness of womanhood and Christianity, had no part in her nature' (p. 69). The connection between 'womanhood and Christianity' is important here. One of the main ways in which notions of real and ideal women became confused in Victorian writing on the

Self-control, willpower and monomania

subject concerned women's supposedly intuitively spiritual nature. For example, the *Quarterly Review* argued that women need not study theology because 'there is no need to teach them wider charities, or more trustful and unaffected piety. Those, in the true woman, are innate.'[12] Olivia's inability to embrace the 'spirit' of Christianity is a further denial of her 'true' womanliness. This explains why, despite Olivia's untiring dedication to the poor, it is not only Mary who feels aversion towards her. Although the parishioners are 'grateful' for her efforts, Olivia does not enjoy 'the love and gratitude, the tenderness and blessings, which usually wait upon the footsteps of those who do good deeds' (p. 67). The narrator identifies 'a lack of personal tenderness in her kindness, which separated her from the people she benefited ... she was always the same,—Church-of-England charity personified ... rigidly just, terribly perfect' (pp. 67–8).

Braddon's depiction of Olivia's benevolent activities is also an engagement with mid-Victorian concerns about the nature and purpose of philanthropic works performed by women. Dickens, for example, parodied women who supposedly directed their charitable energies wrongly in *Bleak House* (1853), with Mrs Jellyby (who neglects her family and the London poor in favour of overseas charities) and Mrs Pardiggle (whose preaching and dispensing of tracts and criticism make no practical difference to the lives of those she visits). In several of Braddon's novels women's charitable acts and the spirit in which they perform them are an indication of moral worth and a means of winning (or losing) reader sympathy. One of the redeeming features of *The Lady Lisle*'s (1862) avaricious Olivia Marmaduke is that she is good to her pensioners during her time as Lady Lisle. Contrastingly, in the later *The Lovels of Arden* (1871) Miss Granger has inherited 'all the commercial faculties of her father' but has 'no other outlet for this mercantile genius' than 'to expend her gifts upon the petty details of a woman's life', which means dictating and enforcing good domestic habits in 'her poor'.[13] To her schoolchildren she seems 'a kind of prophetess, sent upon earth for their correction and abasement' (p. 139). Although the depictions of excessive philanthropy are used to comment on the restrictive nature of women's lives, Miss Granger draws little reader sympathy and the narrator often pokes fun at her po-faced attitude. Braddon's more serious and frequent focalisation through Olivia, and emphasis on the determining factors that mean she cannot feel satisfied with her life, make for a more complicated response to the character.

Indeed, while Braddon's narrator is not as compassionate towards Olivia's internal struggle as Collins's is towards Magdalen's, it is made clear that she is very aware of her shortcomings and is 'for ever fighting against her nature' and 'for ever striving to do right' (p. 69). In one sense, Olivia chooses to do the right thing: caring for her father's parishioners, nursing the sick, offering religious education, acting as a conventional "good woman". But as in this novel 'to do right' means to display the qualities that make 'womanhood beautiful', this is something that Olivia can only ever manage in the most superficial fashion because she is constitutionally unsuited for the role she is playing. She may be 'charitable in thought and word and deed' (to return to *Temple Bar*'s words) but she cannot *feel* it: 'she could be good to her father's parishioners, and she could make sacrifices for them; but she could not love them, any more than they could love her' (p. 69). Similarly, when she becomes Mary's stepmother Olivia 'would have loved her stepdaughter ... if she could have done so; but *she could not* – she could not' (p. 101, emphasis in original).

Olivia's denial of her own nature in favour of conformity is initially presented as admirable; the narrator asks 'and who shall say that such a woman as this, if she persevere unto the end, shall not wear a brighter crown than her more gentle sisters,—the starry circlet of a martyr?' (p. 69). There is even a slight implication that an alternative model of goodness may be put forward when we are told that Olivia is 'not a good woman, in the commoner sense we attach to the phrase' (p. 69). Yet the narrator does not allow us to dwell on such possibilities; there is no doubt that Olivia is doomed to 'fling' down 'her burden' and 'abandon herself to the eager devils who had been watching for her so untiringly' (p. 70). This challenges mid-Victorian advocates of the cultivation of willpower as a key to stability, who claimed that hysteria and other mental derangements were the result of a 'habitual want of self-control' (Carpenter, *Human Physiology*, p. 662). Olivia has an 'iron will' (p. 117), but her constant self-control, her attempts to be "good", take a physical toll: 'the deepening circles about her eyes, the hollowing cheeks, and the feverish restlessness of manner which she could not always control, told how terrible the long struggle had become to her' (p. 69). This depiction of Olivia also contradicts English Christian ideology, which posited 'self-suppression as a means to self-fulfilment' (Reed, p. 83). Braddon in fact anticipates later fictional works about the danger of repression such as Robert Louis Stevenson's *Strange Case of Dr Jekyll and Mr Hyde* (1886). She also looks forward to Thomas Hardy's portrayal of Boldwood in *Far from the Madding Crowd* (1874), whom Ellie Cope reads as a man whose 'long-repressed sexual drives and emotional impulses are stimulated by Bathsheba', leading to monomaniacal obsession (p. 39). Boldwood is therefore a literary descendant of Olivia, although, as argued below, sexual repression is not the only, or even the primary, reason for Olivia's obsession with Edward.

Importantly, even as she acknowledges the damage caused by years of repression, Braddon clearly asserts that there is something fundamentally wrong with Olivia's nature. Even before she has committed any questionable act, we are asked to 'imagine a woman with a wicked heart steadfastly trying to do good, and to be good', and are assured that this 'dark and horrible picture' is 'the only true picture' of Olivia (p. 83). Braddon leaves Olivia with no middle ground: repression is unhealthy and unsustainable, but a failure to live in a way befitting her gender will lead to moral ruin; if she cannot be a good woman, she must be a wicked one. Such melodramatic language correctly forewarns that when Olivia does abandon her course of right living, the consequences will be dire: enraged by jealousy when Edward falls in love with Mary, she mistreats her stepdaughter until she runs away from home; later she allows Mary to be kidnapped and cheated out of her fortune by Paul Marchmont. At this stage in the novel the fault is shown to be within Olivia's original constitution – she is a naturally *un*natural mistake of nature, wicked because unwomanly, and predetermined to be a villain.

Olivia and physiological conceptions of womanhood

Although Braddon does not explain the congenital determining factors that lead to Olivia's mental constitution, her early depiction of Olivia firmly asserts the notion of an original constitution that can only be modified to an extent, whether by the individual herself, or by the environmental influences to which she is exposed. Environmental determinism is important, however, precisely because Olivia's fundamental nature cannot be trained to find satisfaction with her lifestyle and surroundings. Swampington, 'one of the dullest and dampest towns in fenny Lincolnshire' (p. 6), has a definite detrimental impact on Olivia's mental health. Saverio Tomaiuolo's analysis of the early descriptions of Swampington demonstrates how Braddon 'foregrounds the presence of images connected to useless/excessive abundance' that reflect Olivia's mental state.[14] Descriptions of Olivia's personality are interspersed with frequent reminders that she leads 'a fearfully monotonous, narrow, and uneventful life' (*John Marchmont's Legacy*, p. 68):

> She was weary of her life. She sickened under the dull burden which she had borne so long, and carried so patiently. The slow round of duty was

loathsome to her. The horrible, narrow, unchanging existence, shut in by cruel walls, which bounded her on every side and kept her prisoner to herself, was odious to her. The powerful intellect revolted against the fetters that bound and galled it. The proud heart beat with murderous violence against the bonds that kept it captive.

(p. 68)

The use of anaphora and images of captivity, illness and repulsion emphasise the mind-numbingly repetitive and claustrophobic state of Olivia's existence. This continues throughout the chapter; key words such as 'narrow' are repeated multiple times in subsequent paragraphs (and repetition in general is a distinctive feature in Braddon's descriptions of Olivia). To an extent Olivia's suffering is self-inflicted; the 'cruel walls' and 'bonds' to which she chooses to submit are figurative. But she has imprisoned herself, as we have seen, out of an attempt to be the tender Christian woman that society values. Her 'intellect' may be 'powerful', but this is not what is required of a rector's daughter in monotonous Swampington.

Intertwined with the descriptions of Olivia's devotion to duty and boredom with her life are references to another aspect of her character that clashes with both of these, her 'passionate nature':

'Is my life always to be this—always, always, always?' The passionate nature burst forth sometimes, and the voice that had so long been stifled cried aloud in the black stillness of the night, 'Is it to go on for ever and for ever … is the lot of other women never to be mine? Am I never to be loved and admired; never to be sought and chosen? Is my life to be all of one dull, grey, colourless monotony …?'

(pp. 68–9)

Despite Olivia's failure to adhere to the stereotype of the ideal woman, she clearly expresses what most Victorians would accept as a typically feminine desire for romance. Yet Olivia has never received a suitor because her 'inherent want of tenderness … chilled and dispirited the timid young Lincolnshire squires' (p. 70). Her cousin Edward is impressed by her learning, but significantly dismisses Olivia's beauty as having a 'little too much of the Pallas Athenë about it' (p. 78). Such comments would resonate with Victorian readers who had been following contemporary debates over female education and the views of writers such as Herbert Spencer, who asked 'how many conquests does the blue-stocking make through her extensive knowledge of history?'[15]

Olivia's unreciprocated infatuation with Edward is an important phase in her downfall, but also leads to some confusion of characterisation.

Whereas previously womanly tenderness is said to be entirely lacking in Olivia's nature, once her feelings for Edward are introduced this no longer seems to be the case: 'All that was tender or womanly in her nature had been wasted upon her hopeless love for Edward Arundel. The utter wreck of that small freight of affection had left her nature warped and stunted, soured, disappointed, unwomanly' (p. 101). Here her love for Edward is the reason that she has no womanly feelings. Only a few pages later, however, we are told that 'it was not in her nature to love. Her passionate idolatry of her boyish cousin had been the one solitary affection that had ever held a place in her cold heart' (p. 114), and (later still) that Edward is 'the only creature who had ever had the power to awake the instinct of womanhood in her soul' (p. 160). The phrase 'not in her nature' is a telling one: used casually it means that a tendency is unusual (as in 'it was not in her nature to be up before 9am'), but the constant emphasis in this novel on what does and does not constitute Olivia's nature gives it an added weight. These confusions of cause and effect may well be because Braddon made concessions during serialisation, allowing Olivia a 'small freight of affection', just enough to move the plot forward. They also suggest the numerous deterministic paths that may have led to Olivia's current state, but weaken the earlier certainty about her original constitution. Despite the inconsistencies, there is no doubt that Olivia's feelings for Edward are detrimental; they drive her to contravene every personal standard she has striven to uphold.

Although Olivia is unwomanly by Victorian social standards, her excessive passion reflects much Victorian medical writing on female mental physiology. It is notable that, although Olivia is not particularly spiritual, while exhaustively performing good works, she pours her feelings into sermons that are 'fierce denunciatory protests against the inherent wickedness of the human heart' (p. 83). Excessive religious devotion was often viewed with concern by Victorian physicians as it was seen as 'a form of displacement for sexual energy'.[16] For example, the physician J. G. Millingen claimed that women are both highly spiritual, and 'more forcibly under the control of matter' than men, meaning that they are 'subject to all the aberrations of love and religion' and that 'the latter becomes a resource when the excitement of the former is exhausted by disappointment, infidelity and age'.[17] Hughes sees Olivia as 'a study in sexual repression', and her religious zeal as both 'an instrument of self-suppression and self-torture' and 'an indirect outlet for her passion' (pp. 131–2). Medical men often wrote about the problematic effects of sexual repression in women; Henry Maudsley insisted that in unmarried women the 'whole system feels severely the effects of an unsatisfied sexual passion, and exhibits these in irregular bodily functions, in restlessness, irritability, and moodiness of mind, and in a morbid self-feeling, taking a variety of forms'.[18] Carpenter pointed out that propriety often restricted women's ability to express their sexuality: 'in all that relates to sexual love, she is frequently restrained by a sense of decorum from giving outward expression to feelings which she is secretly brooding-over, and whose injurious influence she is exaggerating by the attention she gives to them' (*Human Physiology*, p. 663).

Olivia's struggle to suppress her feelings may well be, therefore, the reason for both her religious zeal and her mental instability. Her passion for Edward is the 'blight of her life', and the narrator speculates that if she had not loved him she 'might have grown out of her natural self by force of her conscientious desire to do right; and might have become, indeed, a good and perfect woman' (p. 86) – i.e. she might have submitted to the constraints of her 'narrow life'. Instead Olivia broods over Edward, exaggerating the 'injurious influence' of her thoughts. Much later on the narrator also hypothesises that if Olivia 'could have been Edward Arundel's wife, she would have been the noblest and truest wife that ever merged her identity into that of another ... She would have been great by reason of her power of self-abnegation' (pp. 356–7). In both cases (if she had never met Edward, or if she had married him) there is the possibility that Olivia could somehow repress or subdue her 'fierce nature' (p. 357). Like the physicians quoted above, Braddon here contradicts another stereotype of womanhood – the idea, upheld by doctors such as William Acton, that women were lacking in sexual feeling.[19] Olivia's mental deterioration is attributable to an excited, but unreleased, sexual desire and the narrator argues that in Olivia 'all the volcanic forces of an impetuous nature, concentrated into one narrow focus, wasted themselves upon this one feeling [for Edward], until that which should have been a sentiment became a madness' (p. 86).

The 'madness' that develops in Olivia is not *directly* identified as monomania, but the language used to describe her mental state is (as with Magdalen) so reliant on the discourse surrounding the condition that readers would undoubtedly have had it in mind. Also like Magdalen, the narrator describes a battle between Olivia's "better" self and her fixed idea:

> It was a madness, an isolated madness, which stood alone in [Olivia's] soul, and fought for mastery over her better aspirations, her wiser thoughts. We are all familiar with strange stories of wise and great minds which have

been ridden by some hobgoblin fancy, some one horrible monomania; a bleeding head upon a dish, a grinning skeleton playing hide-and-seek ... some devilry or other before which the master-spirit shrank and dwindled until the body withered and the victim died.

(p. 116)

Although Olivia does not actually hallucinate, Braddon conjures up images of monomaniacs who do, thereby giving Olivia's love for Edward a destructive and malevolent appearance. Her 'master-spirit' does indeed begin to waste away before the image of Edward Arundel:

> Yes; she thought of him for ever and ever. The narrow life to which she doomed herself, the self-immolation which she called duty, left her a prey to this one thought. Her work was not enough for her. Her powerful mind wasted and shrivelled for want of worthy employment. It was like one vast roll of parchment whereon half the wisdom of the world might have been inscribed, but on which was only written over and over again, in maddening repetition, the name of Edward Arundel.

(pp. 135–6)

Olivia's mind is worn down as it returns again and again to Edward, but it becomes clear here that her obsession with him may be not the cause of her madness, but a symptom of her 'narrow life'. Her great reserves of energy and passion become misdirected towards Edward because she has nowhere else to expend them. It becomes increasingly clear that Olivia's love for Edward is a by-product of unfulfilled potential, that she is wasting 'a world of intellect and passion upon this bright-haired boy' (p. 86). In those passages which most clearly describe the monomaniacal aspects of Olivia's affections, the sense of misspent intellectual capabilities is far more evident than her repressed sexual desires.

The narrator's conjecture that if 'her life had been a wider one, this wasted love would, perhaps, have shrunk into its proper insignificance' undermines a reading of Olivia as merely a slave to her female biology (p. 86). Indeed, even those doctors who wrote about excessive female passion often also commented on the fact that women's restricted existence in Victorian society could exacerbate mental instability. Maudsley, for example, claimed that unmarried women who had 'no aim in life to work for, no outlet for their energies in outward activity, are sometimes driven to a morbid self-brooding, or to an excessive religious devotion' ('On some of the causes', p. 492). As Shuttleworth observes:

> Braddon draws on the contemporary discourse of psychiatry to depict the destructive impact of sexuality on Olivia. This is not some unexplained

monomania, however, but the explicit product of the limited conditions of her life and her willed adherence to ideologies of female self-negation. Female violence and evil, the text asserts, are not the result of physiological aberrations but are directly produced by the social conventions governing Victorian femininity.

('Preaching', p. 217)

Olivia is often likened by the narrator to women with powerful, potentially admirable qualities, but dangerous and morally questionable reputations: she has 'the ambition of a Semiramis, the courage of a Boadicea, the resolution of a Lady Macbeth' (p. 130), 'ambition which might have made her an empress' (p. 85), and is 'by nature dauntless and resolute as the hero of some classic story' (p. 244). Such examples emphasise abilities wasted, distorted, eventually becoming ruinous. The historical and/or legendary nature of many of them suggest the impossibility of Olivia fulfilling her potential in the world as it is. Whilst in an alternative reality Olivia could have been a great (if not a good) woman, her actual situation leaves her 'chained down, bound, trammelled by her love for' Edward (p. 117).

In fact, throughout the novel there seems to be no limit to what Olivia might have been. Braddon gives an array of possible alternatives for Olivia that would fill the same hole in her life as her affection for Edward. Romantic or domestic fulfilment is not the only, or even necessarily the preferable, means of occupation for Olivia:

> If Olivia Marchmont could have gone to America, and entered herself amongst the feminine professors of law or medicine,—if she could have turned field-preacher, like simple Dinah Morris, or set up a printing-press in Bloomsbury, or even written a novel,—I think she might have been saved. The superabundant energy of her mind would have found a new object. As it was, she did none of these things. She had only dreamt one dream, and by force of perpetual repetition the dream had become a madness.
>
> (p. 136)

Again, alternative lifestyles are placed out of Olivia's reach. In some cases Olivia's personality remains a drawback: Braddon's mention of George Eliot's gentle and angelic Dinah Morris simply serves to show how unsuited Olivia is to turn 'field-preacher', and it seems likely that her aversion to frivolous activity would prevent her from writing a novel. As for a medical career, it is true that this passage would have been particularly significant to readers in the early 1860s when the 'image of the first female physician, Elizabeth Garrett', was 'looming over mid-Victorian society' (Mangham, p. 102), but whereas this would not be an entirely impossible dream for some female readers of the novel, *John Marchmont's Legacy* is set from the late 1830s to the mid-1850s, so for Olivia (who in any case could not afford the training) it would have been unattainable.

Ultimately Olivia's dreams remain unfulfilled and she is doomed to repeat the monotonous rounds of visiting that were so damaging to her in the first place: 'day by day she went the same round from cottage to cottage ... exhibiting an unwearying patience that was akin to sublimity' (p. 484). However, there is now an important difference in Olivia. The narrator states that 'passion had burnt itself out in this woman's breast, and there was nothing in her mind now but remorse', and that the people of Swampington believe that she is 'not quite right in her mind' (p. 484). Hughes argues that not only does Braddon 'admire this strange villainess', but she 'seems to warm to her own creation once Olivia has lost all control' (p. 133). Her basis for asserting this is that whilst other characters are either 'killed off' (Mary) or 'sparingly provided' with a happy ending (Edward and Belinda), Olivia is 'never exposed or punished' and in fact ends up respected by the villagers (Hughes, p. 133). And yet, after the many pages dedicated to Olivia's hatred of this lifestyle it seems particularly cruel to leave her where she began. In fact, although Olivia is physically in the dark-haired "Aurora Floyd" mould, her fate is much closer to that of the "buried alive" Lucy Audley than to that of Aurora, who ends her story mature and chastened. I rather agree with Shuttleworth, who thinks that Olivia's fate is perhaps 'even worse' than Lucy's ('Preaching', p. 220), and with Lillian Nayder, who asserts that 'Olivia is conquered by gender expectations and norms.'[20] Olivia is forced into submission; not constitutionally inclined towards any of the female attributes that would make 'womanhood beautiful', she can only fulfil the role of a good woman through the complete effacement of her personality.

Natalie and Ronald A. Schroeder suggest that even though 'Olivia's madness originates in the pressure from those cultural contradictions that both construct and victimize her', Braddon 'dilutes' her social critique through her choice to make Olivia insane because this undermines the 'threat' she poses 'to patriarchal hegemony'.[21] I would take this further, because before Olivia's final defeat, Braddon's characterisation of her is further confused by a change in the narrator's assessment of her mental faculties and the origins of her insanity. Whereas initially the bad combination of narrow lifestyle and vast intellect results in Olivia's dissatisfaction with life, later Olivia's mind is described in terms that reflect aspects of her lifestyle. For example, she is described as one of 'these strong-minded women, whose minds are strong because of their narrowness, and who are the bonden slaves of one idea', in whose 'violent and concentrative natures the line that separates reason from madness is so feeble a demarcation, that very few can perceive the hour in which it is passed' (p. 356). Olivia's mind no longer has room for 'half the wisdom of the world' (p. 135), it is as narrow as her lifestyle, and she is now described as constitutionally predisposed towards monomania. Although Braddon is definitely concerned with explaining Olivia's extreme behaviour, she is not writing with a clear set of deterministic rules in mind. The more Olivia becomes an obviously hopeless case, the more the narrator begins to suggest that she was constitutionally preconditioned for such an outcome all along (we will see this again in the next chapter's discussion of James Arnold). In a sense, Olivia's ending echoes the fates of Dickens's female characters, as read by Wood, 'whose passionate excess seems on the surface of things to parody the model of woman's confinement within the domestic sphere' but who then suffer 'savagely punitive treatment' that works to 're-inscribe', rather than critique, 'the prescriptive doctrines of womanhood' (Wood, p. 10). And yet, while her choices concerning the characterisation of Olivia may partially neutralise Braddon's critique of Victorian patriarchal restraints on women's lives, Braddon's subtle but significant shift in characterisation also demonstrates how much she has warmed to Olivia (to paraphrase Hughes) and is a means of softening the blow; some of Olivia's formidableness, and also the sense of potential tragically wasted in the wrong environment, are lost by the end of the novel, and the distance that she has to fall is not quite so great.

Alternative models of womanhood: the too ideal woman

Olivia's utter unsuitability for her lifestyle, her gender, her moment in history, is further emphasised by comparison with the two heroines of the novel, Mary Marchmont and Belinda Lawford. Influenced by both inherent and environmental determining factors, these women fulfil, to varying extents and in different ways, the role of ideal woman in a manner impossible for Olivia.

Like Olivia, when we first meet Mary there is something about her that strikes the observer, and is revealed through further scrutiny: 'it was impossible to look at her without a vague feeling of pain, that was difficult to understand. You knew, by-and-by, why you were sorry for this little girl. She had never been a child' (p. 18). The narrator goes on to explain that the 'ruthless hand of poverty' has precipitated Mary's development so that 'at eight years old she was a woman,—a woman invested with all that is most beautiful amongst womanly attributes—love, tenderness, compassion, carefulness for others, unselfish devotion, uncomplaining patience, heroic endurance' (p. 18). The latter attributes in the list are also displayed by Olivia before her downfall, but the first three are specifically those that Olivia lacks (excepting her self-destructive love for Edward, of course). Ideal womanliness is a state that Mary achieves prematurely, one that Olivia is unable to achieve. Although environmental determinism in the form of the 'ruthless hand of poverty' has undoubtedly affected Mary, there are a number of indications that she is constitutionally predisposed towards those 'womanly attributes' that *John Marchmont's Legacy* extols. Mary has never been 'vulgarised' by the years of poverty she has endured because of 'her self-contained nature', which 'took no colour from the things that surrounded her'; there is, it seems, an underlying purity that means hardship cannot tarnish Mary's personality (p. 49).

Mary also has a 'capacity' for learning 'far beyond her years' (p. 35), but whereas Olivia's intellect is off-putting, Mary's contributes towards her emotional responsiveness: 'intellect here reigned supreme. Instead of the animal spirits of a thoughtless child, there was a woman's loving carefulness for others, a woman's unselfishness and devotion' (p. 59). As she grows older Mary retains her womanly traits, but also remains 'infantine in her innocence and inexperience of the world outside' (p. 133). This combination of innocent childishness and tender womanliness proves a winning one. When he is reunited with Mary after some years abroad, Edward can 'remember no one as fascinating as this girl, who seemed as childlike now, in her early womanhood, as she had been womanly while she was a child' (pp. 142–3).[22]

As well as being 'delicate like her mother' (p. 26), Mary shares with her father 'an affection that was almost morbid in its intensity', suggesting a hereditary trait (p. 19). Indeed, Mary's 'morbidly sensitive rather than strong' mind is one of her distinguishing features, and one that is partly responsible for her womanly demeanour (p. 22). When her father inherits Marchmont Towers, Mary does 'not forget to be good to the poor', paying visits, reading New Testament stories and distributing 'brandy, and wine, and milk, and woollen stuffs, and grocery' (p. 48). Whereas Olivia diligently but empty-heartedly ministers to her father's parishioners in Swampington, we are told that Mary's 'morbidly sensitive nature adapted her to all charitable offices ... She had a subtle and intuitive comprehension of other people's feelings, derived from the extreme susceptibility of her own' (p. 49). Mary is instinctively the good woman that Olivia tries and fails to be. Her natural 'guilelessness' and 'blind confidence' make another attractive feature, which may be potentially 'dangerous' but is, the narrator assures us, one of the most 'beautiful and pure things upon this earth' (p. 104). Mary's morbid sensitivity proves a threat to her goodness on one occasion, after her father's death, when 'a sudden agony, that was near akin to madness, seized upon this girl, in whose sensitive nature affection had always had a morbid intensity' (p. 110). Mary is inclined towards suicide but her constitutional weakness actually saves her when she faints away before she can perform the act. Whereas Olivia is tried to the point where she sins, Mary is protected by a combination of environmental influences and inherent constitution.

Olivia is aware of the difference between herself and Mary, and wonders 'What had she done, this girl, who had never known what it was to fight a battle with her own rebellious heart? what had she done, that all this wealth of love and happiness should drop into her lap unsought,— comparatively unvalued, perhaps?' (p. 150). Although the narrator is generally admiring of Mary, the use of free indirect discourse here allows the narrative voice to convey empathetically some of Olivia's bitterness. Whilst not necessarily condoning Olivia's behaviour or devaluing womanly virtues it is shows clearly that the temperamentally gentle Mary certainly finds life easier than the naturally dynamic Olivia.

However, Mary's special brand of womanliness comes at a price, and the 'wealth of love and happiness' that Olivia envies is short-lived. Olivia and Mary share the quality of being unsuited to their present surroundings, but whereas the former could display her 'greatness' (p. 117) in another time, another place, another gender, Mary seems unfitted for the mortal world altogether, being described as 'the poor pale neglected flower, the fragile lily, the frail exotic blossom, that was so cruelly out of place upon the bleak pathways of life!' (p. 14). Indeed, Mary's life is short and tragic. She never really gets to experience the material rewards of being a good woman, the 'happiness of a home; the sweet sense of ownership; the delight of dispensing pleasure to others; all the simple domestic joys which make life beautiful' (p. 376). When Mary is about to return to Marchmont Towers as a married woman Edward (again revealing his delight in her childishness) praises her 'pretty, infantine, unworldly spirit', and wishes they could be 'two grown-up babes in the wood, and could wander about gathering wild flowers' (pp. 204–5). The fairy-tale imagery reasserts the sense that Mary is not at home in the world as it is. In true sensational fashion, Mary is prevented from returning to fulfil her role as mistress of Marchmont Towers and a grown 'woman of business' when disaster strikes; Edward is severely injured in a railway accident before their marriage can be made public.

Mary is conditioned for suffering; she is a 'poor broken-hearted girl, whose many sorrows had brought her to look upon life as a thing which was never meant to be joyful, and which was only to be endured patiently' (p. 455). From early on in the novel the narrator wonders whether she is 'already marked out for some womanly martyrdom – already set apart for more than common suffering?' (p. 55). From this point Mary is frequently figured as a martyr and eventually comes to resemble a celestial rather than an earthly being: she herself resolves to be a martyr, convinced that she is willing to suffer and die for her father (p. 97); after her ordeal at the hands of Olivia and Paul Marchmont, her face appears so 'deathly pale ... there was something almost supernal in the brightness of that white, wasted face; something that reminded [Edward] of the countenance of a martyr who has ceased to suffer the anguish of death in a foretaste of the joys of Heaven' (p. 434). Mary dies young and so does not get more than a taste of acting as a wife and mother, but we are assured that 'she was very happy; and her nature, always gentle, seemed sublimated by the sufferings she had endured, and already akin to that of the angels' (p. 480). The overtly religious ending of the novel describes Mary taking her place in heaven, and smiling upon Edward 'from amidst the vast throng of angel faces' (p. 487). The prematurely womanly Mary receives her reward in the end, becoming something she never was on earth (except to the extent to tantalise Edward): 'a child for ever and ever before the throne of God!' (p. 487). Whilst Olivia can only struggle in vain to win the 'starry circlet of a martyr', Mary is predisposed, through constitution and upbringing, towards martyrdom (p. 69).

Alternative models of womanhood: the *ideal* ideal woman

Belinda has received very little critical attention, generally being seen as 'little more than a replica of Mary' (Schroeder and Schroeder, p. 121). While Shuttleworth acknowledges the importance of Mary by suggesting that the role of heroine is 'divided' between her and Olivia, she only briefly describes Belinda as 'a less fragile and childlike bride' for Edward

John Marchmont's Legacy

('Preaching', pp. 215, 219). Certainly, Belinda is introduced more than halfway through the novel, and she does not have much actually to "do", other than fall in love with and (eventually) marry Edward. Nevertheless, it is telling that Braddon felt the need to provide a more robust substitute for Mary. Indeed, whereas Shuttleworth identifies Mary as an 'archetype of womanliness' ('Preaching', p. 216), Belinda, the 'blooming English maiden' (*John Marchmont's Legacy*, p. 315), is in fact the epitome of ideal womanhood, and the characterisation of Olivia and Mary cannot be fully appreciated without comparison to her. When Edward first sees her he feels 'instinctively that she was as good as she was beautiful' (p. 312). Belinda wins love from Edward, and indeed everyone around her. The following passage is worth quoting at length because it is here that we are given a description of the earthly, womanly ideal that neither Mary nor Olivia can fulfil, and of the environment required for creating such an individual. The description is at least as impossible as Ruskin's assessment of the ideal woman, quoted at the start of this chapter:

> She had the beauty of goodness, and to admire her was to do homage to the purest and brightest attributes of womanhood ... the beauties of tenderness, truth, faith, earnestness, hope and charity, were enthroned upon her broad white brow, and crowned her queen by right of divine womanly perfection. A loving and devoted daughter, an affectionate sister, a true and faithful friend, an untiring benefactress to the poor, a gentle mistress, a well-bred Christian lady; in every duty and in every position she bore out and sustained the impression which her beauty made on the minds of those who looked upon her. She was only nineteen years of age, and no sorrow had ever altered the brightness of her nature. She lived a happy life with a father who was proud of her, and with a mother who resembled her in almost every attribute. She led a happy but a busy life, and did her duty to the poor about her as scrupulously as even Olivia had done in the old days at Swampington Rectory; but in such a genial and cheerful spirit as to win, not cold thankfulness, but heartfelt love and devotion from all who partook of her benefits.
>
> (p. 316)

As with Mary, the qualities that Olivia is said to lack are all part of what makes Belinda endearing. The good works that are soul-destroying to Olivia are pleasurable and fulfilling for Belinda. Like Mary, Belinda has done little, it seems, other than be born with a personality type that happens to render her appealing, but also with good health; modest wealth; and a loving, protective family. Whereas Olivia lives a pretence, Belinda, like Mary, is 'a natural, artless, spontaneous creature ... utterly powerless to conceal her emotions, or to pretend a sentiment she did not feel', but she is no fading flower and her father assures her that she is 'as good as a son' (pp. 319, 365). The narrator supports, with qualifications, this declaration: 'she was as good as a son; that is to say she was braver and more outspoken than most women; although she was feminine and gentle withal, and by no means strong-minded' (p. 365). Furthermore, she is 'clever; but only just clever enough to be charming' (p. 378). The image of the ideal woman that is emerging here is of someone useful and opinionated, but only insofar as it will help her to support and bring happiness to those around her. We shall return to this ideal in the final chapter.

The main difference between Belinda and Olivia is that the former is content with her quiet life. As her wedding approaches, Belinda reminisces fondly: 'How often mamma and I have sat under the dear old cedar, making our poor children's frocks! People say monotonous lives are not happy; mine has been the same thing over and over again; and yet how happy, how happy!' (p. 419). Belinda finds contentment where Olivia finds only boredom and frustration. How these women experience love also reflects their intrinsic personalities. Love for Olivia is 'a dark and terrible passion, a thing to be concealed, as monomaniacs have sometimes contrived to keep the secret of their mania, until it burst forth at last, fatal and irrepressible, in some direful work of wreck and ruin' (pp. 144–5). The narrator explicitly compares Belinda's love to that 'which had raged in Olivia's stormy breast'; it comes 'like the gradual dawning of a summer's day,—first a little patch of light far away in the east, very faint and feeble; then a slow widening of the rosy brightness; and at last a great blaze of splendour over all the width of the vast heavens' (p. 319).

Shuttleworth has argued that Braddon exposes 'as a sham the whole ideology of duty and self-effacement that governed Victorian female lives' ('Preaching', p. 217), but Belinda makes for a complication of this argument. On the one hand, Belinda's perfectly complementary temperament, upbringing and environment are too idealised to be taken seriously. If Belinda's character fulfils an impossible paradigm, this reinforces Shuttleworth's argument. There are hints that this may be the case: for example, 'A woman had need to be country-bred, and to have been reared in the narrow circle of a happy home, to feel as Belinda Lawford felt. Such love as hers is only given to bright and innocent spirits, untarnished even by the knowledge of sin' (p. 420). Belinda is both born and raised to be a "good woman", and does not even have 'knowledge of sin' – this is certainly quite a claim. On the other hand, Belinda seems no more unrealistic than the born-for-martyrdom Mary, or the monomaniacal frustrated genius Olivia. *John Marchmont's Legacy* therefore suggests that some women are naturally more suited to lives of 'duty and self-effacement' than others, and exposes 'as a sham' the idea that all females are born with shared womanly attributes.

Joan N. Burstyn argues that the Victorian ideal of womanhood offered a means of social control that 'cast woman as an entity and left little room for variations among individuals'.[23] Although Braddon does depict variations among her female characters, the message is clear that the closer to the ideal of womanhood a woman is in heart and mind, as well as in deed, the better it will be for her. At a time when Herbert Spencer's notions of what came to be known as social Darwinism were being voiced, we can read these three female characters in terms of a struggle for survival of the fittest within patriarchal society. Olivia survives the novel, but remains unmarried and childless – her undesirable traits end with her. The sickly Mary's ethereality makes her physically and mentally unsuited to sustain the Victorian female role of wife and mother; she has only one child (who takes after his healthy father) before dying of 'a lingering pulmonary complaint' (p. 484). Belinda is physically healthy and most suited to her lifestyle and to Victorian ideals of femininity: she marries Edward and provides him with numerous children (p. 487).

This is not to say that Braddon is portraying things as they *should* be. Writing about George Eliot, Moira Gatens responds to arguments that she failed 'to provide her female characters with meaningful or non-traditional life options but rather allowed them to be defeated by circumstance' by pointing out that Eliot felt a 'commitment to portray her characters truthfully and realistically *in situ*'.[24] The same can be said of Olivia, albeit in a more sensational manner, who sees no escape from her miserable life other than the usual route of marriage. Detailed descriptions of Olivia's mental constitution in this novel, along with the many possibilities of what she *could* have been, and *ought* to have been, create ambivalence towards notions of womanliness. Braddon is both portraying the Victorian ideal of womanhood, and suggesting how difficult it is to meet that ideal. Success is arbitrarily reliant on the physiology of, and the environmental influences experienced by, each individual. Only a woman such as Belinda has just the correct temperament and upbringing to ensure perfection. On the one hand Braddon offers the possibility that 'nature makes … mistakes now and then, and the victim expiates the error' (p. 356). Olivia is deprived of the feminine attributes that would make her both attractive and content; her own nature is at the heart of her breakdown. On the other hand, there is an implicit sense that Victorian society also 'makes mistakes' in limiting women's lives and options. As the Victorian notion of womanhood is shown to be socially constructed, and as individual character is revealed to be largely determined before birth – it is purely a stroke of luck if the two prove to be compatible.

This study of character formation in sensation fiction has begun with three novels that depict characters struggling with overwhelming emotions, and whose core personality traits clash dangerously with the circumstances in which they find themselves. In these works we can see the two leading sensation authors of the early 1860s questioning the extent to which an individual can influence their own behaviour in order to fit more appropriately with the expectations of society and conventional morality. Monomania is used to explain extreme behaviour, but also to represent the inner conflict between different aspects of the self: the parts that want to conform, and the (more powerful and compelling) parts that don't. Both authors' works are informed by Victorian theories of the passions and the will, but they do not simply reflect the debates held by physicians and psychologists in this period. Whereas moral management encouraged patients to reintegrate into society by relearning appropriate behaviour, Braddon and Collins ask whether this is desirable (because the surrounding social structures are shown to be as deeply flawed as the characters themselves) or possible. The next section builds on these ideas of core personality traits, and the extent to which they can be modified for better or worse, by discussing two novels in which Braddon and Collins foreground the influence of inherited characteristics in the formation of character.

Notes

1 Mary Elizabeth Braddon, *John Marchmont's Legacy*, ed. Tōru Sasaki and Norman Page (Oxford: Oxford University Press, 1999), p. 356.
2 Karen M. Odden, '"Reading coolly" in *John Marchmont's Legacy*: Reconsidering M. E. Braddon's legacy', *Studies in the Novel*, 36 (2004), 21–40 (p. 24).
3 Jane Wood's chapter on 'Nature's invalids: The medicalization of womanhood' in particular shows how Victorian literature draws (although rarely unquestioningly) on the paradoxical yet simultaneously employed stereotypes of women as 'spiritual' and as troubled by 'their problematic physiology' (Jane Wood, *Passion and Pathology in Victorian Fiction* (Oxford: Oxford University Press, 2001), pp. 8–58 (p. 11)).
4 T. P. Healey, 'Shall we marry her?', *Welcome Guest*, 1 (January 1860), 228–9 (p. 229).

5 John Ruskin, 'Sesame and lilies', in *'Sesame and lilies', 'The two paths' and 'The king of the golden river'* (London: J. M. Dent and Sons, 1907), pp. 1–79 (p. 60). 'Of queens' gardens' (the second lecture in 'Sesame and lilies') does not necessarily encapsulate Ruskin's gender belief system; its importance here is its contribution to the Victorian image of the ideal woman. For revisionist views of Ruskin on womanhood see Dinah Birch and Francis O'Gorman (eds), *Ruskin and Gender* (Basingstoke: Palgrave, 2002).

6 Jeni Curtis, 'The "espaliered" girl: Pruning the docile body in *Aurora Floyd*', in Marlene Tromp, Pamela K. Gilbert and Aeron Haynie (eds), *Beyond Sensation: Mary Elizabeth Braddon in Context* (Albany: State University of New York Press, 2000), pp. 77–92 (p. 79).

7 Anthony Trollope, '"Sesame and lilies"', *Fortnightly Review*, 1 (July 1865), 633–5 (p. 635).

8 Herbert Cowell, 'Sex in mind and education: A commentary', *Blackwood's Edinburgh Magazine*, 115 (June 1874), 736–49 (p. 747).

9 Mary Poovey, *Uneven Developments: The Ideological Work of Gender in Mid-Victorian England* (London: Virago, 1989), p. 1.

10 Jessica Gerard, 'Lady Bountiful: Women of the landed classes and rural philanthropy', *Victorian Studies*, 30 (1987), 183–210 (p. 190).

11 Anon., 'A word to women, by one of themselves', *Temple Bar*, 2 (April 1861), 54–61 (p. 58). Mangham surmises that Braddon wrote this article because *Temple Bar* had two female correspondents in 1861, and the other, Eliza Lynn Linton, did not hold the opinions expressed in the article (Mangham, p. 119). That the article was reprinted in the *Sixpenny Magazine* (2:10 (March 1868), 423–31), which serialised *Lady Audley's Secret*, adds support to Mangham's supposition. *John Marchmont's Legacy* ran in *Temple Bar* from December 1862 to January 1864.

12 James Davies, 'Female education', *Quarterly Review*, 119:238 (April 1866), 499–515 (p. 508).

13 Mary Elizabeth Braddon, *The Lovels of Arden* (Teddington: Echo Library, 2006), p. 139.

14 Saverio Tomaiuolo, *In Lady Audley's Shadow: Mary Elizabeth Braddon and Victorian Literary Genres* (Edinburgh: Edinburgh University Press, 2010), p. 47.

15 Herbert Spencer, *Education: Intellectual, Moral and Physical* (London: Routledge, 1993 [1861]), p. 187.

16 Jenny Bourne Taylor and Sally Shuttleworth (eds), *Embodied Selves: An Anthology of Psychological Texts, 1830–1890* (Oxford: Clarendon Press, 2003 [1998]), p. 167.

17 John Gideon Millingen, '*The Passions; or, Mind and Matter*' (London: J. and D. Darling, 1848), in Taylor and Shuttleworth, *Embodied Selves*, pp. 169–70 (p. 169).

18 Henry Maudsley, 'On some of the causes of insanity', *Journal of Mental Science*, 12 (January 1867), 488–502 (p. 492).

19 Acton asserted that 'in general, women do not feel any great sexual tendencies' (William Acton, *The Functions and Disorders of the Reproductive Organs in Childhood, Youth, Adult Age, and Advanced Life: Considered in Their Physiological, Social, and Moral Relations*, 6th edn (London: J. & A. Churchill, 1875), p. 216. M. Jeanne Peterson warns that Acton's views 'ought not to be accepted as typical' (M. Jeanne Peterson, 'Dr Acton's enemy: Medicine, sex, and society in Victorian England', in Patrick Brantlinger (ed.), *Energy and Entropy: Science and Culture in Victorian Britain* (Bloomington: Indiana University Press, 1989), pp. 248–69 (p. 250)). This view was also challenged in non-medical works: for example, Justin McCarthy, writing about the stereotypical literary heroine, asserted that 'no good end is attained by trying to persuade ourselves that women are all incorporeal, angelic, colourless, passionless, helpless creatures ... who regard the whole end and passion of human life as ethereal, Platonic love, and orderly, parent-sanctioned wedlock' (Justin McCarthy, 'Novels with a purpose', *Westminster Review*, 26:1 (July 1864), 24–49 (p. 48)).
20 Lillian Nayder, 'The empire and sensation', in Pamela K. Gilbert (ed.), *A Companion to Sensation Fiction* (Chichester: John Wiley and Sons, 2011), pp. 442–54 (p. 453).
21 Natalie Schroeder and Ronald A. Schroeder, *From Sensation to Society: Representations of Marriage in the Fiction of Mary Elizabeth Braddon, 1862–1866* (Newark: University of Delaware Press, 2006), p. 132.
22 For a discussion of Braddon's child-women, including Mary, see Anne-Marie Beller, 'Sensational *Bildung*? Infantilization and female maturation in Braddon's 1860s novels', in Jessica Cox (ed.), *New Perspectives on Mary Elizabeth Braddon* (Amsterdam: Rodopi, 2012), pp. 113–32.
23 Joan N. Burstyn, *Victorian Education and the Ideal of Womanhood* (London: Croom Helm, 1980), p. 11.
24 Moira Gatens, 'Freedom and determinism in *Middlemarch*; or, Dorothea, the lunatic', *Sidney Studies in English*, 29 (2003), 31–8 (p. 35).

Part II

Heredity and degeneration

PART 2

3

The Lady Lisle

> Talk as we will and think as we will of the freedom of the will, of moral sense and of moral responsibility ... we cannot escape from the great overhanging cloud of hereditary influences, the fact that moral and intellectual traits follow down a race from father to son, or reappear in more remote descendants, exactly as do peculiarities of feature or diseased states of bodily constitution, such as scrofula and gout.[1]
>
> (G. W. Child, 'Physiological psychology',
> *Westminster Review*, 1868)

Many of the practices, theories and theorists referenced in Part I placed implicit faith in the power of the individual to initiate self-improvement, as long as circumstances allowed, and promoted the possibility of raising a well-balanced, level-headed individual by inculcating a sense of self-discipline from an early age. At the same time, the importance of hereditary influences was not overlooked.

As we have seen, William Benjamin Carpenter placed great emphasis on the training of the willpower as a means of assuring socially acceptable behaviour, but he nevertheless asserted that 'the "original constitution" of each individual is in great part (if not entirely) determined by the conditions ... of the parent-organisms' (*Human Physiology*, p. 592). Questions were asked, additionally, about the extent to which a person's social and physical environment worked with or against heredity in the development of the personality, and about how much education and upbringing could dictate development and behaviour. The relationships and influences among mind, body and environment were, therefore, considered all-important when it came to raising good citizens, but they were often also near-impossible to unravel or even distinguish. In his 1890 discussion of 'criminal heredity', for example, the physician Havelock Ellis acknowledged that there were 'two factors' to bear in mind

> There is the element of innate disposition, and there is the element of contagion from social environment ... Practically, it is not always possible to disentangle these two factors; a bad home will usually mean something bad in the heredity in the strict sense. Frequently the one element alone, whether the heredity or the contagion, is not sufficient to determine the child in the direction of crime.[2]

Ellis was writing at the end of the nineteenth century, when theories of heredity, particularly those concerning dangerous hereditary transmission of physical and moral qualities, were especially dominant. However, Victorian society and sensation novelists were already concerned about, and fascinated by, the idea of negative heredity in the 1860s, and believed that it was possible (as the *Westminster Review* states) for 'moral and intellectual traits [to] follow down a race from father to son' just like physical attributes.

The little-studied *The Lady Lisle* (published in a single volume in 1862, the same year as Braddon made her name with the best-selling *Lady Audley's Secret*) explores, like *John Marchmont's Legacy*, the relationship between an individual's inherent constitution and environmental influences, but makes use of the potential influence of heredity, and its relationship to upbringing and education, to a far greater extent.[3] Themes of class, and especially class boundaries, are central to *The Lady Lisle*, and notions of character formation become crucial to Braddon's depiction of social hierarchy. Both the affluent upper-class Sir Rupert Lisle and the poor lower-class James Arnold begin as unappealing children with several disagreeable, and apparently hereditary, personality traits. They also happen to resemble each other to the extent that the villain, Major Varney, kidnaps Rupert and persuades James's disreputable father to let him present James, some years later, to Rupert's mother Claribel as her missing son in order to take advantage of Rupert's inheritance. Rupert is taken away to be raised as an orphan in a middle-class school, an event that actually leads to a marked improvement in his personality, to his marrying a middle-class rector's daughter and to the revitalisation of his dying family line. In *The Lady Lisle* the aristocracy is characterised by a 'lack of productivity' that Aeron Haynie also identifies in *Lady Audley's Secret*; but whilst *Lady Audley's Secret* 'illustrates mid-Victorian concerns over the sanctity of the aristocratic country estate, the fear that it could be metaphorically invaded and contaminated by the middle class', in *The Lady Lisle* the middle classes are in fact presented as the means of rescue to an increasingly idle and dissolute upper class.[4] James's upbringing under his father and Varney, contrastingly, exacerbates the character flaws he exhibited as a child, and he is unable successfully to ascend the social scale. Moreover, he is increasingly portrayed as *inherently* irredeemable, is increasingly castigated by other characters and the narrator, and eventually dies an ignoble death, being thrown from his dog-cart whilst in a drunken stupor. This novel is an example of a sensation author picking and choosing notions of nature and nurture in order to fit the requirements of the plot, because ultimately Braddon uses heredity as a tool to put an errant working-class member firmly back in his place, and education as a means of introducing middle-class morals and assiduity into the upper classes. The result is a class-inflected engagement with several issues that relate to character formation, including the perceived degeneration of the upper and lower classes, the hereditary nature of morality and criminality, and the possibility of counteracting inherent flaws through education.

A gentleman by nurture

The Lady Lisle immediately establishes links among physical appearance, constitution and temperament. This is apparent from the first character description in the novel, that of Lady Claribel Lisle, Rupert's mother:

> She was tall and slender. Altogether very delicate in appearance. She was dazzlingly fair; she had large, light blue eyes, lovely in colour, but perhaps rather wanting in expression; a small, straight nose; a mouth, which did not promise much decision of character; and long, loose floating curls, of the palest flaxen hair.[5]

Claribel physically resembles the two most famous blonde sensation heroines of the early 1860s, but with some telling differences. One is Braddon's own Lady Audley, whose 'large and liquid blue eyes', 'rosy lips', 'delicate nose' and 'profusion of fair ringlets' play on stereotypes of ideal beauty and the typical Victorian heroine (*Lady Audley's Secret*, p. 52). However, whereas Lady Audley's loveliness masks villainy, Claribel's appearance hides no such surprises. The other heroine is Laura Fairlie in Wilkie Collins's *The Woman in White* (1860), who is altogether a 'fair, delicate girl', with her eyes 'of that soft, limpid, turquoise blue, so often sung by the poets, so seldom seen in real life' (pp. 49–50).[6] However, Laura's 'quietly thoughtful' eyes display a 'clear truthfulness' and reveal 'the light of a purer and a better world', and she is given humanising flaws, such as her 'sensitive lips [which] are subject to a slight nervous contraction, when she smiles' (*Woman in White*, p. 49). Although this reveals a certain mental fragility that develops to the point of breakdown later in the novel, these flaws only serve to endear her further to the sympathetic narrator (her future husband). Whereas Laura's physical appearance concords harmoniously with her appealing personality, Claribel's beauty is in accordance with a *lack* of personality, and her flawlessness is a reflection of her insipidness; the narrator asserts that 'she would have been a beautiful doll, but she was not a beautiful woman' (p. 2).[7]

The description of Claribel as doll-like is particularly appropriate as she is easily manipulated; she is 'entirely at the mercy of those who controlled, or counselled her. She saw with their eyes, thought with their thoughts, and spoke with their words' (p. 16). Claribel's passivity actually makes her a satisfactory wife to her first husband, Reginald; though 'not affectionate' she is 'gentle and tractable' to the point that 'if he had asked her to ascend Mont Blanc, she would have toiled bravely to the summit, though she had died there' (p. 17).[8] The narrator is quick to discourage any admiration for this extreme submissiveness, insisting that 'it was scarcely a virtue, this tacit obedience, this smiling assent; it was rather the constitutional indolence of a lymphatic temperament. Anything was less troublesome to her than resistance' (p. 17). Claribel is not to be praised when her constitutionally predisposed behaviour happens to take the form of acceptable conduct. As well as Claribel being congenitally submissive, her upbringing has compounded this personality trait; she 'had thought for herself so seldom, and had been so used all her life to act upon the opinions of other people, that the most obvious ideas never appeared to occur to her spontaneously' (p. 4). This reflects mid-Victorian notions of the power of habit. Carpenter observed that it was a 'universally admitted fact, that any sequence of mental action which has been frequently repeated, tends to perpetuate itself; so that we find ourselves automatically prompted to *think, feel,* or *do* what we have been before accustomed to think, feel, or do, under like circumstances, without any consciously-formed *purpose*, or anticipation of results' (*Mental Physiology*, p. 344, emphasis in original). Indeed, we are told that Claribel would have married her suitor Walsingham 'at his command, being utterly incapable to resist the influence of a stronger mind than her own, had she not been restrained by the counter influence of her aunt [who wishes her to marry Reginald], which, from the force of long habit, was more powerful still' (pp. 15–16). These depictions of Claribel as the product of "nature" consolidated by "nurture" leave little room for self-determinism, which

The Lady Lisle

sets the tone for much of what follows in *The Lady Lisle*; they also, however, suggest that in *The Lady Lisle* outward signs will accurately represent non-physical characteristics, and this proves to be far less reliable.

Although Claribel's personality is partially the result of inborn characteristics, there is little emphasis on her heredity or ancestry. Claribel's aunt, who pressures her into marrying Reginald, must be a woman capable of pursuing her own agenda, and is therefore quite unlike her niece. We know that Claribel is the 'orphan heiress of a rich East India merchant' (p. 12), and therefore of an affluent (presumably self-made) upper-middle-class background; no information is given about her mother. Contrastingly, Rupert Lisle's aristocratic paternal line is given a sizeable introduction, including prolonged descriptions of the former glory of the Lisles and the current vastness of the Lisle estates. This emphasis on the family history is partly because it is this ancient name, estates and wealth that are at stake in the novel. It is also part of Braddon's differentiation between middle- and upper-class attributes: the latter are associated with ancestry and accumulation over the generations.

The reader is taken on a tour of the 'noble and wide domain' of Lislewood and Sir Rupert's properties, from the 'snug homestead[s] and substantial farmhouse[s]' to the village inns called 'the Lisle Arms, or the Baronet's Head, or the Sir Rupert Lisle' (p. 19). Not only are the extensiveness and affluence of the Lisle family revealed, but its age and prestige; the name goes back to 'the Battle of Hastings itself' and 'the pedigree and grants of the seven years old baronet would have stretched the length of the longest avenue in Lislewood Park, had the great rolls of mouldering parchment been unfolded to their fullest extent' (pp. 19–20). The conditional aspect of the sentence reflects the state of the Lisle family, which, despite its wealth and power, is mouldering in its own way, as the narrator makes clear at the end of our tour:

> It was strange, after this constant recurrence of the ancient name, this wide extension of the grandeur and wealth of the house of Lisle, to come back to Lislewood Park and find the sole owner of so much importance playing drearily in the stiff flower garden, with a pale, sickly face, and languid, girlish manners. Had the captain of the Norman cross bows, the haughty oppressor of the Saxon, the victors of Cressy and Flodden, the noble royalists … had all these strong and valiant men left only this feeble, little, fair-haired child to inherit their wealth and honours? It seemed almost as if the weight of this vast inheritance, falling solely upon this, a helpless orphan, must surely crush and destroy him.
>
> (p. 20)

Heredity and degeneration

Braddon draws a genetic line through ruling English social groups to the Victorian upper classes, stressing a biological and social distinction from those of Saxon lineage, but also an immense fall from action and vitality. Contrasted with his 'gallant' ancestors, the feminised and sickly Rupert symbolises aristocratic decline, and his health is inversely proportionate to his prestige, making him appear a victim of his ancestry; what makes him great will also 'destroy' him. 'There was something sinister and unnatural', the narrator observes, 'in [Rupert's] lonely splendour ... the boy-baronet seemed to languish under a load of grandeur, and to sicken of a surfeit of prosperity' (pp. 20–1).

Indeed, not only Rupert may seem to be sickening. The Lisle family has in fact been deteriorating for some time, and the last three generations of Lisles have 'died of a lingering decline, which had been fatally prevalent in the house of Lisle; for three generations, the heads of the family had died before they had attained their thirtieth year, leaving only sons to inherit the title and property' (p. 16). The Lisles have reached the point where they can only produce one child, and that a sickly one marked out for premature death; Rupert's delicate health seems to foreshadow a similar fate. Primogeniture has become a sort of perverse necessity as the heir of Lislewood takes up his lonely position at the head of a family consisting (as far as the male bloodline is concerned) solely of himself until he can marry and produce the single son who will replace him.

Depictions of an unhealthy aristocracy were a popular source of mid-Victorian satirical humour. In Charles Dickens's *Bleak House* (1853), the Dedlock gout has 'come down, through the illustrious line, like the plate, or the pictures, or the place in Lincolnshire', and (being both hereditary and associated with rich living) is nursed by Sir Leicester Dedlock with perverse pride as 'a demon of the patrician order'.[9] In *John Marchmont's Legacy* Edward Arundel flippantly speculates that members of the upper-class Marchmont family are unlikely to live long, healthy lives:

> The present possessor himself is a middle-aged man; so I shouldn't think *he* can be likely to last long. I dare say he drinks too much port, or hunts, or something of that sort; goes to sleep after dinner, and does all manner of apoplectic things, I'll be bound. Then there's the son, only fifteen, and not yet marriageable; consumptive, I dare say.
>
> (pp. 25–6)

Aristocratic lifestyles and pursuits are depicted as habitually injurious, and indeed not so long after this scene one of the Marchmont heirs *does* die of apoplexy.

The Lady Lisle

Hereditary diseases were also used for more serious and dramatic effect as, for example, with the recurring insanity in Wilkie Collins's 'Mad Monkton' (discussed in Chapter 4). In Ellen Wood's *St Martin's Eve* (1866) the St Johns of Alnwick suffer from a mysterious hereditary affliction (with symptoms reminiscent of those in *The Lady Lisle*) in which family members have 'wasted away without apparent cause; wasted to death' to the extent that they 'never live to see their thirty-third birthday'.[10] Lyn Pykett assumes that the hereditary affliction is consumption (*Sensation Novel*, p. 66), but Wood (like Braddon) leaves it unnamed. This at once adds to the mystery of the wasting disease, makes it appear unique to the families it attacks, and adds to a sense of pervasive enervation rather than a particular condition that can be diagnosed and combated.

Victorian medical literature often blamed aristocratic deterioration on the overindulgence and ennui to which the upper classes' wealth exposed them. One *Lancet* contributor identified the aristocracy as a group in which 'gloomy affections, disease, and excess' resulted in 'unhealthy semen', leading to the degeneration and eventual extinction of the family line.[11] Braddon depicts the idleness of the Lisle family through descriptions of Reginald Lisle's daily activities: he is 'fond of field sports, horses and dogs, gunnery, the turf, all those amusements so dear to gentlemen who have plenty of money and very little to do' (p. 17). Idleness is cited as an actual health threat in Benjamin Brodie's *Psychological Inquiries* (1854):

> The *ennui* which is the necessary result of an over-abundance of leisure is not only painful and a mighty evil in itself, but it leads to still greater evils; the victims of it, in not a few instances, being driven to seek relief by resorting to low and degrading pleasures, while in others the circumstance of the mind preying on itself produces a permanent derangement of the general health, and even to such an extent as to shorten the duration of life.[12]

Braddon's description of Reginald combines the two dangers mentioned by Brodie; he moves from one useless (if not degrading) activity to another before apparently dying of boredom: 'everything wearied him in time; every amusement failed to occupy him; and it almost seemed as if he fell into a decline at last, because he could think of nothing else to do' (p. 17). Reginald's mental weariness translates into physical weariness, and his indolent lifestyle parallels the Lisles' generative unproductivity; the hereditary wasting disease becomes a symbol of the nobility's insularity, idleness and uselessness.[13]

Inheritor of the Lisle name and fortune, Rupert has also inherited many of his parents' unenviable mental and physical traits, resulting in a 'compound of debilitating causes' that mean he is 'clearly ill-equipped to carry the burden of his aristocratic lineage' (Mangham, p. 108). Rupert is 'weak and ailing, small for his age, and very backward with his studies; difficult to amuse, with a dislike to active exercise, and very little love for even childish books and pictures' (p. 30). Rupert possesses his father's short attention span, but does not even *try* to amuse himself. This is perhaps due to the influence of his mother's 'lymphatic temperament' adding another level of languor to the already 'unimpulsive' Lisle temper. Like Claribel he is 'pale-faced' and 'delicate ... resembling his mother both in person and disposition; like her, quiet and unimpulsive; like her, unblest with brilliant talents, or energy of character' (p. 17). Furthermore, Rupert has inherited his parents' limited emotional aptitude. Reginald only experiences short-lived interest in any activity, and only feels desire inspired by covetousness (p. 15); Claribel is rarely troubled by strong emotion, exemplified when she marries Reginald 'without loving him, as passively as she had taken her music lessons without having an ear for melody' (p. 15). Similarly, Rupert 'showed no great capacity for affection, and his love for his mother, who idolized him, was of a feeble and negative order' (p. 30).[14] Rupert's abduction is also the result of inherited personality traits: 'there was a stubborn obstinacy in the Lisle blood, which had often led the sons of that house to do more desperate things than the most courageous men had ever attempted ... Sir Rupert had the true Lisle nature – dull and unimpulsive; but intensely obstinate' (p. 63). Major Varney (deliberately exploiting the boy's weaknesses) dares him to ride his pony down a sheer drop; Rupert nearly dies in the attempt, allowing Varney to abduct him.

As well as contending with being the product of a bad confluence of parental attributes, Rupert spends his first six years 'shut in from the outer world' (p. 20) under the influence of an overindulgent mother and a petty-minded father, not a lifestyle conducive to the counteraction of his inherited defects. Neither Rupert nor Reginald is responsible for creating this situation (although Reginald has perpetuated it), but they seem unworthy of the lands and riches they possess. The unflattering descriptions of the listless Rupert are not so much a critique of *him*, rather a portrayal of familial and class decline and a criticism of the vices associated with the modern nobility.

Despite its weak condition, the Lisle family lingers on, generation after generation. One problem perceived by Victorian eugenicists was that 'aristocrats were notoriously inbred and often mentally weak but,

The Lady Lisle

being rich, could breed as much as they pleased' (Paul, p. 29). This was a concern expressed in Francis Galton's writings on eugenics:

> One of the effects of civilization is to diminish the rigour of the application of the law of natural selection … The sickly children of a wealthy family have a better chance of living and rearing offspring than the stalwart children of a poor one. As with the body, so with the mind. Poverty is more adverse to early marriages than is natural bad temper, or inferiority of intellect. In civilized society, money interposes her aegis between the law of natural selection and very many of its rightful victims.
>
> (Galton, 'Hereditary talent', p. 326)

The Lady Lisle enacts Galton's claim that the poor are left to survive as they will, whilst the rich can buy their way out of the natural selection process. Although Rupert is 'very backward with his studies' (p. 30), this need not concern his family, as Walsingham points out: 'he will be a rich man, and he has no need to be clever. It is we poor fellows, who have the battle of life to fight, who want all the brains' (p. 8). Although Rupert is of delicate health, he is protected by the 'aegis of wealth', having 'escaped many of the scourges common to childhood, through the watchful care of his nurses and his doctors' (p. 30). This is a luxury that others are unable to afford. In this manner, the Lisles have managed to fend off what was seen by doctors such as Maudsley as the likely, even preferable, outcome of hereditary degeneration: the 'ban of sterility' that 'prevents the permanent degradation of the race'.[15] Moreover, despite ill health and unappealing personalities, the Lisle men have little trouble finding wives. Reginald is a particularly unlikeable person who, we are told, 'had never desired to have anything, except for the pleasure of taking it away from somebody else' (p. 15).[16] Yet at the behest of her aunt, Claribel marries Reginald rather than the healthy, devoted, but penniless Captain Walsingham. The even more boorish James Arnold wins the hand of the attractive Olivia who, under the impression that he is Rupert Lisle, openly declares: 'I marry you for your title, and I marry you for your estate, and if you hadn't that, I wouldn't marry you' (p. 153).

Despite being borne up by medical care and mercantile marriages, the Lisle family seems to be at the end of a vicious downward spiral, and, in these early stages of the novel, it seems unclear how the current generation could hope to improve on the past, or even recognise the need for improvement. However, the Lisle deterioration is arrested when Rupert is abducted by Varney so he can be replaced, when he comes of age, with the lower-class James Arnold. Rupert is enrolled under a false name in a respectable middle-class school.[17] Varney's servant Salamons pays occasional visits as his supposed uncle, and convinces Rupert that his memories of being a child baronet are yellow-fever-induced delusions, and that, if he does not want to become mad, he must 'effect [his] own cure' by repressing them (pp. 194–5).[18] Threatened with madness as an alternative, Rupert learns (unlike any other character in the novel) to discipline his own thoughts and behaviour.[19] When we meet him again, at the age of twenty-one, there are still physical reminders of the child he once was. He is 'singularly delicate in appearance' (p. 129), his 'temperament is peculiarly nervous, and his health delicate' (p. 190); in these respects, Rupert does not particularly appear to have changed. However, other personality traits that distinguished him previously (moroseness, languidness, spitefulness, inability to amuse himself, intellectual backwardness) are gone. When we first encounter him again, it is during a visit from Salamons to the school in which he has been housed. Rupert is first observed 'reading' and is so 'absorbed in his book' that he does not notice his visitor's arrival. The principal of the academy assures Salamons that Rupert is perfectly content with 'his books, his botanical studies, his herbal, and his dog ... He is a most amiable youth, and very generally beloved' (p. 129). Rupert is now capable of entertaining himself and of sustained study.

Rupert's studies earn him a reputation as being 'very clever' (p. 190), and he eventually becomes a respected teacher. When the curate Walter Remorden interviews Rupert for the role of schoolmaster, he is initially unimpressed. Remorden observes Rupert's hands, 'white and slender as the hands of a woman', and finds him nervous and monosyllabic, to the extent that he feels bound to view him as being 'as delicate as a girl' and 'sadly deficient in intellect' (pp. 191–2). Once again we are reminded of the Rupert of fourteen years ago. Once Rupert's shyness is overcome, however, his conversation 'grew fluent, nay, almost eloquent. He talked of a great many things; never very brilliantly, but always sensibly' (p. 192). There is consistency here – Rupert is not 'brilliant', but maturity achieved through years of study and discipline has improved his mind. Indeed, his pupils love and respect him, viewing him as 'a great scholar', and he is a devoted reader of the high-brow Quarterlies (pp. 215–16). Here, middle-class education comes to the rescue of the aristocracy, suggesting that environmental influences can counteract what appeared to be inbred flaws. Neither class distinctions nor the influence of heredity are discredited. Rupert is 'not a handsome young man', but he retains 'a delicacy and refinement in his appearance that made him peculiarly attractive ...

The Lady Lisle

wear what he would, he must always have looked a gentleman' (p. 216). Rupert's noble blood shows through, regardless of his surroundings, but it has taken the middle-class environment in which he has been raised to neutralise the negative attributes of the modern aristocracy and display his nobility to its best advantage.

In Victorian advice books the middle classes were often warned that 'idle, artificial habits, copied from a degenerate aristocracy, endangered the health and wealth of the nation' (Shuttleworth, 'Demonic mothers', p. 34). In *The Lady Lisle*, middle-class characters such as Claribel's avaricious aunt are enticed by the thought of forging links with the aristocracy, and Claribel enters into her husband's idle lifestyle, resulting in a listless and sickly child. In the next generation, however, things happen differently: Rupert falls in love with the rector's daughter, Blanche Hayward. Although her mother is a 'ladylike nonentity', Blanche is 'no ordinary girl'; she has been 'educated by her father' and possesses a 'powerful intellect' that, unlike Olivia Marchmont's, is given a suitable outlet, as she teaches at the 'National School' (pp. 185–8). Although her intellectual capacity may be an inborn asset, Blanche's active, dutiful and compassionate personality is due to the influence of her father. While Blanche does not attempt to conform to aristocratic habits, Rupert comes to embrace middle-class attitudes, and she listens to his declaration of love because she believes that they are 'equals by education and feeling, as [they] are most likely equals by birth' (p. 217), and she later learns to love him in return.[20] Characters such as Blanche embody a specific set of middle-class values (including assiduousness, dutifulness and philanthropy) that neither the Lisles nor the Mertons (Claribel's family), who desire to marry into the nobility, possess.

Despite offering a bleak picture of class and ancestral decline, therefore, Braddon implies that this downward spiral can be halted through a careful education and choice of partner. This was something that even the often pessimistic Henry Maudsley admitted may be possible: a 'course of regeneration of the family by happy marriages, wise education, and a prudent conduct of life is possible; the downward tendency may be thus checked, and even perhaps effaced in time' (*Responsibility*, p. 279). More enthusiastically, Galton speculated:

> Neither is there any known limit to the intellectual and moral grandeur of nature that might be introduced into aristocratical families, if their representatives, who have such rare privilege in winning wives that please them best, should invariably, generation after generation, marry with a view of transmitting those noble qualities to their descendants.
>
> ('Hereditary talent', p. 326)

The Lady Lisle makes similarly hopeful suppositions, concluding with the sound of 'childish voices' echoing 'under the long beech avenues in which Sir Rupert Lisle had played seventeen years before', suggesting that Rupert and Blanche have had more than one child (p. 267). The Stereotyped Edition expands upon this, assuring us that Claribel lives 'to see a band of bright children playing merrily in the gardens where Sir Rupert Lisle had wandered listlessly to and fro in his companionless childhood' (*Lady Lisle*, 189[?], pp. 304–5). So at least part of the family curse is broken (tantalisingly, neither version mentions whether Rupert lives beyond his thirtieth year). Major Varney plans to make Rupert believe that he is a different person, but he does not foresee that by removing the boy from his unhealthy environment he gives him the opportunity to become not only a different person, but also a better one.

A scoundrel by nature

So Rupert's personality is salvaged through the acquisition of middle-class values, but for the lower-class James Arnold, who is substituted for Rupert, a bad combination of environment, heredity and class boundaries proves insurmountable. Like Rupert's, James's personality is reflective of his father, the ex-poacher and murderer Gilbert Arnold. Gilbert is 'a sneak and an idler' (p. 26), 'a sulky, dissatisfied man' (p. 27), with a 'capacity for hatred, envy, and malice' that is 'considerably in advance of the generality of his species' (p. 29). It is unclear to what extent James has inherited or acquired Gilbert's personality traits. There are early intimations that Gilbert, who does 'not quite recommend himself as a person whose example it would be well for youth to follow' is a bad influence on his son (p. 29).[21] When James's mother Rachel urges him not to 'tease the pigs or the fowls', Gilbert retorts: 'I don't want him to be a fiddle-faddling girl. Let him tease the pigs and the fowls, if he likes; I did it when I was a boy' (p. 29). On other occasions Braddon gives the impression that Gilbert is more actively training his son to follow in his footsteps, such as when he asks: '[We] won't lie down, and be walked over by rich people's shiny leather boots, eh, Jim?'. James quickly replies 'not if we know it, father', with a 'glance of precocious cunning', as if this is a practised response (p. 52). Like the young Rupert, James is not growing up in the most promising of circumstances. At other times the narrator suggests hereditary influence at work in the development of James's personality, for example when we are told that 'James Arnold inherited his

The Lady Lisle

father's envious temper, without his father's bulldog courage' (p. 54). In either case, paternal influence is paramount.

However, it is James's *lack* of inherited 'bulldog courage' that serves Varney best. As Braddon does not make it explicit, it would be mere speculation to suggest whether James's timidity is inherited or learnt (or both) from his timorous mother Rachel. Nonetheless, it is a core part of his personality, which Varney exploits in the same way that he exploits Rupert's constitutional traits. After James cries in fear at being placed on a pony, Varney declares that 'this boy can't help being frightened … He has a nervous temperament, and a man with a strong will could do whatever he liked with him. I'd make that child follow me like a dog, and look in my face for his words, before he had the pluck to speak them' (p. 55). Varney is proved correct when, fourteen years after having abducted Rupert, he passes James off as the real heir of Lislewood and exerts his influence over him in order to live off the Lisle fortune.

Braddon's description of James's mental abilities also hints at hereditary influences. Hereditary criminality and immorality were increasingly discussed in Victorian medical and popular literature. In an 1856 article for the *Westminster Review*, for example, G. H. Lewes asserted that a range of vices (including alcoholism, gambling and the 'thieving propensity') were inheritable.[22] James's 'precocious cunning' resembles the 'leer of low cunning' in his father's eyes (p. 58). This was seen as a particular attribute of hereditary criminals, whom Maudsley described as being 'of mean and defective intellect, though excessively cunning' (*Responsibility*, p. 30). Braddon makes a similar distinction between intellect and cunning. When the adult James is first described the narrator claims that he has 'rather a delicate, regular face, but it gave no promise of a powerful intellect' (p. 112). Initially this helps to make James look more like the child Rupert who was, it will be remembered, 'backward with his studies' (p. 30). However, the lack of 'powerful intellect' in the countenance of the once precocious James is not a sign that he has lost any mental ability, but that his precocity took the form of cunning, rather than intellect. So, when the hereditary criminal, James, outwits the criminal mastermind, Varney, later in the novel, we are told that 'in the struggle between intellect and cunning, the lower faculty had conquered' (p. 152). Like Rupert, therefore, James has several undesirable traits that are either hereditary or early established.

It is not primarily James's personality that Varney takes advantage of, however, but his physical resemblance to Rupert. James is 'a sickly, precocious boy, six years old, with light flaxen hair, and a pale, sharp face, resembling his mother, and entirely unlike his stalwart, dark-complexioned father' (p. 27). The boys' likeness is due to the physical similarity of their mothers. Rachel tells Gilbert: 'When I was quite a girl ... I was counted rather like Miss Merton, by some of our folks ... Hard work has taken the beauty out of me' (p. 71).[23] Incidentally, this is another type of environmental determinism upon which the novel touches. Between marrying her first and second husbands (she marries Walsingham after Reginald's death), 'Claribel has scarcely changed ... Her delicate beauty has lost none of the purity of its transparent hues. The clear blue eyes are as bright as they were eight years ago' (p. 24). Whilst the women began life resembling each other, Claribel has not been physically taxed over the years, whereas Rachel's life of drudgery has taken its toll. The message that clothes (or lifestyle) make the man is also conveyed when the narrator draws explicit attention to the resemblance between James and Rupert:

> the long curls of the Baronet, and James Arnold's closely-cropped hair, were of the same flaxen shade. Both the boys had light blue eyes, pale faces, and sharp but delicate features; but so great was the distinction made by the rich dress and flowing locks of one, and the ungainly garments of the other, that the careless observer lost sight of the striking resemblance between the children.
>
> (p. 54)

As far as personality is concerned, there is little to choose between the disadvantaged, cowardly James, and the spoiled, intellectually weak heir, Rupert. Neither boy seems to be made of particularly gentlemanly material, and the reader may even feel compelled to agree with Gilbert Arnold when he compares his son with Rupert: 'Look at the little Baronet in his velvet frock, riding his dapple pony ... And then look at my son, in his hob-nailed boots and huckaback pinafore; and yet I know which is the sharpest lad, any day in the week' (pp. 28–9). In the same way that Rachel's lost looks throw into relief Claribel's easy lifestyle, moments like this in the early chapters of the novel highlight the superficiality of differences between rich and poor, often to the former's disadvantage.

Class prejudices are further challenged when Claribel is fooled into believing that James is really her son. Mangham argues that Claribel's 'longing for her son clouds her ability to notice the impostor' (Mangham, p. 111). Certainly Varney's plan works because of Claribel's influence. The sceptical authorities are swayed by 'the testimony of the young man's mother, whose instinct could scarcely be supposed to deceive her, and whose motives were above suspicion' (p. 117). However, whilst Claribel is undoubtedly delighted to be reunited with her son, there are indications in the text that, in at least equal measure to her affections, Claribel's class pride is used against her. When convincing her to declare her belief that the young man he introduces her to is Rupert, Varney asks her to be certain that she is not accidentally mixing him up with James, prompting Claribel to declare emphatically that she 'never believed in the existence of any likeness between the boys' (p. 113). However, James's upbringing has maintained those qualities that made him most similar to Rupert; he looks in delicate health, when he speaks he flushes 'a faint, unhealthy crimson' and 'his thin, bloodless lips [quiver] nervously' (p. 95). Varney has also ensured that James is groomed to have a look of neglected gentility: 'His flaxen hair, which grew rather long, had fallen away from his low, narrow forehead. His clothes, though rather shabby, were of the last fashion, and such as only a gentleman's son would wear. His hands were white and delicate' (p. 111).[24] We are reminded of Rupert's longer curls and his delicate appearance. In fact, James's hair has retained its light colour, whereas Rupert's darkens to 'a pale shade of brown' as he grows up (p. 129). W. F. Rae mocked (and not entirely without cause) the ever-changing hair colour of Braddon's characters, but as children's hair often darkens as they grow up, the change in Rupert's hair from 'fair' to light brown seems deliberate, representing his gradual change and maturation, in contrast to James, whose development has been stalled (pp. 188, 194). This (like Miss Gwilt's imposture as a respectable governess in *Armadale*) suggests the superficiality of class stereotypes, and is supported by later passages, such as when Olivia, James's future wife, declares scornfully 'who would ever think that flaxen-haired stripling came of such a noble house? I fancy a Lisle, of Lislewood, ought to be tall and stalwart, dark and stern' (p. 138).[25] Although the reader, unlike Olivia, knows that James is not a real Lisle, it is also true that Rupert looks equally unlike her ideal image of a baronet (there is no physical description of Reginald to draw comparison with). Moreover, both the criminal, Gilbert Arnold, and Claribel's second, illegitimate, son fit Olivia's description of tall, dark and stalwart (pp. 27, 121).[26] It seems on such occasions that *The Lady Lisle* may be gearing up to dispel class prejudices and challenge a system that favours the dissolute rich over the suffering working classes, regardless of personal merit.

However, in contrast to Rupert, it is never shown what effect a more favourable upbringing may have had on James; after being removed from his home at Lislewood (in preparation for his future imposture) he is raised in near isolation with only his parents and Varney for company. Victorian physiologists debated at length the extent to which an individual could be held responsible for his or her actions in the face of undesirable constitutional traits uncounteracted by education. James's personality has been degraded by his circumstances in life, and Braddon's portrayal of him can be read in the light of Carpenter's reasoning that 'a being entirely governed by the lower passions and instincts, whose higher moral sense has been repressed from its earliest dawn by the degrading influence of the condition in which he is placed, who has never learned to exercise any kind of self-restraint (or, if he has learned it, has only been trained to use it for the lowest purposes)' cannot be held 'morally responsible for his actions' (*Human Physiology*, p. 551). In the popular press the necessity of good environmental influences was often insisted upon when writers tried to invoke sympathy in readers. For example, an article in *Temple Bar* (published in March 1861, two months before *The Lady Lisle* began in *The Welcome Guest*) described a night refuge for the homeless and asked readers to reflect on the living conditions of the unfortunate people:

> As much, God knows, and more than they can bear is theirs of sin and folly and ingratitude; but when one minute's reflection shows us the mere accident of birth, and how that ours might have been the rags, the squalor, the hunger, and the ignorance, and theirs the warmth, the broadcloth, the cheerful home, and the well-stored mind, we should be more readily inclined, not merely to pardon their short-comings, but to think more gratefully of those blessings vouchsafed to us.[27]

In its invocation of a "there but for the grace of God" sentiment, this passage implies that environment and upbringing are the most important determining factors in one's life, because if 'we' were born into a less privileged environment, 'we' would also most probably become victims of 'sin and folly and ingratitude'.

It seems reasonable that James's situation should induce pity, if not sympathy. After all, as the beneficial force of a good upbringing is made apparent in relation to Rupert, it seems necessary to take James's neglected childhood into account. Certainly, when James enters Lislewood as the restored baronet, a lot of emphasis is placed on his unfortunate circumstances, but there is often an element of ambiguity in the manner in which this is done, which may encourage the reader to look for other explanations for James's behaviour. Free indirect speech is frequently used, at once to convey the general opinion of the duped characters that the baronet is the victim of a bad upbringing, and to remind the reader that he is not really the baronet at all. The narrator comments that 'it was only natural that, after fourteen years spent in the society of Gilbert Arnold, Sir Rupert Lisle should be a little awkward at the dinner-table'. James is confused by the cutlery and the servants, gets tipsy on too much 'sparkling Moselle' and 'wind[s] up by quenching his thirst from his finger-glass'. But, as the narrator again assures us, 'this, though very painful to his mother, was only natural' (p. 120). Indeed, regardless of whether it is the "real" baronet we are talking about or not, a person unused to an affluent lifestyle would be uncomfortable in such surroundings. But, as we have seen in the previous discussion of *John Marchmont's Legacy*, references to "nature" and what is "natural" are often ambiguous and can carry multiple meanings when employed by Braddon. Especially as the reader is in on the secret of the substitution, the "naturalness" of James's ineptness may suggest that the son of a lower-class criminal could not, *by nature*, fill the shoes of a true noble.

Similarly, Varney's defence of James's inappropriate behaviour is ostensibly designed to excuse him: 'Poor dear child! it is so like the pupil of that horrible poacher man to prefer port. I daresay he would like it thick and sweet. Injured child! it will take us some time to form him, my dear madam' (p. 121). Although Varney makes a reasonable point, that Gilbert must have had an influence on James as he grew up, because we know Varney is duplicitous, and that James is Gilbert's 'child' as well as his 'pupil', space is created for the reader to speculate that heredity may also be at work.

James also defends himself on grounds of upbringing, declaring during one of his tantrums 'Because my education hasn't been as good as it ought to be for a man of my station and my position in life, I suppose I'm to be bullied and ordered about, and tyrannized over' (p. 144). Yet it is through petty outbursts such as these that Braddon begins to turn the reader against James; after this argument with Varney, James meets Claribel's 'little Blenheim spaniel' in the hall and kicks 'the animal savagely away' (p. 145). This prefigures the Softy's kicking of Aurora Floyd's mastiff (*Aurora Floyd* was serialised the following year), and a similar scene in Collins's *Man and Wife* when Geoffrey Delamayn kicks a dog, breaking its ribs: hurting an innocent animal is a sure sign of villainy.[28] Claribel is deeply disappointed by 'the discovery that her child was no longer worthy of her love', and also blames James's upbringing as the reason for her disappointment in the man her son has become: 'years of association with a cunning villain had so changed the innocent mind that the mother shuddered, as she became every day more familiar with her new-found son' (p. 145).

Despite the comprehension that James has suffered, and the initial feeling that he deserves some tolerance because of this, he increasingly loses the sympathy of the other characters, the narrator and also the reader. As this change happens throughout the second half of the novel there is an adjustment in how James's personality is described, and he is increasingly depicted less as a product of poor nurturing, and more as the result of a bad nature. For example, James woos the scornful Olivia Marmaduke and we are told that 'there seemed to be something craven in his nature, which made him most love and admire this girl when she most openly despised him. He followed her about like a dog' (p. 152). Cravenness 'in his nature' may suggest an acquired characteristic, the quality having become so normal to him during his childhood that it has become an established part of his personality. The phrasing also, though, allows room for the possibility that it pre-exists in him.

James and Olivia honeymoon in Europe, but on their return little has changed:

> Continental travelling had done very little for Sir Rupert Lisle. If there is any particular polish to be attained by contact with the more refined inhabitants of foreign cities, Sir Rupert had failed to attain it. Perhaps this foreign polish, whatever its nature may be, requires a certain smoothness in the surface upon which it is to be spread, and may refuse to adhere to the coarser texture of certain cross-grained woods ... He returned to England, if possible, a greater boor than he had been when he left his native shores.
> (pp. 170–1)

This is a passage full of suggestive phrases – *is* there any particular polish to be had from continental travel? Claribel and Reginald certainly don't profit from their European tours earlier in the novel, being unable 'to distinguish a Titian from a Terniers' (p. 17). However, by this point the focus of the novel has changed and is beginning to fall on James's 'cross-grained' nature, which is apparently incapable of receiving elevating influences. Henry Maudsley argued that although 'the training which a person undergoes must have a great influence on the growth of his intellect and the formation of his character', the influence of education was 'limited by the capacity of the individual nature, and can only work within this larger or smaller circle of necessity'. At the end of the day, Maudsley asserted, men differ, 'and this is not a difference which is due to education or circumstances, but a fundamental difference of nature which neither education nor circumstances can eradicate' (*Responsibility*, pp. 20–1). Braddon, writing some thirteen years before Maudsley, shares this assessment of the limited pliability of the inherent personality in her depiction of James, who, as the narrative progresses, is presented as constitutionally incapable of change. His new life is not counteracting the influence of his old one, it is throwing his flaws into relief, perhaps even intensifying them. Braddon adds more and more references in a similar vein in order to suggest that while it may have seemed 'only natural' that James did not know how to behave in polite society because of his upbringing, it was actually natural because it was in his nature. For example, his 'nature' is once again used to explain his behaviour, when the narrator describes how James lives in fear of his headstrong wife, and yet still congratulates himself on the fact that 'She was his! To his coarse and low nature all was said in this. However she might rule him, she was, after all, but a part of his wealth' (pp. 174–5).

James's worst action occurs towards the end of the story, when he murders (and, it is implied, rapes) a gipsy girl, but this is told in retrospect by another gipsy. The most *shocking* display of his increasingly bad behaviour is the moment when he strikes his mother Rachel who, having fallen into poverty, has come to beg of him in front of his guests, an action described in painful detail:

> The poor creature, still kneeling on the ground and clinging to his hand, lifted up her face in supplication as she spoke. In a mad fury the Baronet, with his disengaged fist, struck the wretched woman full in the face; so violently, that the blood gushed in a torrent from a cut across her upper lip. Rachel Arnold fell to the ground with a stifled shriek.
>
> (pp. 179–80)

This is the truly damning moment of the novel when the reader, and the characters around him, realise the extent of James's viciousness.[29] The reaction of the characters is significantly different from their worried but sympathetic reactions to his earlier harmless blunders. Varney declares James to be a 'contemptible villain! without one redeeming touch of common humanity': 'if I had known what you really are, you might have rotted piece-meal in the garret where I found you before I would have soiled my hands by lifting a finger of them to help you' (p. 180). Although it is unclear how real Varney's shock is (he has, after all, watched and influenced James's upbringing), his words – 'what you really are' – are significant. James is no longer an 'injured child', but innately bad. A guest who witness James's assault on Rachel declares that his behaviour is 'a sign of the deterioration in the blood of our great county families. The Lisles, sir, have been accounted the noblest gentlemen in Sussex for upwards of six hundred years, and I can assure you the conduct of that young man to-day was a severe blow to my feelings' (p. 182). On the one hand, the hypocrisy of the guest may come to mind: Sir Reginald was hardly a fine example of a noble gentleman. On the other hand, James's behaviour has gone far beyond Reginald's worst moments, and once again the reader is aware that it is not a true Lisle behaving in such a way. James does not have noble blood, and it seems more and more that he may be incapable of acting nobly. James's upbringing ceases to be used as an explanation; his flaws are increasingly referred to as inherent rather than acquired; and he is portrayed as a scoundrel by nature, rather than by nurture.

This change in narrative treatment is similar to the previously discussed shift in the description of Olivia Marchmont, as she ceases to be portrayed as an unfulfilled genius constrained by a narrow existence, and instead is spoken of as a woman with a narrow mind, constitutionally predisposed towards insanity. In both cases, as the characters' flaws are more explicitly shown to be inherent, they are also shown to be hopeless cases. As *The Lady Lisle* progresses, James inspires not sympathy or understanding, but contempt, especially from those characters who know, or discover, his true identity – perhaps, most importantly, from the narrator. When Olivia discovers that James is an impostor, she declares: 'look at him, drunken and stupid,—more brutal than the oxen that sleep in his fields,—lower than the lowest brute in his stables. Good heavens! what a pitiful dupe I must have been to have been deceived by such a thing as that!' (p. 209). The narrator, also drawing on animalistic imagery, likens James to a 'tiresome dog' (p. 172), an 'ill-conditioned cur' (p. 246) and a 'guilty hound' (p. 197). Remorden (unaware of James's true identity) describes him to Blanche as a 'low-minded vulgarian', explaining that although he was high-born 'there were peculiar circumstances attending his childhood and youth, which, as some said, accounted for his loutish manners and paltry mind' (pp. 221–2), but by this point the reference to James's upbringing seems like a poor excuse, and once again, Walter's affirmation that James is high-born reminds the reader that he is *not*. The gipsies are also scornful: 'If fine clothes and a great fortune could make a gentleman, he'd be one; and if a bitter, black, treacherous, and cowardly heart can make a scoundrel, he *is* one' (p. 232). The gipsy's words ring true; in James's case clothes have not made the gentleman in anything but a superficial sense, and he is without doubt a scoundrel. In him we see the image of his father (also a murderer), but with wealth and power to corrupt him further. After James meets his end, Rupert eventually returns to his rightful place at Lislewood. Once again motherly instinct is relied upon to judge the validity of the apparent heir's claim, but this time we are assured that Claribel welcomes Rupert 'with a wild cry of delight and a thrill of affection such as she had never felt for the impostor, James Arnold' (p. 265).

Inherent constitution and heredity hold a lot of potential power in this novel. Braddon does not portray hereditary decline as entirely intractable, or as an irrefutable means of categorising society and measuring individual worth – Rupert, after all, is capable of personal improvement. But Braddon does employ heredity selectively, calling it into play differently depending on whether it is related to James or Rupert. Heredity functions in this novel to protect the middle and upper classes from the possibility of incursion by the lower classes, as James is portrayed as increasingly incapable, by nature, of being a gentleman. But, whilst hereditary degeneracy results in the segregation of the lower classes, the hereditary degeneracy of the upper classes is curable with a good dose of middle-class moral and social principles. When Rupert brings his acquired middle-class practices and his middle-class bride home to Lislewood with him, *The Lady Lisle* offers its middle-class readership the aspiration of upward class mobility, and suggests the desirability of merging the values of the one class with the affluence and antiquity of the other. *The Lady Lisle* is, in this sense, more conservative than *Lady Audley's Secret*. Winifred Hughes observes that Lucy Audley is a 'social climber' who 'embodies an internal threat to the respectable classes because she identifies with them; she wants what they value and brilliantly parodies their ideal. It is the validity of this ideal that Braddon repeatedly calls into question' (p. 127). In *The Lady Lisle*, the 'ideal' of the 'respectable classes' is represented by the middle rather than upper classes, and it is an ideal that is firmly endorsed.[30]

The Welcome Guest was intended for a middle-class readership but was eventually sold on to become a working-class magazine, offering the 'stronger class of fiction' that such readers desired; the editorial staff moved on to work on *Robin Goodfellow*, in which *Lady Audley's Secret* appeared.[31] Periodicals aimed at the lower classes often adopted a rather didactic tone towards the working and lower-middle classes. For example, the *Halfpenny Journal* (which serialised Braddon's *The Black Band* from 1861 to 1862, so concurrent with *The Lady Lisle* and *Lady Audley's Secret*), styled itself in the subtitle as *A Magazine for All who Can Read; Containing Novels, Romances, Tales and Sketches, Poetry, Miscellaneous Articles, Essays, Interesting Items, Family Helps, Golden Gleanings, Merry Moments, &c., &c.*,

which gives a sense of the journal's paternalistic tone. It included snippets with titles such as 'Be punctual', and pages 'To correspondents' that offered help and advice to readers. Although *The Welcome Guest* is slightly more high-brow, it shares a tendency to praise the working (especially the servant) classes for industry and service that could earn them respectability firmly within class boundaries. Hence, in *The Lady Lisle*, James is punished for his social climbing, but his mother Rachel, who is misled by her scoundrel husband but knows (and does not seek to exceed) her place as a servant, is also rewarded at the end of the novel by returning to the 'pretty Gothic lodge at the gates of Lislewood' where she started (p. 267).

Some ambiguity remains at the end of the novel. Ideas of hereditary and environmental determinism, once released into a text, are not easily controlled, and may initiate trains of thought that contradict the overall current of the novel. James's hopelessly awful upbringing remains difficult to forget, even when he is at his most despicable. Nevertheless, *The Lady Lisle* is not a work that generally offers sympathetic readings of its characters, and Braddon's portrayal of James is designed to inspire increasing contempt. In *The Lady Lisle* Braddon is appropriating notions of inherent constitution and heredity, as well as ideas about upbringing and education, to control the direction of her story and reader responses to the characters. As we shall see in the next chapter, in *Armadale* Collins also explicitly draws attention to issues of nature and nurture. However, unlike Braddon in *The Lady Lisle*, Collins often invites the reader to sympathise with characters who are morally, socially and possibly hereditarily dubious.

Notes

1 G. W. Child, 'Physiological psychology', *Westminster Review*, 33:1 (January 1868), 37–65 (p. 63).
2 Havelock Ellis, *The Criminal* (New York: Scribner and Welford, 1890), pp. 91–2.
3 The only other critic who has written (briefly) on *The Lady Lisle* is Mangham, pp. 108–13.
4 Aeron Haynie, '"An idle handle that was never turned, and a lazy rope so rotten": The decay of the country estate in *Lady Audley's Secret*', in Tromp, Gilbert and Haynie, *Beyond Sensation*, pp. 63–76 (pp. 66, 64).
5 Mary Elizabeth Braddon, *The Lady Lisle* (London: Ward and Lock, 1862), p. 2. All further references, unless otherwise stated, are to this edition. In the

The Lady Lisle

1890s Braddon's publishers produced a 'Stereotyped Edition' of her works so far. *Lady Lisle* ('*The*' was abandoned) includes some revisions; here the addition of 'a rosy little mouth' reinforces Claribel's doll-like beauty. Mary Elizabeth Braddon, *Lady Lisle* (London: Simpkin, Marshall, Hamilton, Kent, 189[?]), p. 6.

6 Braddon may have been capitalising on Collins's success. Both novels share a preoccupation with doubling and substitutions that breach class boundaries; both have charismatic villains with a seemingly near-preternatural understanding of human nature; both have two heroines, one feisty and strong-minded, one lovely, fair, and a little bit bland. Braddon certainly regarded Collins as competition to keep an eye upon, as she told Bulwer-Lytton (Wolff, 'Devoted disciple' (November or December 1864), p. 26).

7 The superficially attractive Lady Audley is also described as 'wax-dollish' (*Lady Audley's Secret*, p. 33).

8 Pliable women recur throughout Braddon's fiction. Millicent Markham in *The Captain of the Vulture* (1863) would learn Homer if asked, although she is driven by affection, Claribel by lethargy (Mary Elizabeth Braddon, *The Captain of the Vulture* (London: Simpkin, Marshall, Hamilton, Kent, 189[?]), p. 53). Georgy Sheldon in *Birds of Prey* (1867) also accepts 'all things as they were presented to her by a stronger mind than her own', and has 'no exalted capacity for happiness or misery' (Mary Elizabeth Braddon, *Birds of Prey* (Whitefish, MT: Kessinger Publishing, 2004), p. 95).

9 Charles Dickens, *Bleak House* (Oxford: Oxford University Press, 1998), p. 234.

10 Mrs Henry [Ellen] Wood, *St Martin's Eve* (London: Macmillan, 1907), pp. 51, 53. *St Martin's Eve* began as a *New Monthly Magazine* short story from 1853, but the family "curse" is not mentioned. Braddon's revisions to *Lady Lisle* add that the 'lingering decline' is 'a slow wasting away; a kind of disease', making the Lisles' condition closer to that described by Wood (*Lady Lisle*, 189[?], p. 22).

11 K. Corbet, 'The degeneration of race', *Lancet*, 78:1981 (17 August 1861), 170.

12 Benjamin Collins Brodie, *Psychological Inquiries, Part II* (1862), in *The Works of Sir Benjamin Collins Brodie: With an Autobiography*, 3 vols (London: Longman, Green, Longman, Roberts and Green, 1865), Vol. I, pp. 259–385 (p. 302).

13 Affluent, idle and unhealthy men are also a feature of Collins's fiction: *The Woman in White*'s Mr Fairlie has a 'frail, languidly-fretful, over-refined' look (p. 39); *No Name*'s Noel Vanstone suffers from 'a wearing and obstinate malady' (p. 118).

14 Claribel's being 'passionately fond of her son' (p. 18) may seem a redeeming feature, but Victorian doctors warned that 'emotional immoderation in the mother' could lead to effeminate 'offspring', and Claribel's idolisation of Rupert may be read as a contributing factor to his languidness (Sally Shuttleworth, 'Demonic mothers: Ideologies of bourgeois motherhood in the

mid-Victorian era', in Linda M. Shires (ed.), *Rewriting the Victorians: Theory, History, and the Politics of Gender* (London: Routledge, 1992), pp. 31–51 (p. 43)).

15 Henry Maudsley, *Body and Mind: An Inquiry into Their Connection and Mutual Influence, Specially in Reference to Mental Disorders* (London: Macmillan, 1870), in Taylor and Shuttleworth, *Embodied Selves*, pp. 326–9 (p. 327).

16 The Stereotyped Edition is even more scathing, reading: '*rarely in the whole course of his brief and useless existence* had [Reginald] desired to possess himself of anything, except …' (*Lady Lisle*, 189[?], p. 20, my emphasis).

17 Rupert Lisle and James Arnold are referred to by their real names except in quotations, when the original text is maintained.

18 The novel has a continuity flaw: Salamons begins as Uncle Alfred and Rupert begins as George (p. 130), but Salamons becomes Uncle George (p. 194), whilst Rupert becomes Richard (p. 191).

19 Threatened madness recurs throughout Braddon's work. For example, Lady Audley threatens Robert Audley (*Lady Audley's Secret*, p. 273), and later in *The Lady Lisle* Varney threatens Olivia, after she discovers James is an impostor (p. 214). Here, Rupert actually believes he was on the brink of madness.

20 In the Stereotyped Edition Braddon adds the reassurance that Blanche fell for Rupert 'before the discovery of the young man's real position' (*Lady Lisle*, 189[?], p. 304).

21 The Stereotyped Edition further emphasises Gilbert's influence on James when the boy looks at Rupert with an 'envious glance' because 'Master Arnold had acquired some of his father's propensities, and thought it a very hard thing that this other boy should wear a velvet tunic and a plume of feathers' (*Lady Lisle*, 189[?], p. 47). Bad father figures are common in Braddon's early novels: in *The Captain of the Vulture* Henry Masterson's lower-class father teaches him 'his own bad ways', and he eventually becomes a highwayman (p. 89).

22 George Henry Lewes, 'Hereditary influence, animal and human', *Westminster Review*, 66:129 (July 1856), 135–62 (p. 143).

23 Whereas in *The Woman in White* Laura Fairlie and Anne Catherick's resemblance is explained by their being half-sisters, no reason is given in *The Lady Lisle*.

24 The *Welcome Guest* (in which *The Lady Lisle* was serialised from May to September 1861) enhances the superficiality of James's appearance, describing his hands as 'white and delicate, and evidently unused to work of any kind' (Mary Elizabeth Braddon, *The Lady Lisle*, *The Welcome Guest*, 4 (July 1861) 239–43 (p. 241)).

25 Miss Gwilt infiltrates Thorpe Ambrose society by fulfilling the external requirements of a reputable, and therefore supposedly morally respectable, lady. Both *Armadale* and *The Lady Lisle* discredit such conventional measures of virtue and propriety. The Stereotyped Edition further emphasises the

The Lady Lisle

theme of class as Olivia adds 'That sickly effeminate face and low forehead of his have such a plebeian look' (*The Lady Lisle*, 189[?], p. 160).

26 In true sensational style, it turns out that Claribel's second husband, Walsingham, actually legally married Mrs Varney before Claribel.
27 Anon., 'The houseless poor', *Temple Bar*, 1 (March 1861), 225–9 (p. 227).
28 Mary Elizabeth Braddon, *Aurora Floyd* (Oxford: Oxford University Press, 1996), p. 138; Wilkie Collins, *Man and Wife* (Oxford: Oxford University Press, 1998), p. 171. Comparatively, the upbringing of Collins's Ozias Midwinter is almost as awful as James's, but he comes to feel compassion for his 'brother' dogs, and this core of seemingly inherent "goodness" is never lost (*Armadale*, p. 107).
29 The young man's striking of his own mother whilst she kneels before him, so hard that he draws blood, is as memorable and unsettling as Aurora Floyd's famous whipping of the Softy (provoked by the latter's kicking of the mastiff) (*Aurora Floyd*, pp. 138–9).
30 This is in contrast to Collins's *The Woman in White*, in which, as Janice Allan points out, the 'honest efforts of the middle-class hero' are rewarded by marriage to an upper-class woman in a 'typical narrative of bourgeois ascendancy' (Allan, p. 102).
31 Anon., 'Preface', *Welcome Guest*, 4 (May 1861), iii.

4

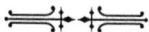

Armadale

> There is absolutely no limit to this law of material and immaterial heredity. The physical defects, the physical beauty; the meanness of spirit, the nobility of soul; all things that make us petty and despicable, all that make us wise and excellent—are alike to be derived through this channel.[1]
> (Nathan Sheppard, 'Genesis', *Temple Bar*, 1874)

The previous chapter began with G. W. Child's rather ominous description of the 'the great overhanging cloud of hereditary influences' that challenges a faith in 'the freedom of the will'. Six years later Nathan Sheppard's claim that 'there is absolutely no limit' to the rule of heredity, that 'all things' good and bad are the result of its effects, seems even more portentous, and this is indicative of a trend in thought about hereditary influence that would continue to the end of the century. Theories of degeneration and eugenics were increasingly entertained, although not always endorsed, by doctors, scientists and policy makers, and were circulated in periodicals aimed at both specialist and popular readerships. B. A. Morel's *Traité des dégénérescences physiques, intellectuelles et morales de l'espèce humaine* (1857) influenced British psychiatrists such as Henry Maudsley, whilst Francis Galton publicly speculated about selective human breeding from the 1860s.[2] These theories did not necessarily discount the possibility of influencing personal behaviour through upbringing or education, but the extent of that influence was seen to be distinctly limited; instead, the force of hereditary factors was emphasised in deciding the development of an individual's physical and mental constitution. Although there was not one cohesive theory of degeneration, they all shared a bleak outlook for the possibility of improving the degenerate individual. Degenerationists asserted that offspring would inherit parental flaws in a more virulent or transmuted form, and that the effects of upbringing and education would be, at best, a means of postponing an inevitable decline and probable demise. Eugenicists also perceived around them a growing number of weak, sickly, mentally limited and otherwise hereditarily undesirable offspring. It was therefore theorised that either good characteristics had to be bred into the race (positive eugenics), or bad characteristics bred out (negative eugenics).

Like *No Name* and *The Lady Lisle*, Wilkie Collins's *Armadale* (1866) is a novel of confused identities and a fortune pursued by disreputable con artists. Unlike Collins's earlier novel, and even more so than Braddon's, it engages extensively with ongoing Victorian debates about heredity. Written before most theories of eugenics and degeneration were crystallised, the novel does not clearly distinguish between the two, but does demonstrate Collins's awareness of the dangerous potential of heredity; importantly, however, he does not accept these theories unquestioningly.[3] This chapter begins with a reading of Collins's early story 'Mad Monkton' (1855), which provides a useful link between previous chapters and *Armadale* as it combines themes of monomania, family illness (possibly a curse) and heredity. Both texts make connections early on between heredity and morality. In 'Mad Monkton' the hereditary insanity that afflicts each generation of the Monkton family is triggered by incest. In *Armadale*, the first of many Allan Armadales we are introduced to (hereafter Armadale Senior) is dying of syphilis, a sexually transmitted disease that carried moral connotations, and he fears that his sins (profligacy and murder) may be passed on to his son. In both texts, Collins speculates about the consequences of hereditary transmission in its most negative sense. In the novel, the character of Ozias Midwinter (son of Armadale Senior, and himself originally named Allan Armadale) is a mixed-race, potentially criminal, nervous, sometimes hysterical social outsider and a prospective degenerate in numerous ways, who refers to his childhood self as 'an ill-conditioned brat, with my mother's negro blood in my face, and my murdering father's passions in my heart' (*Armadale*, p. 105). Through him especially, *Armadale* engages with a whole conflation of issues concerning moral and social undesirability that distinguished emerging theories of degeneration.

Midwinter, and also the villainous Miss Gwilt (who wants to marry her way to winning the fortune), view and describe themselves in degenerate terms because they perceive themselves, and their unconventional behaviour, as deviant or immoral (which, in Miss Gwilt's case, they often are). This immorality is expressed in terms of contagion and disease, and as something that, once acquired, cannot be removed. However, whereas degeneration and eugenics allowed little space for the development, and therefore, arguably, the importance, of the individual post-conception, Collins, who 'was fascinated with defending difference, valorizing the idiosyncratic or marginal over the "typical"', significantly focuses upon Midwinter and Miss Gwilt as individuals.[4] Collins spends considerable time describing the nervous vacillations of Midwinter's psyche and, as with Marion Halcombe in *The Woman in White* (1860), the reader is allowed to read extracts of Miss Gwilt's diary. In fact, Miss Gwilt has a more direct connection to the reader, as her diary is not 'appropriated and annotated' by male characters as Marion's is.[5] This 'independent stance', as Catherine Delafield argues, reinforces 'her criminality' but also means that 'despite her death, Lydia [Gwilt] still looks boldly out from the pages of *Armadale*'.[6] In her work on *fin-de-siècle* Gothic fiction Kelly Hurley observes that 'by dehumanizing ... the degenerate, the normative subject humanized itself' (p. 79). However, Collins prioritises the experience of the supposed degenerate and, by focusing on and focalising through such characters, depicts in very personal terms the struggle to overcome whatever it is in them that threatens an impending decline. This leads the reader to view potentially degenerate characters with pity, sympathy and sometimes even empathy.

Alfred Monkton in 'Mad Monkton' is also sympathetically portrayed, although a certain distance is maintained by the choice of a concerned, but never fully comprehending, friend as narrator.[7] Significantly, however, 'Mad Monkton' portrays the consequences of hereditary insanity as devastating and inescapable, while *Armadale*'s engagement with a broader range of hereditary threats does not depict them as insurmountable. This may have something to do with the changing climate surrounding theories of heredity, and also with Collins's growing sense of moral responsibility as an author (which led towards his later "novels with a purpose", such as *Man and Wife*). Jenny Bourne Taylor points out that in the 1860s Collins 'could draw on a range of psychological and experimental scientific methods, speculatively and hypothetically', but as degeneration came in later decades to be 'a dominant discursive model' Collins chose to 'overturn [its] assumptions' (p. 211). This is most evident in his 1888 novel *The Legacy of Cain*, in which a murderer's daughter, Eunice, is at times of extreme stress tempted to do 'dreadful things!', but overcomes these urges by drawing on the beneficial effects of her loving upbringing and 'the counterbalancing influences for good which had been part of [her] birthright'.[8] However, I suggest that in *Armadale* Collins was already showing a greater awareness of the potential consequences of unequivocally accepting theories of degeneration, and that although he was willing to push notions of negative heredity to their destructive limits in the earlier short story 'Mad Monkton', he was not willing to do so in *Armadale*.

In the same way that Braddon's treatment of James Gilbert can be usefully read alongside work of Henry Maudsley's from the 1870s, this chapter draws comparisons between Collins's fiction and a number of works on heredity that were unpublished at the time it was written. This shows that sensation fiction and medical writing about heredity responded to the same concerns about society, family and the nation, and that sensation authors were contributing to changing public awareness of heredity. Whereas with *The Lady Lisle* heredity is used by Braddon to bring about a certain outcome in the plot, in *Armadale*, Collins is far more concerned with the fear that can be generated by the thought of hereditary decline. Although Collins was not submerged in the cultural discourse of degeneration (unlike later writers such as Thomas Hardy and Bram Stoker[9]), he had (as a sensation author should) an eye for the more alarming implications of hereditary transmission. This means that even though Collins's plot challenges the inevitability of hereditary decline, *Armadale* is suffused with hereditary discourse and anxiety, creating a distinctively degenerationist atmosphere.

Mid-Victorian theories of heredity and degeneration

Theories of physical and moral heredity and its dangers were present in medical discourse throughout the nineteenth century, and physicians acknowledged the 'direct and immediate relation between Mental and Corporeal agency' (Carpenter, *Mental Physiology*, p. x). This meant that non-corporeal aspects, which had been traditionally seen as separate from and superior to the body – the mind and morality – were influenced by the physical transmission of constitutional traits. John C. Waller's work on pre-Galtonian 'discourses on hereditary transmission and "prudent" reproduction' demonstrates that 'by the mid-Victorian period notions of the inheritance of insanity and moral debasement were well established'.[10] In 1814 Joseph Adams was so concerned about what he perceived to be excessive public fears about 'the apprehension of hereditary diseases' that he published *A Treatise on the Supposed Hereditary Properties of Diseases: Containing Remarks on the Unfounded Terrors and Ill-Judged Cautions Consequent on Such Erroneous Opinions*.[11] Adams argued that hereditary disease was less prevalent than was generally believed, and he called for a level-headed approach to the choosing of one's (or one's child's) partner in marriage. Adams took a generally sanguine attitude towards human progress. Anticipating Darwinian natural selection, he assumed that in the same way that the strongest male animal would be 'father of the most offspring', 'health and intellect' would play a similar role in human society (Adams, p. 32). This differs from eugenicist thought, which encouraged an interventionist approach to human breeding on the basis that, as discussed in the previous chapter, society had reached a stage when it could avoid the evolutionary favouring of the fit and the clever. Nevertheless, although Adams argued that, in general, there was no need to interfere 'with the dictates of Nature', he also suggested that, in order to 'lessen anxiety' about hereditary diseases, 'family peculiarities, instead of being carefully concealed, should be accurately traced and faithfully recorded' so that imprudent marriages could be avoided and vulnerable offspring be identified (p. 41).

The most important difference, in terms of this discussion, between Adams and later eugenicist or degenerationist texts is a change of tone, which becomes generally more alarmist. Adams argued that if correct precautions were taken against a hereditary taint such as gout, generations could pass 'without any appearance of the disease' as long as the individual did not 'yield to habits of indulgence' (p. 25). Contrastingly, the *Lancet* in 1860, discussing degeneration resulting from marriages of consanguinity, warns readers to 'remember that the seeds of disease are slow to germinate, and may possibly be restrained from development by skilful management, fortunate circumstances, and care'; even if a child of a consanguineous marriage appears healthy, 'the laws of Nature work secretly and silently, but not capriciously', and 'it is perfectly certain that not one of the children, offspring of that union, can escape from that law'.[12] Whilst Adams views the non-appearance of a hereditary flaw in a generation as a result of good management, the *Lancet* gives a sinister slant to the same occurrence – the flaw may be hiding, but it is always there. Rather than emphasising the possibility of controlling defects, the later article focuses on their ineradicable nature. One of the most discussed forms of biological transmission was hereditary insanity. Falling somewhere between the two works cited above (both in tone and chronologically), G. H. Lewes reminded readers of the *Westminster Review* in 1856 that

> insanity is not only transmissible, but may suddenly manifest itself in persons who have hitherto shown no predisposition to it. The fact forces upon every mind an awful sense of responsibility, when a parent or guardian has to decide on permitting a marriage where the "hereditary taint" exists.
>
> ('Hereditary influence', p. 158)

Like Adams, Lewes attempted to deal with the subject in a non-alarmist manner, and asserted that the hereditary transmission of insanity was by no means assured. Nevertheless, the threat of atavistic insanity suddenly rearing its head, and the 'awful sense of responsibility' that it leads to, gives a greater impression of potential danger than Adams's work.

Escalating fears of negative heredity were accompanied by more emphasis being placed on the hereditary nature of morality. In 1865 Galton made it clear to readers of *Macmillan's Magazine* that hereditary defects covered a wide spectrum. Beginning with a range of physical diseases such as tuberculosis, Galton moves towards non-physical traits that carry ethical connotations: 'A morbid susceptibility to contagious disease, or to the poisonous effects of opium, or of calomel, and an aversion to the taste of meat, are all found to be inherited. So is a craving for drink, for gambling, strong sexual passion, a proclivity to pauperism, to crimes of violence, and to crimes of fraud' ('Hereditary talent', p. 320). There is a specificity to these examples – an inclination towards not just deceit, but 'crimes of fraud' – which helped to create the sense of inexorableness that characterised degenerationist thinking. This attitude led Galton to exclaim later in the article: 'how differently are the principles of virtue measured out to different natures!' (p. 324). He consequently speculated that selecting partners for breeding with a 'regard to their moral nature' would lead to a 'marked improvement' of people's 'natural disposition' (p. 325).

The hereditary nature of criminality attracted especial attention in both popular and medical journals. As noted in the previous chapter, Lewes believed that 'the "thieving propensity"' was transmissible from parent to child. In an 1860 article on 'Thieves and thieving' for the *Cornhill Magazine*, the clergyman H. W. Holland addressed this particular trait more fully and voiced the opinion that 'very few [criminals] adopt a life of crime from the sheer love of wrong-doing, and though they have, and must have, evil tendencies, the initiation of a criminal career is often wrought by the force of circumstances'. While he acknowledges that child criminals are influenced by their parents and environment, his reference to 'evil tendencies' gives the impression of something irremovable, and Holland tellingly speaks of the 'suppressing' of crime, rather than its eradication. He goes on more explicitly to assert that 'there is in some a *natural tendency* and *strong bias* towards dishonesty', and that 'thieving, and some other crimes seem to be hereditary, running in the same families for generations'.[13] Holland's language is very similar to the narrator of *No Name*'s musings on 'inbred forces', but while Collins's novel emphasises that 'we' all have the capacity for 'Good and Evil' within us (*No Name*, p. 116), here the emphasis falls fully on the 'evil tendencies' of children born of criminals.

In 1870, prison surgeon J. B. Thomson addressed a similar topic but adopted an even more extreme view-point, asserting that a distinct '*criminal class*', comprising physically and mentally degenerate individuals, had been produced through years of criminals breeding amongst themselves. Thomson asserted that, because of its hereditary nature, crime was 'intractable in the highest degree', and that prison reform would never work whilst criminals were still inter-breeding. Thomson asserts that because criminals interact only 'with those of their own nature and habits, they must beget a depraved and criminal class hereditarily disposed to crime'; habits acquired from lives amongst criminals are then 'superinduced upon their original moral depravity'. Thomson assures his readers that even when 'brought under very early training' to get them into good habits, the children of criminals are 'apt to lapse into their hereditary tendency'.[14] Thomson sees heredity as the predominant determinant for human action, and so moves towards eugenics as the only possibility for improvement.

Another way in which heredity came to appear more and more dangerous was the negative spin that was given to the notion of acquired characteristics. While J. B. Lamarck had theorised that habits acquired through life could be passed on to aid survival in the next generation, emerging degenerationist thought focused on the idea that undesirable behaviour that became habitual could be transmitted to children. Although some eugenicists, like Galton, argued that 'there are but few instances in which habit even seems to be inherited' (Galton, 'Hereditary talent', p. 322), 'Lamarckism' was 'essential' to the concept of degeneration because 'conscious indulgence in vice or excess' was seen as an initiator of decline (Oppenheim, pp. 269, 276). In 1859, a *British Quarterly Review* article warned its readers that

> *inherent*, intellectual, or moral qualities may not always be transmitted; but an *acquired and habitual vice will rarely fail to leave its trace upon one or more of the offspring, either in its original form or one closely allied.* The habit of the parent becomes the all but irresistible instinct of the child; the voluntarily adopted and cherished vice of the father or mother becomes the overpowering impulse of the son or daughter.[15]

Maudsley speculated that 'certain unfavourable conditions of life tend unquestionably to produce degeneracy of the individual; the morbid predisposition so generated is then transmitted to the next generation' (*Body and Mind*, p. 327). Maudsley gives the example of intemperance developing into dipsomania, which could lead to 'idiocy, suicide or insanity' in later generations (*Responsibility*, p. 43). Similarly, Sheppard asserted that a husband may contribute 'to his offspring many and unmistakable impresses', which 'may be evolved from traits and characteristics which are enduring, or from temporary conditions, the result of imprudence and excess' (p. 185). Such works cautioned parents that it was not only their own health and moral worth at stake if they slipped into socially unacceptable habits. Deviant behaviour was therefore often perceived as an instigator as well as a sign of degeneration (much as sensation fiction was seen as a cause and effect of social decline), and 'symptoms became increasingly confused with causes as degeneration theory became a tool for measuring the moral health of society as well as the health of the individual' (Hurley, p. 71).

Theories of degeneration and eugenics also stressed that individuals were responsible not only for their offspring's behaviour, but for the good of the nation, and concern about 'national fitness' became a defining aspect of eugenics (Waller, p. 463). Daniel Pick similarly notes a

> general shift from notions of the individual degenerate ... towards a biomedical conception of crowd and mass civilisation as regression; the "individual" was reconceived in relation to the mesh of evolutionary, racial and environmental forces which, it was now insisted, constituted and constrained his or her condition.
>
> (p. 222)

This change was partially because hopes of hereditary improvement related to children, society and the race; the individual's hereditary lot was already, irrevocably, cast. It was therefore essential to raise each generation with an awareness of any 'disastrous proclivities' and 'hereditary virtues' that might have been 'derived from the parental stock' (Sheppard, p. 180). Equally importantly, new generations must be made aware of the 'laws of health' when choosing a partner, because the 'evil results' of a bad marriage 'may be inexhaustible, and run on through the coming ages with augmented force and in multiplying channels' (Sheppard, pp. 181–2). This overlooking of the good of the individual in favour of the nation or the race is one of the ways in which Collins, who sympathetically explores individual suffering, conspicuously diverges from degenerationist thought. However, as the rest of the chapter will demonstrate, there is still a kind of literary eugenics at work which means that however sympathetically the potential degenerate is viewed, he or she is still prevented from breeding and passing on his or her dangerous potential.

'Mad Monkton'

Alfred Monkton is the last in the line of a family plagued by hereditary insanity. He believes that he must prevent the fulfilment of an ancient prophecy about his family's extinction by finding and burying the lost body of his uncle. Monkton's plans are thwarted when the recovered body is lost at sea; he fails to get over the shock of his adventure and dies before marrying his childhood sweetheart. The first-person narrator, despite his scepticism, cannot entirely explain the strange course of events that lead to the destruction of the Monkton line. In 'Mad Monkton', the reader is consistently faced with alternative means of interpretation: is the prophecy of the destruction of the Monkton line supernaturally fulfilled, is it the natural result of hereditary insanity, and do these two options necessarily oppose each other? As Norman Page observes, 'Collins's art in this story lies in creating an area of uncertainty in which, without necessarily giving full credence to the kind of experience enacted, we may find it difficult to dismiss it with the comforting label of "coincidence" or the more desperate one of "madness".'[16] Whilst Collins goes to undeniable lengths in order to offer the reader the possibility of a supernatural explanation, he makes an equally determined effort, in both 'Mad Monkton' and *Armadale*, to offer non-supernatural justifications for events by drawing on Victorian discourses of heredity that are just as disconcerting. In fact, as Mariaconcetta Costantini observes, 'fate and spiritism are inextricably intertwined with the psychic disorder that condemns Alfred', and 'No easy exit from this fatal legacy is indicated in the text.' Costantini reads this in connection with the story's drive to 'invalidate the idea of the self as a unitary, balanced entity',[17] but the notion of supernatural forces dictating the behaviour of a victim whose fate is already decided becomes a metaphor for degeneration in which the future conduct of the individual is already partially determined by his or her ancestry: act how they may, the final outcome is inevitable.

Monomania is the particular form of insanity that manifests itself in Alfred Monkton, but unlike Mannion or Magdalen, his condition is unquestionably hereditary, supposedly traceable back to a 'crime committed in past times by two of the Monktons, [who were] near relatives'.[18] Victorian medical texts frequently warned against incestuous and consanguineous unions. The *Lancet*, for example, asserted that 'marriages of consanguinity lead to the intellectual degradation and physical degeneration of the offspring of such unions' (Corbet, pp. 619–20). In 'Mad Monkton' the supernatural alternative could actually be seen as the less disturbing explanation, as Dickens's unwillingness to print the story in *Household Words* out of 'consideration for those numerous families in which there is such a taint' of hereditary insanity suggests.[19]

As with *No Name* and *Basil*, Collins's description of Monkton's behaviour shows striking similarities to contemporary medical accounts of monomania. As explained in Chapter 1, early accounts of monomania described sufferers experiencing a 'hallucination [that] is confined to a single point, while, on every other subject, the patient speaks and acts like a rational man'.[20] For example, Monkton appears sane under normal circumstances, as one of his acquaintances informs the narrator: 'When you can get him to say anything, which is not often, he talks like a sensible, well-educated man ... But touch the subject of his vagabond of an uncle, and the Monkton madness comes out directly' ('Mad Monkton', p. 47). The narrator soon has the opportunity of corroborating this account and observes that at the mention of his uncle, Monkton's 'eyes wandered away, and fixed themselves intensely, almost fiercely, either on the perfectly empty wall at our side, or on the vacant space between the wall and ourselves' (p. 48). It is subsequently revealed that Monkton believes he is looking at his dead uncle's spectre, the expression of a growing obsession with his family and his family's past.

Monkton is hereditarily and constitutionally vulnerable. The need to control the passions, extolled by early Victorian physicians, was seen as doubly important when hereditary insanity was involved. Families predisposed to insanity were advised that the education of children should aim for 'a character remarkable for sedateness, for the strict discipline of the feelings, and, as far as this is attainable, for the abolition of strong passions and emotions' (Prichard, *Treatise*, p. 172). Such a course of action could allow some control over the development of the personality, which would in turn inculcate the child with the ability to control his or her own behaviour. Monkton's descriptions of his childhood and young adulthood reveal that, like Magdalen Vanstone, he was not raised in a situation conducive to counteracting any dangerous tendencies.

Monkton's sensitive and excitable nature is shown by his childhood fear of his Uncle Stephen, whose visits instigate a strange fascination in the boy, who 'used to dream of him long after he had gone away' (p. 63). Furthermore, as a child Monkton hears something of the prophecy that tells of his family's decline and extinction, and when he discovers some of it in an 'antiquarian book' he is shocked to see a wood carving of a man 'strangely like' his uncle (p. 64). Collins therefore gives the reader a means of tracing the basis and development of Monkton's monomaniacal attachment to his uncle. Monkton tells the narrator he was warned 'that I must not waste time in thinking of such trifles, that I had more imagination than was good for me, and must suppress instead of exciting it', but this only irritates his 'curiosity' (p. 64). Monkton embarks on a search through the family records that takes him into the long-deserted depths of his ancestral home: 'such tempting suspense, such strange discoveries, such wild fancies, such enthralling terrors, all belonged to that life!' (p. 64). In this account of his experience (which, incidentally, sounds somewhat like a Victorian critic's description of reading sensation fiction) we can see that Monkton's nerves are thrilled, his imagination is fired, and he is entranced by the whole experience. He is, in short, living in a 'fascination of suspense and terror' (p. 65). This is reminiscent of the 'horrible joy' Mannion experiences when he is driven to pursue Basil (*Basil*, p. 257). Monkton's description of his own life repels the narrator, who can see the 'results' of such an existence, the crazed Monkton, before him (p. 65). For Monkton, however, the search for the prophecy is entirely addictive:

> I always found something to lure me on. Terrible confessions of past crimes, shocking proofs of secret wickedness that had been hidden securely from all eyes but mine, came to light ... There were periods when the results of this search of mine so horrified me, that I determined to give it up entirely; but I never could persevere in my resolution, the temptation to go on seemed at certain intervals to get too strong for me, and then I yielded to it again and again.
>
> (p. 65)

By indulging and exciting his morbid inquisitiveness Monkton is actively seeking out the dark centre of his family shame. By moving deeper into the rooms of his family home he is increasingly entrapped, and enraptured, by the threat of the hereditary taint. Although he attempts self-restraint, Monkton fails 'again and again'. This obsessive delving into his family's past uncovers a full written version of the prophecy. The fatal pull of hereditary insanity, and the way in which an individual can become complicit in their own downfall, is made apparent: Monkton cultivates his own morbid excitement, which then focuses on the family prophecy and later conjures up the spectre of his uncle. Monkton is caught in a vicious circle: constitutionally predisposed towards morbid fascinations, he is constitutionally incapable of avoiding temptation and therefore seeks it out, bringing himself closer and closer to insanity.

Lewes used 'Mad Monkton' as one example of stories that 'assume that the transmission of the malady [insanity] is inevitable, and hence they insist on the duty of renunciation'. In his attempt to offer a balanced account of the potential dangers of heredity, he warned his readers that 'artists are not bound to be physiologists, and are assuredly bad lawgivers in such cases' because they offered too extreme an image of hereditary insanity ('Hereditary influence', p. 158). Monkton does indeed suffer for the sins of his fathers, but although his behaviour is dictated by the insanity he has inherited, 'Mad Monkton' significantly does not carry the anxiety about *moral* heredity that is explored in *Armadale*. It is true that the family madness is initiated by a socially unacceptable act, that members of his ancestry were morally dubious and also that Monkton's fascination with his family's dark past could be read as a sign of his own inherent depravity. However, Monkton is a perfectly upright young man whose quest to retrieve his uncle's body is undertaken so that he can return home and faithfully marry his true love with an easy mind. 'Mad Monkton', therefore, offers a rather bleak outlook for sufferers of hereditary insanity, but does not imply that morality will necessarily be transmitted as well. The story both reflects contemporary concerns about heredity, and anticipates later, more severe anxieties. It also looks forward to *Armadale*, in which the influence of biological and moral determinism is realised to its fullest, yet most ambiguous, extent in Collins's fiction.

Armadale

Whereas Alfred Monkton is the last in a long line of hereditarily afflicted individuals, and 'Mad Monkton' depicts the final destruction of the family, Collins's *Armadale* begins with the possible initiation of a hereditary affliction: Midwinter's father has led a 'wild' and 'vicious' life, and is now dying from a 'paralytic affection' (p. 15). Here, Collins draws on the reader's recognition of the physical signs of syphilis, and its connection to a dissolute lifestyle. As Andrew Smith explains, syphilis was 'both a medical problem and a trope for social and cultural degeneration. In other words, there was the reality of the disease and a cultural fear of it' (p. 95). Collins employs this trope to create an atmosphere of moral infection. Armadale Senior fears that reprisal for his sins will be meted out to his son:

> I see the vices which have contaminated the father, descending, and contaminating the child; I see the shame which has disgraced the father's name, descending, and disgracing the child's. I look in on myself—and I see My Crime, ripening again for the future in the self-same circumstance which first sowed the seeds of it in the past; and descending in inherited contamination of Evil, from me to my son.
>
> (p. 55)

The language that Collins uses here taps directly into discourses of degenerative heredity and acquired characteristics. The biblical warning about the sins of the father (Exodus 25.5, 34.7) was a favourite reference point of the degenerationists when referring to acquired characteristics, and was often used to emphasise that individuals were responsible not merely for their own behaviour, but for any generations that came after them. Maudsley, for example, reminded his reader that 'it has been declared that the sins of the father shall be visited upon the children unto the third and fourth generations', and that the 'failing of the father ... will run on in the stream of family descent' (*Responsibility*, p. 22). In a similar spirit, Armadale Senior believes that his 'wild' lifestyle and murderous act have initiated Midwinter's own moral degeneration. His behaviour as a young man was, according to him, largely socially determined because his 'boyhood and youth were passed in idleness and self-indulgence' and his 'passions were left ... entirely without control of any kind' (p. 31). He therefore sees himself as the source of the hereditary moral decline of the family.

Armadale Senior's words share the dramatic tones of degenerationist texts that seemed designed to shock and dismay the reader. T. A. Ribot, in 1873, for example, attributed the 'decline of nations' to heredity, and declared that in looking back to the ancient Greeks 'we discern the slow, blind, unconscious working of nature in the millions of human beings who were decayed, though they knew it not, and who transmitted to their descendants a germ of death, each generation adding to it somewhat of its own'.[21] Despite the difference in scope, there is an atmospheric similarity between this and the passage from *Armadale*: 'Evil' and 'death' respectively are invisibly transmitted from one generation to the next like 'seeds' or 'germs' that bring decay rather than life, making for a terrifying account of hereditary degeneration. In both passages there is also the sense of a privileged retrospective view-point. Ribot is looking back into the ancient past and discerning what those living at the time could not see; he uses this knowledge to awaken his reader's awareness of the fact that they may suffer a similar fate. Midwinter's father sees his former life with a new awareness, not available to him when he was a young man.

One significant way in which Collins's depiction of hereditary transmission differs from that of degenerationists is his emphasis on replication rather than decline or accumulation of flaws. Oppenheim points out that in 'older hereditarian theories of nervous temperament' the hereditary flaw was generally replicated in each generation and 'did not automatically assume a graver pathological form in offspring', whereas later, 'nervous degeneration was something altogether more frightening and more disgraceful. Once set in motion, virtually everyone assumed that it was an irreversible process, dragging entire families into an inexorable downward spiral of declining physical and mental powers' (p. 272). Armadale Senior's language ('descending') suggests evolutionary "descent", but he envisions the immorality being passed on, 'ripening again for the future in the self-same circumstance', which suggests that Midwinter will literally duplicate his father's debauched and murderous behaviour.[22] 'Mad Monkton' also deviates from degenerationist theories in this sense, because whilst insanity is certainly hereditary in the Monkton family, it does not appear to be intensifying with each generation. In a sense, Collins's vision of heredity is more disconcerting than the degenerationist version. Degenerationists assumed that degeneracy in a family would get worse and worse until it led to sterility, a much reduced lifespan, or a condition such as idiocy, in which a person was unlikely to leave offspring: 'the common assumption that the degenerate was a marked departure from the normal and tending, more or less rapidly, towards extinction medicalized a notion of "the fall from grace" in which the progeny of degenerates exhibited a progressive moral and physical deterioration' (Rimke and Hunt, p. 74). In Collins's fiction, however, the fear is that the same situation will occur again and again with little hope of arresting the process.

All this build-up, however, proves to be deceptive; Midwinter does not follow in his father's footsteps. Neither does Allan Armadale, the son of the man that Midwinter's father killed (and whom, it is implied, Midwinter is destined to harm). The sons do bear a physical resemblance to their fathers: Allan and his father are both bigger and stronger than Midwinter and his father (pp. 40, 150). Furthermore, Midwinter's unprepossessing social conduct presents an unattractive impression that is ostensibly suggestive of his father's immorality: 'a stranger who had heard his story, and who saw him now, would have said, "His look is lurking, his manner is bad; he is, every inch of him, his father's son"' (p. 120). This only serves to emphasise, however, the fact that appearances are deceptive. Allan (whose father 'left his home an outlaw' (p. 31) and used deception to marry the woman Armadale Senior loved) may be 'heedless to the last degree', but has a 'disposition' as 'open as the day' (p. 62); Midwinter is unwaveringly loyal to those he cares for. Furthermore, although the events of the past certainly affect the present, there is no literal mirroring of events such as Midwinter's father fears: his 'vices' are not Midwinter's vices; the shame that has 'disgraced the father's name' does not disgrace the child's; even though Midwinter and Allan fall for the same woman, Miss Gwilt, his 'Crime' is not repeated. All in all, the sons could not lead their lives any more differently from their fathers; everything that happens to them is a result of the events in the past, not a recreation of them.

However, Midwinter is described (by both himself and the narrator) as having inherited his father's superstitious nature; he suggests that 'the inheritance of my father's heathen belief in Fate is one of the inheritances he has left to me' (p. 120). Midwinter attempts to combat this 'heathen belief' by convincing himself that it is unreasonable to believe that 'a friendship which has grown out of nothing but kindness on one side, and nothing but gratitude on the other, is destined to lead to an evil end' (pp. 121–2). However, this faith in his own good nature occurs early on in *Armadale*, and Midwinter vacillates between many levels of belief in his father's prophecy, especially after Allan's dream, which consists of a series of visions that may or may not prophesy evil events to come, and appear to come true during the course of the novel (pp. 170–2). Only moments after declaring his faith in his love for Allan, Midwinter's suspicions are reawakened by the news that Miss Gwilt has visited Allan's mother (whom she helped to elope with Allan's father). At this point, the narrator implicitly supports an interpretation of Midwinter's fatalistic tendencies as inherent by asking whether he felt 'the horror of his hereditary superstition creeping over him again?' (p. 124).

Midwinter is unable to dispose entirely of his 'hereditary superstition' during the course of the novel, but in the end he manages to sublimate it into the Christian faith advocated by the clergyman Mr Brock, who assures Midwinter that 'God is all-merciful, God is all-wise: natural or supernatural, it happens through Him' (p. 623). It is Mr Brock's 'belief in rational religion' that 'finally cancels out the opening of the scriptural [*sic*] denunciation of the absent father in the Prologue' (Taylor, p. 162). Mr Brock suggests to Midwinter that he 'may be the man whom the providence of God has appointed to save' Allan (p. 624), and so encourages a revisioning of events through a Christian faith in providence, as opposed to a 'heathen', superstitious belief in fate. Midwinter claims that he cannot accept coincidences as an explanation for the fulfilment of the Visions, but he tells Allan that he has 'learnt to view the purpose of the Dream with a new mind ... I once believed that it was sent to rouse your distrust of the friendless man whom you had taken as a brother to your heart. I now *know* that it came to you as a timely warning to take him closer still' (p. 815). The possibility of a hereditary belief in fate is not discounted, nor is the possibility that fate may indeed play a role in the workings of the world, but the degenerationist tone that characterised Midwinter's previous belief in the dream, and in his father's prophecy, is gone, and Midwinter's natural tendencies are modified into healthier ends.

Nevertheless, Midwinter is the character in *Armadale* most readily connected with ideas of "bad" heredity, both as a victim and as a potential propagator of degeneration. Beyond the very fact that he is his father's son, his physically undersized appearance, his 'sensitive self-tormenting nature' (p. 233) and his part-African background all serve to make him hereditarily "undesirable". If Midwinter's excessive love for Allan is perceived as homosexual, which Maria K. Bachman and Don Richard Cox argue it could have been, then in the eyes of conventional Victorian England this becomes another detrimental trait.[23] It does not help that Midwinter is initially introduced to the reader when suffering from brain fever, and is nursed back to health (p. 67). Midwinter's nervousness is noted by the doctor, Mr Hawbury, who sees 'his varying colour, and the incessant restlessness of his hands', and concludes 'I wouldn't change nervous systems with that man, for the largest fortune that could be offered me' (p. 166). In 1872 Charles Kingsley, who frequently lectured on social issues, observed (much like Galton did in a more class-conscious manner, as noted in the previous chapter) that modern social developments had resulted in the ability to 'save alive those who – looking at them from a merely physical point of view – are most fit to die'.[24] Although such constitutional weaknesses are not necessarily hereditary, they are certainly not hereditarily desirable; Midwinter's frail constitution is preserved to be passed down the family line, should he ever breed.

Despite Midwinter's fragile nervous system, and although he is 'undersized' (p. 67), he is physically tough, as he explains: 'From the time when I was a child, I have been used to hardship and exposure. Night and day, sometimes for months together, I never had my head under a roof. For years and years, the life of a wild animal—perhaps I ought to say, the life of a savage—was the life I led' (p. 367). From the choice of language, his physical hardihood becomes another potential source of degeneration; although Midwinter says he lived *like* a savage, not that he *is* a savage, in the light of his mixed-race heritage the use of the word would be telling for Victorian readers interested in "racial science". Less civilised cultures (which to the conventional Victorian mind meant non-white, non-European cultures) were often described as 'savage', which in post-Darwinian Victorian society meant less evolved and closer to an animal state. Charles Kingsley argued that our 'forefathers ... were hardy, just as the savage is usually hardy, because none but the hardy lived' ('The science of health', p. 21). Midwinter, for all his nervousness and physical slightness, is certainly 'hardy', and this could lead him to appear either atavistic (a throwback to his 'forefathers') or 'savage'. Midwinter's tendency to refer to himself as a 'dog', and the narrator's description of him following Allan 'like a dog' (p. 166), are also significant, as this again could intimate a less evolved, animalistic, state.

The references to Midwinter as "doglike" have echoes in the final decades of the century, when criminologists such as Cesare Lombroso would describe the born criminal as 'an atavistic being who reproduces in his person the ferocious instincts of primitive humanity and the inferior animals'.[25] Havelock Ellis's *The Criminal* (1890) drew comparisons between 'the instinctive criminal [and] the lower animals as well as the lower races of man', as they were both less sensible to physical pain and quicker to heal than Europeans (p. 114). Although criminality came to be associated with animalistic traits and 'primitive man', I am not arguing that Collins is anticipating such lines of thought in the same way that I *do* think he is anticipating other degenerationist ideas. Although Greta Olson has shown that Lombroso acknowledged his debt to 'great artists such as Shakespeare [who] had identified and depicted the criminal type [as atavistic] long before he did so',[26] Collins's repeated references to Midwinter's doglike nature actually help to reinforce his honest loyalty to Allan as he assumes a non-threatening attitude of submission towards him. What is most significant here is that Midwinter (who was literally raised with dogs for part of his childhood, coming to see them as his 'poor little four-footed brothers' (p. 107)) is not claiming that he is *innately* animalistic, but the sense of his own animalism has a perceptible impact on his self-conception, and helps to keep him subordinated to Allan; we shall shortly see a similar process at work in the character of Miss Gwilt.

Armadale

This characterization of Midwinter may have brought one of many common, but contrasting, racial stereotypes to the mind of some Victorian readers: that of the placid negro. An 1863 article in the *Reader*, for example, informed its readers that 'it has been said that the present slave-holders of America no more think of rebellion amongst their full-blooded slaves than they do of rebellion amongst their cows and horses. That was because the tranquillity of negroes in their approach to civilization resembled the content of domestic animals.'[27] Herman Melville made ironic use of this stereotype in the earlier 'Benito Cereno' (1855): his narrator explains that 'most negroes are natural valets', who possess 'the great gift of good-humor', and have the 'repute of making the most pleasing body servant in the world ... less a servant than a devoted companion'.[28] Although Collins does not directly reference this stereotype, the loyalty to Allan that wins the favour of Mr Brock can also be read as Midwinter's tame, "doglike" acceptance of his place.

Midwinter's racial heritage is not only important in relation to the language that is used. Bachman and Cox claim that although Midwinter's 'darker skin could be an issue or a cause for alarm, this radical distinction is never mentioned by any of the characters, and it apparently goes unnoticed by all the novel's narrators' (p. 327). There are, however, several references to Midwinter's racial heritage that are crucial for his characterisation, and important to this discussion. Mr Brock's initial suspicion of Midwinter, a stranger found 'wandering ... in a disordered state of mind' (p. 67), is understandable, but it is also indicated that he experiences feelings of apparent revulsion: 'the rector's healthy Anglo-Saxon flesh crept responsively at every casual movement of the usher's supple brown fingers' (p. 73). Collins has loaded this sentence with racial awareness: Mr Brock's English body seems to be acutely sensitive to the difference in colour, instinctively creeping of its own accord.

In contrast, the initial description of Midwinter's mother is reasonably flattering: 'a woman of the mixed blood of the European and the African race, with the northern delicacy in the shape of her face, and the southern richness in its colour ... who moved with an inbred grace' (p. 23).[29] Her behaviour occasionally suggests a struggle with self-control, but, considering that, at this point, her husband is dying and confessing a secret he has kept throughout their marriage, neither her 'hungering suspense' (p. 46) to hear the truth nor her hysterical tears appear particularly excessive. What wilfulness she shows, however, is explicitly related to her race: when she asks if her husband's first love was 'fair' or 'dark', the 'hot African blood' is visible in her cheeks (p. 35). Collins depicts innate "hot" blood as something that Midwinter struggles with: when Miss Gwilt, hoping to pass herself off as Allan Armadale's widow, denies her marriage to him 'the savage blood that he had inherited from his mother rose dark and slow in his ashy cheeks' (p. 757); when he resists striking her the 'black flush died out of his face' (p. 758). Here Collins clearly draws on another racial stereotype as the supposed savagery of African races is portrayed as hereditary and dangerous.

A number of critics have explored the ways in which, and the extent to which, Midwinter is integrated into respectable English society by the end of the novel; this is important to the current discussion because it reveals how Collins at once positions Midwinter as hero, and contains his potentially degenerate traits. Piya Pal-Lapinski perceives Midwinter as finding himself, through 'his relationship with Allan', engaged in a 'process of domestication, which seeks to homogenize and manage the plurality of his nomadic identity, distancing him from his mixed heritage and his mother's "negro blood"'.[30] Midwinter, by attempting to make himself worthy of Allan's friendship, undertakes a normative process, appearing to become less degenerate as he conforms to social expectations. Audrey Fisch argues that *Armadale* is not entirely 'sanguine about the possibility for peaceful assimilation of mixed-race people into English society' because Midwinter must commit an act of sacrifice in order to 'restore a degraded white society to its rightful position'.[31] Fisch goes on to point out that

> while both [Midwinter and Allan] share a criminal inheritance born of the corruption of West Indian slavery on their white fathers, Armadale lives in complete ignorance. The mixed-race Midwinter is aware of and needs to do psychological battle with his inheritances: black blood on one side and white criminality on the other.
>
> (Fisch, p. 324)

Allan's ignorance is maintained through Midwinter's effort, and, as Fisch observes, 'literally, the mixed-race character takes the poison for the white one here and, in so doing, enables the white man's continued success' (p. 324).

However, Fisch also argues that Midwinter 'remains alive only as a marginal character' at the end of *Armadale* (p. 324). Certainly, it is notable that Midwinter's marriage to Miss Gwilt remains childless, and he therefore fails to fulfil any biological threat he poses to 'healthy Anglo-Saxon' blood.[32] In a form of literary eugenics, Midwinter may play the role of the hero, but successful marriage is reserved for the 'thoroughly English'

Allan (p. 62). Critics such as Greenslade have explored the normative drive of degeneration theories, which 'facilitated discourses of sometimes crude differentiation: between the normal and the abnormal, the healthy and morbid, the "fit" and "unfit", the civilised and the primitive' (p. 2). Degeneration theories worked towards the fixation of such bipolar categories, and the policing of the border between them. In terms of procreation, Midwinter's role in English society continues to be marginalised at the end of the novel and he can continue to be viewed as Other. However, he is not marginal as far as the focal points of the novel are concerned. While attention is often drawn to his racially othered state, the reader is also often invited to relate to Midwinter, and his actions are explained by the mediating voice of the narrator. His inappropriate decision to accompany Miss Gwilt into her home, for example, is defended by an appeal to general manhood: 'At his age, and in his position, who could have left her? The man (with a man's temperament) doesn't live who could have left her. Midwinter went in' (p. 461). Moreover, it is Midwinter's battle that has been fought and won (at a cost), he has a promising career ahead of him, the final chapter is entitled 'Midwinter', and the description of his words and emotions closes the narrative. Here, although Collins polices the borders to some extent, Midwinter's ability to sublimate the hereditary threats of his father's superstitious nature, and his mother's 'hot blood', allows him to emerge (in striking contrast to Braddon's treatment of a murderer's son in *The Lady Lisle*) as *Armadale*'s hero. The outsider is brought to the foreground and portrayed in a positive light literally as the novel ends with the 'light of the new day' shining 'tenderly on his face' (p. 816).

In contrast to Midwinter, Allan is, physically, an ideal candidate to procreate, his constitution receiving a favourable assessment from Mr Hawbury (p. 169). Allan also lives away from an unhealthy city atmosphere. City living, with its frantic pace, polluted atmosphere and opportunities for unhealthy indulgences, was often seen as an initiator of degeneration. Kingsley, for example, observed the healthiest men were 'country-bred' ('The science of health', p. 25). Benjamin Brodie (whose *Psychological Inquiries* Collins owned[33]) speculated that it was 'not to be expected that the artisans in crowded cities, living in close habitations, and to a great extent indulging in intemperate and thriftless habits, can enjoy the robust health and physical powers of a rural population', and expressed concern that, because of increased relocation to cities, 'after a few more generations have passed away, the race will degenerate' (p. 313). Allan has also, despite being the product of two landed families, been

Heredity and degeneration

raised away from an upper-class environment (which, as discussed in the previous chapter, was often considered physically and morally debilitating) because of his mother's rejection by her family (after her elopement) and her desire to raise Allan away 'from all contact with the temptations and the dangers of the world' (p. 61). Allan's isolated upbringing has (in a similar way to Rupert Lisle's middle-class education) ensured that he does not pick up the bad, potentially degenerative habits of the upper classes, so when he inherits the Blanchard Estate of Thorpe Ambrose he may not win the approval of the local gentry (because of his dislike of hunting and visiting) but he does supply 'the manly vigour' that Kingsley desired to see in society ('The science of health', p. 25). At the beginning of the novel the Armadale name is in moral and economic decline: the original Armadale disinherits his son (Allan's father), who has 'disgraced himself beyond all redemption' (p. 31); the value of the Caribbean land of both the Armadales and the Wrentmores (Midwinter's father's original name) is threatened by the coming slave emancipation (p. 53). Allan brings the Blanchard fortune to the Armadale name, as well as the advantages of his upbringing; physical health; and honest, amiable nature.

However, in the paranoid spirit of degenerationist thought, and in the knowledge that there were many varied, often conflicting notions of degeneration, it is worth considering whether this fine young Englishman is as hereditarily desirable as he may appear. Allan's fitness for procreation becomes questionable in relation to Edwin Ray Lankester's definition of degeneration as an organism becoming 'adapted to *less* varied and *less* complex conditions of life'.[34] In comparison to the highly strung but assiduous Midwinter, Allan is somewhat lacking in intelligence and diligence, being 'slow over his books – but more from a constitutional inability to fix his attention to his tasks than from want of capacity to understand them' (pp. 61–2). There are examples throughout the novel that show that, although honourable, Allan is morally simplistic, such as his choosing the Milroys as his tenants at the spin of a coin (p. 135). Lankester's example of 'an active healthy man' who 'degenerates when he becomes suddenly possessed of a fortune' is particularly pertinent (p. 33). Allan's upbringing away from society, his possession of the Blanchard fortune, and the number of people who assist him in difficult situations (notably Mr Brock, Pedgift Junior and Midwinter) ensure he encounters few challenges requiring him to struggle or adapt in his life. Kingsley similarly spoke of men living a 'lap-dog' existence, which he saw as 'unfavourable to the growth of the higher virtues', because for many 'safety and comfort may, and actually do, merely make their lives mean and petty, effeminate and dull'.[35]

Gabrielle Ceraldi's discussion of *The Woman in White* is pertinent here, as she explores the novel in the light of the theory of natural selection and social Darwinism. Ceraldi argues that Collins portrays England as culturally and evolutionarily superior to the rest of the world, but 'undermined from within by its growing ability to shelter itself from the rigors of evolutionary struggle'; because of this, according to Ceraldi, Collins suggests that 'biological stagnation is inevitable'.[36] This is also apparent in the character of Allan, who cannot compete against, or even perceive the real danger of, his enemies. As Caroline Reitz pithily puts it, Allan is 'long on pluck and short on almost everything else, including a sense of the complexities of the modern world'.[37] Reitz's choice of 'complexity' is particularly applicable to this discussion, as Midwinter does not only represent a triumph of the individual over a particularly hard hereditary lot; because he is able to endure, and is hardened by, difficult experiences, he is the more complex organism.

Rafaella Antinucci also notes 'Midwinter's more complex character'. As part of her comparison of the two heroes she considers the novel's addressing of 'the question of nature as opposed to nurture' and aligns Allan with the former: 'Brought up in an isolated and rural environment, Allan incarnates the Rousseauvian model uncorrupted by society ... Allan's inborn goodness assimilates him to ... heroes whose gentlemanly status is not so much the result of a process or an education, as a preordained, almost ontological condition.' Antinucci associates Midwinter with nurture, as he 'embodies the negative effects an inhuman society can have on a young man', and his 'personality is shaped by a long chain of events and circumstances, which make him become a reclusive and isolated man'.[38] This is a convincing reading (and certainly fits with Collins's tendency to depict characters with 'inborn goodness', such as Magdalen), but Allan's personality does not have to be perceived solely in terms of what has *not* affected his inherent constitution, and can also be seen as a product of his upbringing. Moreover, while Midwinter's life experiences have definitely affected his character, his complexity does not have to be purely a result of these; even though he ran away from school, his literary tastes include Sophocles and Goethe in their original languages (p. 68), a potential sign of a naturally more refined mind than Allan's, whose isolated situation leads to more physical pursuits.

However, complexity itself could be seen as a cause of degeneration. Members of supposedly more evolved societies were believed to have more complex, but therefore more delicate, brains. Maudsley (writing about insanity) claimed that 'as is the height so is the depth, as is the development so is the degeneration' ('On some of the causes', p. 490). Certainly Collins's depiction of Midwinter's behaviour and physiology – his mental anxieties and highly strung nervous system, his brain fever and hysteria, his obsessive overanalysing and moral vacillations – gives the impression that he is teetering, much of the time, on the brink of another breakdown. This is exactly the type of "modern", "civilised" degeneration that, according to Maudsley, "savages" (with their less developed brains) were not capable of experiencing – the kind of mental instability that was 'a result of the necessary and positive intricacy of being at the apex of creation' (Davis, p. 71). In Midwinter, Collins has created a character who carries the potential for numerous types of degeneracy: on the one hand his "savage" blood could enter, and therefore cause to degenerate, the white race (the very fact of his existence shows this has already happened to an extent); on the other hand he represents the fear of degeneration as something generated within civilised society itself.[39] Allan, contrastingly, is an admirable physical specimen, bringing vitality to the failing upper classes. Yet this educated, affluent, white English male threatens a different type of degeneration again (although also a threat from within society), and can be seen as a confirmation of Lankester's warning that 'we are all drifting, tending to the condition of intellectual Barnacles or Ascidians' (Lankester, p. 60).

While Allan is open and honest, if not particularly morally sophisticated, and while Midwinter appears shifty, but is actually honourable, the other major character in the novel, Lydia Gwilt, is a deceiver and a criminal, and it is therefore not surprising that she is described in terms of moral degeneracy. Miss Gwilt's family background is a mystery even to herself, but she is initially described by Midwinter's father as 'innately deceitful' and 'innately pitiless', 'a marvel of precocious ability' with 'wicked dexterity', suggesting she has inborn immoral tendencies and natural criminal ability (p. 39).[40] However, the ultimate discrediting of Midwinter's father's belief in his own moral contagion casts doubt upon his assessment of Miss Gwilt. She has, furthermore, been exposed to many morally detrimental social forces. She is abandoned by her parents; by the Oldershaws, who used her as a child advertisement for quack beauty products; and by Allan's mother, Miss Blanchard (after being encouraged to commit forgery). Her subsequent exposure to increasingly dissolute influences (as Bashwood Junior's tale reveals (pp. 632–44)) gives validity to her final supposition that she might have been a 'better woman ... if [she] had not lived a miserable life' (p. 806).

Miss Gwilt's criminality may well be a result of upbringing rather than being innate, but she describes herself in terms associated with discourses of degeneration and acquired characteristics. In a diary entry she tries to understand how her marriage to Midwinter has failed to fulfil its early promise:

> I have thought and thought about it, till a horrible fancy has taken possession of me. He has been noble and good in his past life, and I have been wicked and disgraced. Who can tell what a gap that dreadful distance may make between us, unknown to him and unknown to me ... Is there an unutterable Something left by the horror of my past life, which clings invisibly to me still? And is *he* feeling the influence of it, sensibly, and yet incomprehensibly to himself? Oh me! Is there no purifying power in such love as mine? Are there plague-spots of past wickedness on my heart which no after-repentance can wash out?
>
> (pp. 660–1)

Miss Gwilt fears that her actions have set her irredeemably apart from Midwinter. Because the narrator remains silent about the reasons why Midwinter seems to lose interest in his new wife, we have only the suspicions of Miss Gwilt to extrapolate from and, like Midwinter's father, the fear of her own immorality renders her narrative voice compelling, but extreme and unreliable. Criminal behaviour was exactly the kind of conduct that could supposedly initiate degeneration, and it is the fear that her previous immoral ways may have changed her in a fundamental, irreversible manner that is particularly important here. Miss Gwilt's description of the sinister 'unutterable Something', the irremovable 'plague-spots' of wickedness she may have acquired, is expressive of the same fearful, anxiety-ridden atmosphere that was often generated by descriptions of degeneration.

The sheer number of degeneration theories that can be linked to this novel results in a complex net of possibilities in which any form of weakness is a potential future threat and no character is free from the possible taint of degeneration in one of its many forms. This gives an impression of how oppressive and all-encompassing the concept of degeneration could become, but also of how comfortably sensation fiction can accommodate ideas of negative heredity. Sensation fiction is in fact the ideal genre for addressing, and exploiting, concerns about degeneration. In his review of *No Name*, Alexander Smith commented upon the ultra-tight plotting of sensation novels: 'every trifling incident is charged with an oppressive importance: if a tea-cup is broken, it has a meaning, it is a link in a chain; you are certain to hear of it afterwards'.[41] This is equally true for degeneration in its most extreme form – every deed, every mistake or weakness will affect an individual's future progeny. Degeneration theorists saw potential danger everywhere. Just over six months after *Armadale* finished its run in the *Cornhill* (from November 1864 to June 1866) Henry Maudsley warned readers of the *Journal of Mental Science* that:

> all evil habits of life—habits of luxurious effeminacy, of indolence, and of excess in the indulgence of any appetite—as well as all unfavourable external conditions of life which deteriorate the mental and bodily health of individuals, are so far predisposing causes of the degeneracy of the race which individuals constitute.
>
> ('On some of the causes', p. 495)

The repetition of 'all' makes degeneracy seem almost unavoidable (and echoes the quotation with which this chapter opened). The atmosphere of destructive fatality that appears to be at work in *Armadale* complements that of destructive heredity. Even the marriage of Allan Armadale to Neelie is problematic, not only because Allan himself can be seen as degenerate, but because Mrs Milroy suffers from a mysterious illness. Although Neelie seems particularly fit, having the 'blessed exuberance of youth and health' (p. 206), her mother's condition did not manifest itself until later in life, and there is no indication in the text as to how hereditary it may be (pp. 374–5).

Armadale is a novel full of instances of potential mental, physical and moral decline. Because of the way in which Collins employs degenerationist discourse from the very start of the novel, behaviour and character traits that may have passed unnoticed come to seem worrying. Indeed, degeneration is, in many ways, seemingly only restrained through the 'renunciation' of the supposed degenerates (Lewes, 'Hereditary influence', p. 158). Midwinter ends the novel single and childless, devoted to his soon-to-be-married friend; Miss Gwilt commits suicide, purging the degenerate threat she poses. However, by showing admirable qualities in Midwinter, and even in Miss Gwilt (who dies, to some extent, for love), and by revealing Allan Armadale to be in some senses morally and intellectually inferior, Collins blurs the boundaries between fit and unfit, desirable and undesirable; a hereditarily suspect and vulnerable individual such as Midwinter may be able to overcome and improve on the imperfections of his parents. In fact, *Armadale* is in many ways about the factors that *do not* determine an individual's behaviour. Rather than heredity or fatality proving the true danger, the accidents and coincidences with which characters are faced during their lives, and the choices they make in response to them, are what really matter. This looks forward to the next chapter and Collins's later novel, *Man and Wife* (1870), in which there is no longer such a subtle blending of deterministic factors, and the rule of "circumstance" is increasingly enforced.

The emergence of the sensation genre was contemporaneous with the emergence and dissemination of nascent theories of eugenics and degeneration in England. Novelists, just as much as physicians and scientists, perceived the alarming possibilities implied in the thought that one's hereditary or constitutional lot may be inescapable, and in fact anticipated in their imaginative depictions of negative hereditary and innate influences the disconcerting writings of people such as Maudsley, who spoke of the overwhelming 'tyranny' of man's 'organization' (*Responsibility*, p. 22). Neither Braddon nor Collins suggests that the influence of heredity can *never* be counteracted; for characters such as Rupert Lisle and Midwinter, improvement or avoidance of an apparently biologically preordained fate is possible. Although the fear of degeneration sometimes proves false, for James Gilbert it appears increasingly true, while for Miss Gwilt the fear that it *might* be true is enough to precipitate self-destruction. In fact we could wonder whether, even if they don't endorse it, Braddon's and Collins's sensational anticipation of the bleak outlook of late Victorian degenerationists may actually have brought such thinking to public attention, helping to pave the way for acceptance of their theories.

Notes

1 Nathan Sheppard, 'Genesis', *Temple Bar*, 41 (May 1874), 175–93 (p. 179).
2 Galton coined the term 'eugenic' in Francis Galton, *Inquiries into Human Faculty and Its Development* (London: Macmillan, 1883). For a concise account of Galton's career see Raymond E. Fancher, 'Scientific cousins: The relationship between Charles Darwin and Francis Galton', *American Psychologist*, 64:2 (February–March 2009), 84–92. For responses to Galton's theories see Paul, pp. 31–9.
3 For some (particularly later) theorists, degeneration and eugenics were separate and even antagonistic ways of thinking. For example, the degenerationist Edwin Ray Lankester and H. G. Wells advocated improved education as opposed to eugenics as a plan for improving society (see Richard Barnett, 'Education or degeneration: E. Ray Lankester, H. G. Wells and *The Outline of*

History', *Studies in History and Philosophy of Biological and Biomedical Sciences*, 37:2 (June 2006), 203–29 (esp. pp. 216–19)).

4 Nathan K. Hensley, '*Armadale* and the logic of liberalism', *Victorian Studies*, 51 (2009), 607–32 (p. 620). As I have similarly argued about sensation fiction more generally in the introduction, Hensley points out that 'critics who have focused on *Armadale*'s apparent preference for plot over character fail to notice that its plot is about character'; Hensley goes on, however, to think about the instability of identity, and how character 'can be falsified, how names do or don't match it, how one individual (in disguise) might inhabit several of them in sequence' (p. 608).

5 Lyn Pykett, 'Collins and the sensation novel', in Jenny Bourne Taylor (ed.), *The Cambridge Companion to Wilkie Collins* (Cambridge: Cambridge University Press, 2006), pp. 50–64 (p. 57).

6 Catherine Delafield, *Women's Diaries as Narrative in the Nineteenth-Century Novel* (Farnham: Ashgate, 2009), pp. 49, 143.

7 With a rationally minded but perplexed first-person narrator observing a mentally unstable friend who is the end of his family line, this story has clear similarities to Edgar Allan Poe's 'The Fall of the House of Usher' (1839). For Collins's adaptations of Poe's work, see John Bowen, 'Collins's shorter fiction', in Taylor, *The Cambridge Companion to Wilkie Collins*, pp. 37–49.

8 Wilkie Collins, *The Legacy of Cain* (Stroud: Sutton Publishing, 1993), pp. 199, 201. *The Legacy of Cain*'s villainess is Eunice's adopted sister, the attempted poisoner Helena. Helena functions as a contrast to Eunice, as proof that a murderer's daughter can be better than a child of "respectable" parents. The reason for Helena's behaviour is not entirely explained, but the fact that Helena acts far worse than her petty-minded and 'wicked' (p. 35) mother ever does makes her the moral degenerate, which Collins takes pains to prove that Eunice is not. The sisters serve as a warning that a person's true nature cannot be assumed based on their parentage or nurture, but in delivering this message Collins complicates his assertion that negative hereditary traits can be overcome.

9 See, for example, Greenslade on Hardy (Chapter 8), Hurley (*passim*) and Andrew Smith on Stoker (Chapter 5).

10 John C. Waller, 'Ideas of heredity, reproduction and eugenics in Britain, 1800–1875', *Studies in History and Philosophy of Biological and Biomedical Sciences*, 32:3 (September 2001), 457–89 (pp. 458, 463).

11 Joseph Adams, *A Treatise on the Supposed Hereditary Properties of Diseases: Containing Remarks on the Unfounded Terrors and Ill-Judged Cautions Consequent on Such Erroneous Opinions* (London: Callow, 1814), p. v.

12 Anon., 'The degeneration of race', *Lancet*, 76:1947 (22 December 1860), 619–20 (p. 620).

13 H. W. Holland, 'Thieves and thieving', *Cornhill Magazine*, 2:9 (September 1860), 326–44 (pp. 326–30), emphasis in original.

14 J. B. Thomson, 'The hereditary nature of crime', *Journal of Mental Science*, 15 (January 1870), 487–98 (pp. 488–98). Maudsley, who was an editor for the *Journal of Mental Science* between 1863 and 1878, uses this article to support his own degenerationist arguments (*Responsibility*, p. 30). See Trevor Turner, 'Henry Maudsley – psychiatrist, philosopher and entrepreneur', *Psychological Medicine*, 18:3 (August 1988), 551–74 (p. 555).
15 Anon., 'Physical and moral heritage', *British Quarterly Review*, 29:57 (January 1859), 3–56 (pp. 5–6). Emphasis in original.
16 Norman Page, 'Introduction', in Wilkie Collins, *'Mad Monkton' and Other Stories*, ed. Norman Page (Oxford: Oxford University Press, 1994), pp. vii–xxx (p. xv).
17 Mariaconcetta Costantini, *Venturing into Unknown Waters: Wilkie Collins and the Challenge of Modernity* (Pescara: Tracce, 2008), pp. 76, 75.
18 Wilkie Collins, 'Mad Monkton', in *'Mad Monkton' and Other Stories*, pp. 39–104 (p. 39).
19 Letter from Charles Dickens to W. H. Wills (subeditor of *Household Words*), 8 February 1853, in *Letters*, p. 23. 'Mad Monkton' was eventually published with the title 'The Monktons of Wincot Abbey' in *Fraser's Magazine for Town and Country*, November and December 1855.
20 John Abercrombie, *Inquiries Concerning the Intellectual Powers and the Investigation of Truth*, 2nd edn (Edinburgh: Waugh and Innes, 1831 [1830]), p. 330.
21 Théodule A. Ribot, *Heredity: A Psychological Study of Its Phenomena, Laws, Causes and Consequences*, 2nd edn (London: King, 1875), in Taylor and Shuttleworth, *Embodied Selves*, pp. 306–8 (p. 308). The morbidity of tone is apparent when compared with an article such as G. H. Lewes's 'The two aspects of history', which also sees the destruction of ancient civilisations as likely to be repeated in the future, but optimistically declares that 'nations perish, individuals vanish, but the Race survives, and, surviving, advances towards completer life' (G. H. Lewes, 'The two aspects of history', *Cornhill Magazine*, 9:51 (March 1864), 292–6 (p. 292)).
22 Armadale Senior's fear of degeneration is compounded with a supernatural fear of divine retribution: the murder has remained 'unpunished and unatoned', and for this reason 'Evil' is to be Midwinter's legacy (p. 54).
23 Maria K. Bachman and Don Richard Cox, 'Wilkie Collins's villainous Miss Gwilt, criminality, and the unspeakable truth', *Dickens Studies Annual*, 32 (2002), 319–37.
24 Charles Kingsley, 'The science of health', in *Sanitary and Social Lectures* (London: Macmillan, 1880), pp. 21–45 (p. 27). Kingsley asserted that society should take responsibility for the existence of its weak members and should preserve and improve them as much as possible, but also try to improve the race at the same time (p. 28).

25 Cesare Lombroso, 'Introduction', in Gina Lombroso-Ferrero, *Criminal Man: According to the Classification of Cesare Lombroso* (New York and London: Knickerbocker Press, 1911), pp. xi–xx (p. xv).
26 Greta Olson, *Criminals as Animals from Shakespeare to Lombroso* (Boston: De Gruyter, 2013), p. 106.
27 Anon., 'On the physical and mental characters of the Negro', *Reader*, 2 (1863), 324. Although there is not space to discuss it here, it is interesting that this was published during the American Civil War.
28 Herman Melville, 'Benito Cereno', in Nina Baym and Robert S. Levine (eds), *The Norton Anthology of American Literature, Volume B, 1820–1865*, 8th edn (New York: W. W. Norton, 2012), pp. 1526–82 (pp. 1556, 1531).
29 African blood, especially in women, is something Collins employs elsewhere for aesthetic purposes. Natalie Graybrooke in 'Miss or Mrs?' (1873) has a 'mixture of Negro blood and French blood' from her mother's side, and therefore has 'her mother's superb black hair, and her mother's melting lazy lovely brown eyes'. Natalie is certainly no "savage", having 'the gentle, innocent manner of a young girl' (Wilkie Collins, 'Miss or Mrs?', in *'Miss or Mrs?', 'The Haunted Hotel', 'The Guilty River'* (Oxford: Oxford University Press, 1999), pp. 1–83 (pp. 9–10)).
30 Piya Pal-Lapinski, 'Chemical seductions: Exoticism, toxicology, and the female poisoner in *Armadale* and *The Legacy of Cain*', in Bachman and Cox, *Reality's Dark Light*, pp. 94–130 (p. 107).
31 Audrey Fisch, 'Collins, race, and slavery', in Bachman and Cox, *Reality's Dark Light*, pp. 313–28 (p. 319).
32 For a discussion of Victorian theories of racial hybridity see Nancy Stepan, 'Biological degeneration: Races and proper places', in J. Edward Chamberlin and Sander L. Gilman (eds), *Degeneration: The Dark Side of Progress* (New York: Columbia University Press, 1985), pp. 97–120 (esp. pp. 104–12). Midwinter is the child of a mixed-race woman, suggesting Collins accepted (unlike some Victorians) that different racial types could breed successfully. Although 'mulattoes' could be seen as infirm and 'in the long run unproductive', Midwinter's various weaknesses more clearly fit (as discussed presently) the degeneration associated with white, civilised societies (Stepan, p. 108).
33 William Baker, *Wilkie Collins's Library: A Reconstruction* (London: Greenwood Press, 2002), p. 82.
34 Edwin Ray Lankester, *Degeneration: A Chapter in Darwinism* (London: Macmillan, 1880), p. 32.
35 Charles Kingsley, 'Heroism' (1873), in *Sanitary and Social Lectures* (London: Macmillan, 1880), pp. 225–54 (p. 226). In fact, Midwinter's saving of Allan at the end of the novel, and the final decision to keep Allan ignorant of the full story in order to protect his mother's memory, puts Allan in the position of the innocent heroine.

36 Gabrielle Ceraldi, 'The Crystal Palace, imperialism, and the "struggle for existence": Victorian evolutionary discourse in Collins's *The Woman in White*', in Bachman and Cox, *Reality's Dark Light*, pp. 173–94 (pp. 176, 186).
37 Caroline Reitz, 'Colonial "Gwilt": In and around Wilkie Collins's *Armadale*', *Victorian Periodicals Review*, 33:1 (2000), 92–103 (p. 98).
38 Rafaella Antinucci, '"Not another like him in the world": Wilkie Collins and the gentleman within', in Mariaconcetta Costantini (ed.), *'Armadale': Wilkie Collins and the Dark Threads of Life* (Roma: Aracne, 2009), pp. 133–54 (pp. 139–40).
39 The "savage" and "modern" combine, as Midwinter's moral and intellectual anxieties (which make him 'complex') are based in part on his superstitious beliefs, a state of mind connected to less evolved races. The nineteenth-century craze for spiritualism was often seen as a sign that modern society had not reached the height of civilisation, and as late as 1900 periodicals were asking why 'in almost every respect the civilised human being is unlike the savage' and yet still displays the superstitious feelings of 'the men of the primeval world' (D. F. Hannigan, 'The tenacity of superstition', *Westminster Review*, 154:1 (July 1900), 69–72 (p. 69)).
40 Descriptions of Lydia as 'tigerish' (pp. 438, 668) render her (like Midwinter) potentially atavistic.
41 Alexander Smith, 'Novels and novelists of the day', *North British Review*, 38:75 (February 1863), 168–90 (p. 184).

Part III

Education, environment and circumstance

5

Man and Wife

It seems to me that, wherever we begin, we are always brought back to the same point, and compelled to acknowledge that we are but the creatures of circumstances, these circumstances being, up to a certain point, at least, independent of anything that we ourselves can do.[1]

(Benjamin Brodie, *Psychological Inquiries*, 1862)

In Benjamin Brodie's mid-century philosophical dialogue, *Psychological Inquiries*, his interlocutors Eubulus and Crites find themselves discussing whether, 'if Nelson or Wellington had been brought up in the Court of Louis XIV', they would have turned out 'profligate and idle' because of an 'over-abundance of leisure' (Brodie, p. 302). This leads Crites to declare that we are all 'creatures of circumstances' that we can only partially control. Eubulus seeks to change the topic at this point, as it is drifting too close to 'the metaphysical question as to necessity and free-will', which he does not feel 'disposed to enter further' (p. 303). Much of the discussion in the previous chapters of *Creating Character* has shown how, more or less explicitly, the sensation fiction of Braddon and Collins depicts characters in the midst of a mass of circumstances that are out of their control: from inborn disposition; to parental influences; to aspects of class, race and gender.

The prevailing trend in thinking about character formation in the second half of the nineteenth century, which turned progressively towards theories of hereditary degeneration to explain deviant behaviour and social problems such as crime and alcoholism, put notions of personal agency and responsibility under further pressure. If a person's biological and psychological makeup was almost entirely determined before birth, then there was little that he or she could do to change in any significant way during the course of his or her life. Although some expressed concern that certain forms of degeneration were the result of the pressures of modern life, and that it could manifest in the heart of respectable society (Robert Louis Stevenson's *Strange Case of Dr Jekyll and Mr Hyde* (1886) and Bram Stoker's *Dracula* (1897), amongst others, play with this idea), it was also a means of allowing 'the late Victorian establishment and the propertied classes' to find 'plausible explanations for disturbing social changes' relating to their 'anxieties about poverty and crime, about public health and national and imperial fitness' (Greenslade, pp. 1–2). By citing heredity as the unstoppable cause of social ills (barring eugenic intervention), Victorian society could avoid finding blame in its own systems (whether it be educational, housing, criminal or other policies), presenting supposed degenerates as victims of biological rather than social circumstance. This also meant that whole groups or types could be labelled as degenerate, whether it be the brutal lower classes, the debauched upper classes, or the decadents and homosexuals that (amongst others) Max Nordau castigated in his bestselling *Entartung* (1892), published in English as *Degeneration* in 1895. Figuring the degenerate as different by nature from respectable and normal people meant that to view them with sympathy was difficult, and even unnecessary. In the West, such trains of thought would lead to extreme eugenic practices such as sterilisation in the early twentieth century.[2]

The previous sections have shown that Braddon's and Collins's fiction of the 1860s portrayed powerful innate forces influencing the behaviour of individuals, but often resisted depicting heredity as necessarily the predominant determinant in behaviour. This final section of *Creating Character* looks at how and why Collins and Braddon more trenchantly (even if sometimes implicitly) resist and deviate from this prevalent attitude in the two examples of 1870s fiction included here. In each case the author constructs their characters to emphasise the importance of social and environmental factors on people, and to show that upbringing and education are key in making or marring the individual. Neither Braddon nor Collins entirely abandons the idea that every person has innate characteristics, and they are not denying the existence of hereditary influences, but they both address topics relating to social reform that were drawing attention in the press, and they use their fiction to demonstrate the need for change by insisting that individuals are capable of improvement (or the opposite) in response to the way they are treated by others and to the quality of their environment. In the final chapter, Braddon's intervention into debates about women's higher education will be discussed in relation to *Lost for Love* (1874), but first Collins's *Man and Wife* (1870) will be read as a work that revisits previous themes, tropes and devices (particularly heredity and monomania) whilst placing greater emphasis on the influence of environmental, non-congenital determining circumstances.

This shift in focus towards environmental factors is linked to the fact that Collins uses *Man and Wife* to address particular social grievances; Margaret Oliphant found *Man and Wife* to be the most 'distinctly didactic' of Collins's novels up to that point.[3] The social-purpose novel was by no means a new creation; earlier examples include Elizabeth Gaskell's *Mary Barton* (1848) and Charles Dickens's *Hard Times* (1854). The *Westminster Review* described 'novels with a purpose' as ones in which the author wrote 'not because he or she felt inspired to tell a story, but because certain meditations, or convictions, or doubts, on some subject connected with human society, seemed to find convenient and emphatic expression through the medium of a work of fiction' (McCarthy, p. 29). Collins's preface declares that he intended the novel to 'afford what help it may towards hastening the reform of certain abuses which have been too long suffered to exist among us unchecked' (*Man and Wife*, p. 5), but also that he intended the story to be more than just the means of conveying his message. He hoped that his reader would 'find that the purpose of the story is always an integral part of the story itself', and explained that he had tried to write a work in which 'the fact and the fiction' were 'never separable one from the other' (p. 7). *Man and Wife*'s main purpose is to censure the 'scandalous condition of the Marriage Laws of the United Kingdom' (p. 7), and the plot is reliant on the state of the marriage laws as they stood at the time; in this sense 'fact' and 'fiction' are intertwined. Collins uses his plot and characterisation to show the harmful impact of these legal and social conditions. The parents of the heroine, Anne Silvester, discover that by Irish law their marriage is illegitimate because the husband failed to convert to Catholicism at the correct time. Anne herself twice falls foul of the Scottish marriage laws: first when she inadvertently marries her friend Blanche's fiancé, Arnold, by (innocently) spending the night with him in a hotel room and allowing the staff to believe they are married for propriety's sake; second when it turns out that she is previously married to the villain Geoffrey Delamayn because they have exchanged a written 'promise of marriage' (p. 523). The injustice of the English marriage laws, which denied a wife control over her own earnings, is also revealed through the story of Hester Dethridge, whose abusive, alcoholic husband legally claims and spends all of her wages until she is driven to murder and insanity. Demands to change the laws had been voiced for some time when Collins was writing. Almost twenty years previously the early feminist Harriet Taylor Mill had added a note to her essay 'The enfranchisement of women':

> The truly horrible effects of the present state of the law among the lowest of the working population, is exhibited in those cases of hideous maltreatment of their wives by working men, with which every newspaper, every police report, teems. Wretches unfit to have the smallest authority over any living thing, have a helpless woman for their household slave. These excuses could not exist, if women both earned, and had the right to possess, a part of the income of the family.[4]

The issue remained topical, however, and in his preface Collins references the 'Report of the Royal Commission' that had been 'appointed to examine the working of [the marriage] laws' (p. 5); some progress was in fact made just after the publication of *Man and Wife* with the passing of the 1870 Married Women's Property Act. Hester is actually in a "worse" position than the woman in Mill's description, because she does earn a living, but it is taken from her and spent on alcohol by her husband.

The novel's other purpose is the disparagement of what Collins perceived as a harmful national 'mania for muscular cultivation' (p. 5) at the expense of intellectual and moral development. Geoffrey Delamayn represents what Collins calls the 'washed Rough in broadcloth' (p. 6). Although he is from an affluent and privileged family, Geoffrey's education has led him to prize his physical prowess over his intellectual or moral development, and as a result he is a brutal villain who ends up planning to murder Anne so that he can make a better marriage. In order to convey these messages about the deleterious influence of certain legal and social practices, Collins highlights socially constructed determinants and their damaging consequences on individuals.

The 1870s are often seen as the beginning of a downturn in the quality, complexity and readability of Collins's fiction.[5] Algernon Charles Swinburne's much quoted assessment of Collins's later work accords with (and perhaps influenced) that of many subsequent critics: 'What brought good Wilkie's genius nigh perdition? / Some demon whispered – "Wilkie! have a mission."'[6] Although Oliphant felt that Collins's 'strength, which lies in plot and complication of incident, does not lend itself successfully to polemics' ('New books', p. 628), *Man and Wife* received reasonable reviews elsewhere: the *Contemporary Review* found it 'weirdly fascinating' and 'forcibly written'; the *Saturday Review* critic admitted to taking it 'at one draught' because it was 'too amusing to be laid down unfinished'.[7] Certainly the characterisation is less nuanced, the social message is conveyed more emphatically than in previous novels and there is less complex engagement with Victorian psycho-physiological theories of determinism. Nevertheless, *Man and Wife* does not mark a sudden shift (or, necessarily, a downwards one either) in Collins's work, and this chapter looks at how he continues to make use, with a few significant differences, of the themes, devices and notions of character formation that we have already seen at work in earlier novels. This includes his portrayal of innate moral potential, particularly in his depiction of Anne Silvester and other "good" characters, his insistence on the importance of education and upbringing in order to control negative characteristics, his evocation of the fear of moral heredity, his references to the sensation fiction staple of "chance" and his employment of monomania. In each case these elements are used to progress the moral and social messages of *Man and Wife*.

'Inbred nobility' and innate moral potential

In *No Name*, Magdalen Vanstone is depicted as possessing 'inborn nobility' (p. 236) that ultimately triumphs over her (also innate) potential for 'Evil', and this, the narrator suggests, is just once instance of the 'infinitely varying ... inbred forces of Good and Evil in all of us' (p. 116). In *Man and Wife*, Collins continues to assert that people possess innate characteristics: Blanche, for example, has 'a substance of sincerity and truth and feeling' (p. 57), and Arnold has an 'affectionate nature—simple, loyal, clinging where it once fastened' (p. 274). The character whose 'inbred nobility' is most significant in terms of characterisation and the novel's message is Anne Silvester (p. 168). Anne is certainly not, by the standards of conventional Victorian morality, an obvious candidate for the role of virtuous heroine, as she has, before the novel begins, been the mistress of Geoffrey Delamayn (she suffers a stillbirth during the course of the novel).

However, Anne is in some ways a less controversial figure than Magdalen; not only did she believe that Geoffrey was sincere in his affections (as she was sincere in hers), but she desires to rectify her mistakes by marrying him, or to end her life if this does not happen (which, although technically sinful, certainly shows her remorse).[8] Because in his later fiction Collins often chose to champion controversial heroines in order to make a social point (1873's *The New Magdalen* is the story of the ex-prostitute Mercy Merrick, for example), he found, as Jenny Bourne Taylor notes, the 'need to strip away much of [the novels'] psychological and cognitive equivocation in order to elicit their reader's sympathy' (p. 221). So Anne must appear to be very, *very* good during the course of the novel if we are to forgive her for her previous transgressions. Her 'inbred nobility' never significantly fails her, nor does she struggle against her own nature as Magdalen does; indeed, she has 'moral courage' (p. 566), which is repeatedly referenced in favourable terms, particularly when she resigns herself to going with Geoffrey as his wife (p. 524).

Furthermore, the narrator lets his readers know early on exactly how they should react to Anne through an "aside":

> Is there no atoning suffering to be seen here? Do your sympathies shrink from such a character as this? Follow her, good friends of virtue, on the pilgrimage that leads, by steep and thorny ways, to the purer atmosphere and the nobler life. Your fellow creature, who has sinned and has repented—you have the authority of the Divine Teacher for it—is your fellow-creature, purified and ennobled. A joy among the angels of Heaven—oh, my brothers and sisters of the earth, have I not laid my hand on a fit companion for You?
> (pp. 77–8)[9]

Through preaching a doctrine of Christian tolerance, Collins makes it clear that the reader is intended to accept Anne, despite her breaching of accepted social and moral codes, as the heroine of the novel. Even more so than with Magdalen, Oliphant was thoroughly annoyed that Collins let Anne 'do that which, in a woman's code, is the last and vilest of all evils, without being any the worse for it', and found it entirely improbable that a woman like Anne would degrade herself with a 'brutal, brainless villain' like Geoffrey ('New Books', p. 629). Indeed, unlike other fictional fallen women, such as the eponymous heroines of Gaskell's earlier *Ruth* (1853), or Hardy's later *Tess of the D'Urbervilles* (1892), Anne is not only allowed to survive to the end of the novel, but marries Sir Patrick Lundie, who has been impressed by her 'moral courage' throughout her ordeal.

Another reason that Anne is shown to be such an innately good character in this novel is because it was written at a period in Collins's career when he was frequently engaged with writing melodramatic adaptations of his novels for the stage, and because it was originally intended as a play (Peters, p. 314). Whereas some adaptations (such as *The Woman in White* (1871)) did not actually require a radical adaptation of the main characters to fit this genre of spotless heroines and dastardly villains because they already fell neatly enough into the requisite categories, Collins often had to reconcile the moral absolutes of melodrama with heroines who (like Anne Silvester) commit morally dubious acts.[10]

Man and Wife

No Name is particularly interesting, as it was dramatised in 1870, the same year as *Man and Wife* was published, and received a substantial alteration of tone and characterisation. Some of the controversial aspects of the novel are maintained as Magdalen continues to pursue the Trust as single-mindedly as in the novel. Also, several of Magdalen's speeches are kept almost intact as they already suit the heightened register of melodrama: for example, 'Oh, my father! my father! the wrong your brother has done us haunts me like a possession of the devil. The resolution to right it burns in me like fire.'[11] However, in the play, Magdalen is addressing the spirit of her father when she says this, rather than threatening Noel Vanstone whilst in disguise, to impress on the audience the fact that she is righting a wrong done to the dead. Indeed, throughout the play, Magdalen is given clearer reasons (which could be seen as justifications) for her behaviour. For instance, Norah has become 'a bedridden invalid, suffering from a spinal complaint' (*No Name* (1870), p. 10), who may be cured if the money can be found for her treatment. Moreover, Magdalen's remorse is emphasised; although she still goes through with the marriage to Noel Vanstone, she not only buys the laudanum, she actually takes it and declares 'placed between death and degradation, I have chosen death' (*No Name* (1870), p. 56). Luckily, the concerned chemist has given her a harmless liquid. Additionally, George Bertram (who replaces Magdalen's two lovers in the novel: Frank, who deserts her, and Captain Kirke, who saves her) is the constant hero and lover of Magdalen, who refuses to lose faith in her:

> BERTRAM [Magdalen's] noble nature ... may fall, on the hard journey of life, but it has in it the capacity to rise again ... *I* can see that her own keen sense of the wrong that she has suffered is her own worst enemy. *I* can make allowance for generous impulses led astray by temptation and bad advice. In one word, *I* can sympathise with her.
>
> (*No Name* (1870), p. 52)

In a manner that closely echoes the narrator's defence of Anne in *Man and Wife*, Bertram exemplifies and dictates how the audience should react to Magdalen, and her increased guilt and good motives smooth the way towards our feeling 'sympathy' with her. Both Anne and the stage version of Magdalen have been led into bad behaviour by 'temptation' but are innately 'noble' and so redeemable heroines.[12]

In *Man and Wife*, therefore, Collins's insistence that we accept Anne as our heroine because of her innate goodness is in part an adaptation of the stock character types of melodrama. It also, however, allows him to convey his moral message because we are supposed to sympathise with Anne's terrible situation as she finds herself a sorrowful but courageous victim of the marriage laws, and of Geoffrey Delamayn, which, as the aghast Margaret Oliphant reported to her readers, made Anne 'an angel recognised by everybody concerned' in the novel ('New books', p. 629).

Physical and moral education

If Anne takes the role of melodramatic heroine despite her fallen status, Geoffrey far more easily fulfils the role of melodramatic villain. He is uncouth, stupid and treacherous, lacking the charisma of a Fosco or the glamour of a Miss Gwilt, and apparently morally irredeemable, making him one of the most utterly unsympathetic villains in Collins's oeuvre. His function in the novel is in part to support Collins's critique of the marriage laws, as the fact that Anne ends up "married" to him is depicted as clearly unfair. He is also, however, used to comment upon the outcome of a deficient education. Whereas Anne's character is reliant on her inner core of goodness, Geoffrey's is reliant on the fact that he is nothing but a 'savage' underneath his gentlemanly exterior.

The quality of education became an increasing matter of concern throughout the 1860s, as a number of nationwide Schools' Inquiries Commissions were set up to investigate teaching and learning at all social levels: 'The Newcastle commission of 1858, the Clarendon commission of 1861, and the Taunton commission of 1864 investigated respectively ordinary elementary schools, the great public schools, and the varied schools for "those large classes of English society which are comprised between the humblest and the very highest".'[13] The results of these inquiries led to a general questioning of the quality of national education and concluded that the standard of teaching that children received was lacking on a number of levels. One aspect of education that drew particular attention was the balance of mental and physical development practised in schools and universities. John Bale notes that although some 'negativities of "athletic games" were circulating as early as the 1830s' it was in 'the second half of the nineteenth century' that arguments really started to emerge 'that sport per se had achieved dominance over intelligence'.[14] Several works of prominent writers and thinkers, many of whom have already been cited in this study as contributing to notions of character formation, reflect this change. At the end of the 1850s, Herbert Spencer advocated less emphasis on intellectual labour and more attention to health and fitness. Spencer argued that men of past generations were stronger than those of the present generation, and that the next generation looked as though it would be even weaker (p. 173).[15] Spencer attributed much of this degeneration to an 'excess of mental application' at the expense of physical development (p. 174). He observed that the importance of physical development was beginning to be recognised, and cited Charles Kingsley's writings as evidence of this. Kingsley, spearheading what came to be known as 'muscular Christianity', promoted boys' and men's pursuit of physical fitness, participation in team sports and a generally active lifestyle. Spencer acknowledged the need for balance, however, and thought perhaps Kingsley went a bit 'too far' (Spencer, p. 147).[16] Throughout the 1860s worry was expressed that the emphasis on physical fitness had indeed gone 'too far', particularly in upper-class boys' schools. In 1861 *Temple Bar* published an article on various forms of quackery and attacked 'the quack on the muscular Christianity basis' who

> makes the playground of more importance than the class-room or the study; whose end and aim of masculine education is a manly bearing at football, and who ranks a good batter or a swift stroke before a Smith's prizeman or a double first; who places animal forces higher than brain power, and makes muscle of more account than mind.[17]

An 1864 *Cornhill Magazine* article about the standard of education at Eton observed that 'influence and distinction in the school are only to be acquired by intense devotion to the oar or the bat'.[18] Similarly, in an 1868 address to a working men's college, Huxley suggested that some might well ask whether 'the richest of our public schools might not well be made to supply knowledge, as well as gentlemanly habits, a strong class feeling, and eminent proficiency in cricket'.[19]

Collins makes Geoffrey an extreme example of the outcome of the 'mania for muscular cultivation'. Geoffrey's excessive physical exertions not only lead him to go 'stale' (p. 345) and lose a foot-race for which he has been in serious training, but also culminate in a 'paralytic stroke' (p. 610), which allows Hester Dethridge to strangle him in a monomaniacal rage (p. 636). Also, Geoffrey's lifestyle reflects Charles Kingsley's regret that 'athletic exercises' had become 'mixed up with drinking, gambling, and other evils'.[20] He frequently visits drinking establishments, at one point for a training session where he considers how best to deal with the problem posed by Anne Silvester. He and others gamble in dishonourable ways over his performance in sporting events (his own manager bets against him when he suspects his failing health). He socialises with university-educated young 'gentlemen by birth', who are 'all profoundly versed in horse-racing, in athletic sports, in pipes, beer, billiards, and betting. All profoundly ignorant of every thing else under the sun' (p. 205).

Geoffrey is not merely 'ignorant', he is entirely unscrupulous, and this moral element is what attracts the most attention and criticism from Collins. The possibility of moulding the developing moral personality through education was frequently discussed in Victorian scientific and medical circles. Carpenter, for example, felt that education was key to developing an individual's 'self-directing power', which was integral to his theories about human agency and self-determination:

> The whole theory and practice of Education, indeed, involves the distinct recognition of external influences, as having a most important share in the formation of the character; whilst it is the object of every enlightened Educator to foster the development, and to promote the right exercise, of that power by which each individual becomes the director of his own conduct.
>
> (*Human Physiology*, pp. 550–1)

With his stunted moral and intellectual development, Geoffrey lacks any 'self-directing' power beyond that which will achieve his basic desires (for fame, money and a suitable wife). Whereas Spencer in 1859 argued that 'we see infinite pains taken to produce a racer that shall win the Derby: none to produce a modern athlete' (p. 146), Collins in 1870 attacks the cult of athleticism by showing what happens when men are raised and trained like animals, describing Geoffrey as at best 'a magnificent human animal' (p. 61), and at worst a 'wild beast' (p. 495).

These animalistic descriptive terms are coupled with atavistic ones: for example, when Geoffrey's anger is roused as he speaks to Anne, 'the savage element in humanity—let the modern optimists who doubt its existence, look at any uncultivated man (no matter how muscular), woman (no matter how beautiful), or child (no matter how young)—began to show itself furtively in his eyes; to utter itself furtively in his voice' (pp. 79–80). Whilst, in *Armadale*, the label of 'savage' is mainly associated with Midwinter so as to allude to his racial heritage, here Collins chooses to point out that even members of supposedly civilised societies have an underlying 'savage' element that will come out if the individual is not sufficiently 'cultivated'. By referring to this innate savagery, Collins actually places more importance on external factors that can be used to counteract it. This is what Collins felt was no longer happening in modern

England, as the elderly, refined Patrick Lundie (who represents the older generation, and often acts as Collins's mouthpiece) complains: 'there is far too much glorification in England, just now, of the mere physical qualities which an Englishman shares with the savage and the brute' (p. 68). Collins argues that the 'savage element in humanity' must be counteracted by cultivation, achieved through the kind of education that Geoffrey conspicuously lacks, as the narrator goes on to make clear: 'Was he to blame[?] ... Not he! What had there been in the training of *his* life (at school or at college) to soften and subdue the savage element in him? About as much as there had been in the training of his ancestors (without the school or the college) five hundred years since' (p. 80, emphasis in original). Here human society is responsible for failing to take control of the development of its members; Geoffrey is not 'to blame' because his personality has been moulded by his early and youthful experiences. Collins re-emphasises this point, with an important difference, at the moment when Geoffrey has decided to 'desert Anne, on the infamous pretext that she was Arnold's wife' (p. 234) and feels no 'remorse'. The narrator explains that

> remorse springs, more or less directly, from the action of two sentiments, which are neither of them inbred in the natural man. The first of these sentiments is the product of the respect which we learn to feel for ourselves. The second is the product of the respect which we learn to feel for others ... No such sense as that exists among the instincts of the natural man. And no such feelings as these troubled Geoffrey Delamayn; for Geoffrey Delamayn was the natural man.
> (pp. 235–6)

This is quite different from depictions of characters such as Magdalen or Midwinter, who, although they are affected by their upbringings, and often in negative ways, have a core of goodness with the ability at least to struggle against those parts of themselves that are considered immoral or undesirable. It is also unlike Collins's portrayal of Anne (and the other "good" characters in the novel) with her 'innate nobility', which is intended to retain the sympathy of the reader. Geoffrey does not have even a hint of innate nobility that could urge him to do good; he is shown to be utterly the victim of environmental determinism. Similarly, when showing the physical deterioration that is the eventual result of Geoffrey's excessive training, it is explicitly denied by a medical expert that he loses his race because of any hereditary infirmity: 'His rowing and his running, for the last four years, are alone answerable for what has happened today'

(p. 500). Like Braddon, Collins is willing to modify his portrayal of character formation in order to suit his literary and moral purposes.

As Reed explains, many Victorian thinkers (such as Huxley) 'believed that humanity, not the individual human, could improve itself through education' (Reed, p. 116). The individual may be largely incapable of self-determination, but human societies could take control of their collective development. This reflects, although with a different emphasis, the views of eugenicists who felt that selective breeding needed to be employed to alter the "race", rather than placing the onus on individuals' capacities for self-improvement. Collins here advocates such a view-point: Geoffrey is a villain because of his defective upbringing; he cannot alter his own behaviour, but a good education would have made a difference.

Both the narrator and Sir Patrick offer critical assessments of the circumstances that have resulted in Geoffrey's dishonourable character. In a lengthy lecture to several young men of the "present" generation, Sir Patrick warns of the dangers of praising physical over mental training; because an individual who has not been suitably educated is found 'defenceless, when temptation passes his way ... he is to all moral intents and purposes, an Animal, and nothing more' (p. 214). So on the one hand, an individual such as Geoffrey Delamayn has no choice in his conduct, as he has not been properly prepared for the moral challenges that life throws at him. However, whereas Geoffrey has been previously absolved of blame, here Sir Patrick goes on to state that such an 'animal' will kill not 'in the character of a victim to irresistible fatality, or to blind chance; but in the character of a man who has sown the seed, and reaps the harvest' (p. 214). Later, when Geoffrey feels no qualms about committing a murder, the narrator again reminds us to 'look back at him in the past' (p. 577) and realise that he is a product of his experiences and, when faced with an uncommon 'temptation', is no more than 'what his training has left him, in the presence of any temptation small or great—a defenceless man' (p. 578). Despite the ways in which Geoffrey has arrived at his current state, he has been faced with 'temptation' and must make a moral choice – from the moment he abandons Anne to the moment he attempts to murder her he is entirely aware that what he is doing is wrong. This is also reminiscent of the controversies over lunatic responsibility that were discussed in Part I: Geoffrey is 'defenceless', and cannot help his actions, but he has made his choices and must still be held responsible for them on some level. It also brings us back to Brodie's *Psychological Inquiries*, which introduced this chapter. After claiming that he does not want to enter into the 'metaphysical question [of] free-will',

Eubulus goes on to add that such questions are 'beyond the reach of our limited capacities', but that he nevertheless feels that

> We may make an allowance for the external influences which operate on men's minds; we may excuse altogether those who labour under the illusions of actual insanity; but otherwise we cannot get rid of the feeling of responsibility as regards either ourselves or others: and the most thoroughgoing Necessarian, when he quits the loftier regions of Metaphysics to mix in the ordinary affairs of life, thinks and reasons precisely in the same way as the most unhesitating believer in free-will.
>
> (p. 303)

The paradox that people are at once formed by environments and circumstances they cannot control, and yet are still in some way responsible for their actions, is at the heart of many discussions of free will. The only solution Collins can offer is that it is of paramount importance that society (whose 'material tone' has 'tacitly encouraged' the creation of such men as Geoffrey (p. 578)) rethink its attitude towards education and morality.

Heredity

Despite the increased emphasis on social and circumstantial determining factors in *Man and Wife*, Collins includes some references to negative heredity that are reminiscent of *Armadale*. As in the earlier novel, the growing Victorian tendency to associate heredity with morality is taken to extremes by evoking intimations of the workings of fate. It is not merely that children will inherit their parents' personalities and moral nature; rather it is insinuated that the events of the past will somehow mysteriously recreate themselves in the next generation. As with Midwinter's father in *Armadale*, *Man and Wife* begins with a dying parent's fear that her child is fated to repeat her mistakes (a career on the stage and an unhappy marriage). Anne Silvester Senior sees her daughter as her 'second self' and anxiously speculates 'She is Anne Silvester— as I was. *Will she end like Me?*' (pp. 42–3, emphasis in original). The fear is that children do not merely resemble their parents, they become them. Unlike Midwinter's father, however, Anne Senior hopes that some of the past will be positively recreated in the shape of her enduring friendship with her school friend Blanche:

> We two mothers ... seem literally to live again in our children. I have an only child. My friend has an only child. My daughter is little Anne—as *I*

was. My friend's daughter is little Blanche—as *she* was. And, to crown it all, those two girls have taken the same fancy to each other, which *we* took to each other, in the bygone days at school. One has often heard of hereditary hatred. Is there such a thing as hereditary love as well?

(p. 18)

The possibility of 'hereditary love' and 'hatred' reflects the increasing emphasis on morality that was applied to theories of heredity, but without the unremittingly negative tone that accompanied theories of degeneration. Anne's hopes seem to be fulfilled as the younger Anne and Blanche become the best of friends.

Whilst the love between the older Anne and Blanche is replicated in their daughters, Anne Senior's fears (like those of Midwinter's father) do not prove entirely warranted. Anne never pursues a career on the stage and the exact circumstances of her mother's life are never repeated: whereas it is the dissolution of Anne Senior's marriage that initiates her misery, the commencement of Anne's supposed marriages (first to Arnold, then to Geoffrey) brings about her suffering. However, as the narrative often makes clear, there are some strange similarities between Anne's situation and her mother's. For example, when Geoffrey tells Anne she is married to Arnold, 'she dropped senseless at his feet: as her mother had dropped at his father's feet, in the bygone time' (p. 252). Anne begins to share her mother's fears for her future when she realises that Geoffrey's father was the man who discovered the 'flaw' in her mother's marriage that led to her father's choosing another wife: 'she felt the shock of the revelation with a chill of superstitious dread. Was the chain of a fatality wound invisibly round her? Turn which way she might, was she still going darkly on, in the track of her dead mother, to an appointed and *hereditary* doom?' (p. 424, emphasis added). Once again there are similarities with *Armadale*'s Midwinter, as the supposedly ill-fated character appears to have inherited, if nothing else, the 'superstitious' nature of the parent. The narrative continues to reveal the supposed resemblances between the lives of mother and daughter:

> The parallel between her mother's position and her own position, was now complete. Both married to husbands who hated them; to husbands whose interests pointed to mercenary alliances with other women; to husbands whose one want and one purpose was to be free from their wives. Strange, what different ways had led mother and daughter both to the same fate! Would the parallel hold to the end? 'Shall I die', she wondered, thinking of her mother's last moments, 'in Blanche's arms?'

(p. 551)

The use of free indirect speech in this passage tinges it with Anne's anxiety about the future, and allows the narrator to suggest that fatality is stalking her without confirming it. Despite some similarities between the positions of mother and daughter, it seems an exaggeration to suggest that the 'parallel' between them is 'complete', and it certainly does not 'hold' to the end. As with *Armadale*, Collins invokes the fear of negative heredity, only to show members of the current generation eventually overcoming the threat of the past and forging their own futures.

Chance, destiny and circumstances

The futures that the characters forge, however, are not necessarily formed intentionally or willingly, as most of the circumstances that come about in *Man and Wife* are the seeming result of chance and accident. Coincidences are a common feature of sensation fiction. Braddon felt compelled to question the use of 'accident in art' in a letter to Bulwer-Lytton, asking 'why not admit accident in a story when almost all the great tragedies of real life hinge upon accident[?]' (Wolff, 'Devoted disciple', p. 26). To note two famous examples, *The Woman in White*'s Walter Hartright just happens to meet the half-sister of the woman he is soon to act as drawing master to on Hampstead Heath in the middle of the night, while Lady Audley bigamously marries the uncle of the best friend of her first husband, leading to attempted murder and the eventual revelation of her secrets.

Man and Wife is no exception in its liberal employment of coincidental happenings that occur to drive the plot to its conclusion, but whereas Braddon defends the use of chance occurrence in fiction by essentially pointing out that "accidents happen", Collins goes to great pains to show that, often, what may seem chance occurrences to characters within the story are not entirely random happenings, but arise out of unforeseen or misunderstood circumstances. Moreover, the seemingly arbitrary actions of characters are always shown to be reliant on the context of any particular situation. Early on in the novel, 'by a strange coincidence', both Anne and Geoffrey try to get out of the game of croquet; this is quickly revealed to be irony, as they are planning a secret meeting. On another occasion, Blanche fails to see Geoffrey (who has just told Anne that she is married to Arnold) leaving the library. The narrator tells us that 'making that one discovery, might have altered the whole course of events, not in her coming life only, but in the coming lives of others. So do we shape our own destinies, blindfold. So do we hold our poor little tenure of happiness at the capricious mercy of Chance' (p. 253). Even as the narrator uses the word 'Chance', he tells us that there is a perfectly logical reason that Blanche missed Geoffrey. She sees Anne in a swoon, but because Anne has already said that she feels unwell, Blanche is unconcerned: 'her own previous observation of her friend necessarily prevented her from being at any loss to account for the fainting fit'. For this reason she does not bother to go 'to the window to see if any thing had happened, out-of-doors, to frighten Anne', and Geoffrey gets away (p. 253).

Blanche's choice is just one of many examples of Collins's referring to destiny in such a way as to emphasise how small things can have a big impact, and how each person's outcome is formed by a series of events that he or she cannot know the importance of at the time. Blanche's decision to take Sir Patrick into her confidence about Anne's situation is 'a resolution, destined to lead to far more serious results, in the future, than any previsions of hers could anticipate' (p. 165). Similarly, when Geoffrey approaches Sir Patrick for information about Scottish law, their discussion is 'so trifling in appearance, so terrible in its destined influence' (p. 225). There is always a chain of cause and effect, but characters are unable to perceive it in its entirety and therefore repeatedly miss each other, misconstrue each other or the situation, or make bad decisions based on poor information. In the same way that he invokes a fear of heredity, Collins invokes the teleological grandeur of 'destiny' at the same time as he shows it to arise naturally out of human motives, actions and errors such as Blanche's affection for, and Geoffrey's dislike of, Anne, and the characters' ignorance (or sometimes misapplied knowledge) of the law.

Throughout the novel, although the characters are free to make their own choices, free will can only ever be exercised on incomplete information and using inadequate powers of perception, in response to events that the individual may never see coming, or may inadvertently create. Reed sums this up in relation to Collins's fiction generally, by asserting that Collins's outlook is 'that life has no inherent design to be fathomed by the interpretation of this or that set of signs but is a complex union of human motive and external circumstance guiding a very limited yet free will to make choices in the face of mystery' (p. 294). Collins depicts 'the face of mystery' extensively in *Man and Wife*. For example, when Blanche and Sir Patrick wonder who the man in Anne's hotel room could have been and Arnold walks through the door, the narrator exclaims:

> there stood the Discovery, presenting itself unconsciously to eyes incapable of seeing it ... The terrible caprice of Chance, the merciless irony of

> Circumstance, could go no further than this. The three had their feet on the brink of the precipice at that moment. And two of them were smiling at an odd coincidence; and one of them was shuffling a pack of cards!
>
> (p. 285)

Here, Collins reveals the emphasis that he is placing on men and women's inability to understand fully their own place in the world. 'Discovery', 'Chance' and 'Circumstance' hover around the unwitting human players, unknowable to them, and unalterable because they are unknowable. However much (or little) free will characters possess in this novel is almost irrelevant because they so rarely have enough knowledge to put it to effective use, as Collins places increased weight upon human beings' helplessness in the face of circumstance.

This is all part of Collins's strategy for demanding social change by demonstrating that people are what circumstances make of them. The growing interest in degeneration and eugenics theories was marked, as discussed in the previous chapter, by an increasing emphasis on the health of the nation, rather than individuals or individual families. Although Collins still does not adhere to ideas of unassailable negative heredity, *Man and Wife* is full of references to 'the nation' and the 'present generation'. Hester, Anne and Anne's mother are all victims of current national marriage laws (of England, Scotland and Ireland, respectively), and Geoffrey is the product of the prevailing system of boys' education. These characters may be extreme examples but they are still representative of entire sections of society.

Even characters who do not fall neatly into social categories are still described in terms of social influences. Arnold Brinkworth's father gambled his social position away, and as a result 'ruined his children's prospects'; Arnold has since earned his living 'in a roughish way' at sea (p. 66). Sir Patrick admires his ability to support himself and declares 'you're not like the other young fellows of the present time' (p. 66). The distinction between Arnold and a typical fellow 'of the present time' is exemplified when he asks to be allowed to spend the night in the hotel with Anne rather than brave the storm: Arnold wants 'tact, poor fellow—but who could expect him to have learnt that always superficial (and sometimes dangerous) accomplishment, in the life he had led at sea?' (p. 151). Arnold is direct and honest, if indiscreet, not only because of his innate good nature, but because he has not lived in mainstream modern British society (although, like Allan Armadale, this also makes him vulnerable to manipulation by less scrupulous people such as Geoffrey).

Education, environment and circumstance

Characters are also shaped by their generational status, and there is an overall sense that the current generation is not up to the same standard as the older one, with which Collins implicitly aligns himself through his repeated use of Sir Patrick as his spokesperson (even though Sir Patrick is considerably older than Collins, who was in his forties at the time of writing *Man and Wife*). Often this generational difference is employed for humorous ends. Sir Patrick is 'a gentleman of the byegone [*sic*] time' who is 'distinguished by a pliant grace and courtesy, unknown to the present generation ... The talk of this gentleman ran in an easy flow—revealing an independent habit of mind, and exhibiting a carefully-polished capacity for satirical retort—dreaded and disliked by the present generation' (pp. 57–8). This is in contrast to the caricatured description of Blanche, a young lady who dresses in 'the height of the fashion' including a hat 'like a cheese-plate', 'fully inflated' hair, excessive jewellery, and 'striped stockings' (p. 56): 'Position, excellent. Money, certain. Temper, quick. Disposition, variable. In a word, a child of the modern time—with the merits of the age we live in, and the failings of the age we live in' (p. 57). The humour in Collins poking fun at the latest fashion fads and the supposed quick tempers of modern young ladies is reliant on an acceptance of environmental determinism: the idea that people will act the way they do largely because of the world in which they have been raised, and that people of a certain rank, gender and generation will share certain attributes.

On a more serious note, when Sir Patrick addresses Anne at a delicate moment his behaviour is reliant on his status as one of the older generation: whereas a modern man would 'strike an attitude' and affect excessive sympathy, he is 'courteous as usual' (p. 143). The narrator goes on to inform us that in Sir Patrick's time, it was usual to practise the 'habitual concealment of our better selves', but that this was 'upon the whole, a far less dangerous national error than the habitual advertisement of our better selves, which has become the practice, publicly and privately, of society in this age' (p. 143). Here again are references to the 'nation': certain personality traits are widespread, for better or for worse. Environmental factors such as social status and surroundings, education and experience are by far the most deterministic forces in this novel. Collins is tapping into the increasing sense of mental, moral and physical national health, and in fact asserting that the structure and methods of society, particularly its educational practices, need to change: degenerate types are produced by society rather than breeding, and must be managed by social policies, not eugenics.

Man and Wife

Social circumstance and monomania

Social determinism is also used to illustrate Collins's point about the unfairness of the marriage laws through the story of Hester Dethridge. Driven to despair over the years, Hester premeditates the murder of her abusive alcoholic husband. Having planned the murder Hester describes how she attempts to leave the scene of her intended crime, but her wanderings through the city repeatedly bring her back to her own house: 'the house held me chained to it, like a dog to his kennel. I couldn't keep away from it' (p. 601). This can be read as the onset of her insanity, as an unconscious homing in on the place she is trying to avoid, as the work of fate or as a massive coincidence; in any case it is a literal or metaphorical indication that ongoing abuse can lead to retaliation that may not be fully controlled.

After successfully completing the act, Hester rapidly loses control of her sanity in a particularly dramatic manner. Apparently dumb during the course of the novel following a blow from her husband, it is not until her written confession is discovered by Geoffrey that it is revealed that, at the prompting of a vision, she ceased speaking as an act of penance for her husband's murder (p. 603). Shortly after her vow of silence Hester begins to see an 'Appearance', which she describes as 'the vision of MY OWN SELF—repeated as if I was standing before a glass' (p. 605), and which instructs her to kill innocent people. Nevertheless, like those monomaniacs discussed in Part I of this book, Hester can behave in a sane manner for the majority of the time, and when she makes her appearance in the novel she is working as a cook for the Lundies and seems to be a 'steady, trustworthy woman' (p. 113).

Once again, Collins is drawing for dramatic effect on a form of the commonly recogniaed medical condition of partial insanity. Esquirol described 'instinctive monomania' as a condition in which the patient 'is drawn way from his accustomed course, to the commission of acts, to [*sic*] which neither reason nor sentiment determine, which conscience rebukes, and which the will no longer has the power to restrain. The acts are involuntary, instinctive, irresistible' (p. 320). More specifically, in 'homicidal monomania' the sufferers became 'the blind instruments of an involuntary, and instinctive impulse, which impels them to the commission of murder' against their will, and despite any attempts to restrain their own behaviour (Esquirol, p. 362). Prichard used the term 'homicidal madness', and explained that 'the murderer is driven, as it were, by an irresistible power; he is under an influence which he cannot overcome, a blind impulse without reason' (*Treatise*, p. 388). Such terms continued to be used throughout the nineteenth century. Henry Maudsley used the phrases 'impulsive' and 'homicidal insanity', describing it as 'a certain state of mental disease' in which 'a morbid impulse may take such despotic possession of the patient as to drive him, in spite of reason and against his will, to a desperate act of suicide or homicide' (*Responsibility*, pp. 133, 140).

All three of the above medical writers note the failure of willpower or reason to control behaviour as the murderous urge takes hold. The person may be aware that what they are doing is wrong, but 'the will cannot always restrain, however much it may strive to do so, a morbid idea which has reached a convulsive activity, although there may be all the while a clear consciousness of its morbid nature' (Maudsley, *Responsibility*, p. 138). Hester describes similar overwhelming sensations: 'I can only describe the overpowering strength of the temptation that tried me in one way. It was like tearing the life out of me, to tear myself from killing the boy' (*Man and Wife*, p. 606). Medical descriptions of the condition were usually accompanied by examples with which Hester shares various similarities. One particularly striking and often reported case was the account of a young maid who pleaded with her mistress to be removed from the house as she felt an overwhelming compulsion to tear to pieces the white flesh of her mistress's baby (Maudsley, *Responsibility*, pp. 145–6; Prichard, *Treatise*, pp. 385–6). John Barlow also used this case, although because he, unlike the others cited here, did not hold with the idea of reasoning insanity he used it as an example of how one can suffer from 'mental derangement' but still be considered sane: for Barlow it was only if the girl had succumbed to her impulse that she would have been truly insane (pp. 42–3). The incident was also reprinted in popular periodicals such as *Chambers's Edinburgh Journal*.[21] Like the maid, Hester initially manages to resist her urge, until she begins to see her apparition repeatedly when in proximity to Geoffrey. Maudsley gives an example of an elderly woman who, like Hester, displays great strength when undergoing a sudden compulsion towards strangulation, although in this case the target is her own daughter ('Practical observations', p. 679). Like Alfred Monkton, although in a far more sinister way, Hester experiences a clear delusion – the apparition of herself, which indicates her victims to her. This was also a common feature of homicidal monomania; Esquirol describes a man, for example, who 'hears a voice, which says to him: *slay, slay; this is thine enemy; slay him, and thou shalt be free*' (p. 363, emphasis in original). Hester finally succumbs to her impulse, and in a 'homicidal frency [*sic*]' strangles Geoffrey (p. 636).[22] Collins's choice of mental illness combines with his employment of environmental determinism to support his social point about the injustice of the marriage laws, and also furthers the plot: by insanely despatching Geoffrey, Hester enacts the violent revenge that Anne Sylvester, as the noble-hearted heroine, cannot.

In the end, Hester's monomania deteriorates into mania and she spends the remainder of her days in an asylum (p. 639). Although this is certainly an outcome fitting for a villain, it is significant that Hester is not convicted for murder. As we have seen in Chapter 3, the treatment and punishment of criminal lunatics were much debated in the Victorian period. The question of whether or not the maniac was aware that his or her actions were wrong, and whether that did or did not change the extent of their responsibility, was particularly discussed in cases of impulsive insanity, when the sufferer might know right from wrong but be unable to resist committing a murderous act. For example, in the *Lancet* Harrington Tuke expressed shock that a man who had 'cut the throat of the woman with whom he had lived for thirteen years, and had intended to kill his three children by her, and afterwards himself' was sentenced to be hanged with no consideration of his mental state beyond whether he knew right from wrong when he committed the act. Tuke asserted that the man's 'disease of brain' was 'shown by insane letters, by insane words, by insane intentions, and an insane act'.[23] Collins's decision to leave Hester in an asylum rather than a prison (or on the scaffold) reflects these debates about the appropriate treatment for the criminally insane.

Like Geoffrey, Hester's life experiences have left her a hopeless victim to her own darker nature, hence her visions are of herself, the result of a moral corruption engendered through her husband's victimisation of her. There is no gleam of goodness in Collins's portrayal of Geoffrey, and there is, correspondingly, no gleam of hope in his portrayal of Hester: the cook only resists her urges for long enough that her actions ultimately serve the plot by saving Anne. In this way Collins shows the devastating effects of marital abuse.

Collins's novels of the 1860s evoke multiple forms of determinism as converging forces that create an atmosphere in which the reader is never entirely certain how much the characters are either responsible for, or capable of making, their own decisions. In *No Name*, for example, Magdalen is monomaniacal, but she makes a final moral choice that may be due to the satisfying of her "dominant idea", the influence of Captain Kirke, the fact that she is an inherently noble person who will necessarily make the right choice in the end, or all of the above. These novels reflect the quandaries that many nineteenth-century thinkers found themselves facing as they reflected on humanity's position in the universe. *Man and Wife* largely abandons such explorations of multiple determinants in order to focus on a portrayal of character formation that supports the novel's social critique. Whilst Collins does not go so far as to renounce his earlier claim in *No Name* that 'infants are not born with blank tempers' (p. 116), and although neither heredity nor fate is actually discredited in *Man and Wife*, they take a back seat to the influence of socially constructed determinants and the determining power of circumstance. Collins's characterisation combines a melodramatic dichotomy between good and evil (intended to ensure his reader's sympathy with the correct characters), with a portrayal of individuals at the mercy of their social environment in both a long-term and a more immediate sense. Whilst characters can make choices and act on their own volition, their vision of their own circumstances is often too narrow for them to make informed decisions. The best hope for the improvement of individual lives and characters lies with the improvement of society and the social institutions that provide many of life's chances. This reading of the novel shows, therefore, that while Collins's authorial aims and style began to change direction from the 1870s, notions of character formation remained an intrinsic and functional part of his fiction, which he both explored and employed to deliver his social messages.

Notes

1 Brodie, *Psychological Inquiries, Part II*, Vol. I, p. 302.
2 See Paul, Chapter 5.
3 Margaret Oliphant, 'New books', *Blackwood's Edinburgh Magazine*, 108:661 (November 1870), 607–31 (p. 628).
4 Harriet Taylor Mill, 'The enfranchisement of women', *Westminster Review*, 55:2 (July 1851), 289–311 (p. 299).
5 See Lonoff, *Wilkie Collins and His Victorian Readers*, pp. 52–3.
6 Algernon Charles Swinburne, 'Wilkie Collins', *Fortnightly Review*, 46:275 (November 1889), 589–99 (p. 598).
7 A. H. Japp, [H. A. P.] '*Man and Wife*', *Contemporary Review*, 15 (August 1870), 317–19 (p. 319); Anon., '*Man and Wife*', *Saturday Review*, 30:767 (July 1870), 52–3 (p. 52).
8 Although suicide was considered a sin, Wiener explains that as the nineteenth century progressed it was seen less as a crime and more as an unfortunate sign of an unsound mind. It was no longer 'classed as homicide' from 1879 (p. 267).

9 Collins also evokes New Testament morality as a defence of his subject matter in his preface to *Armadale* (p. 4). As is typical of Collins's fiction, however, his appeal to the religious sentiments of his readers is not accompanied by overt religiosity in the story itself. For Collins's attitude towards religion see Catherine Peters, *The King of Inventors: A Life of Wilkie Collins* (London: Secker and Warburg, 1991), p. 108; Keith Lawrence, 'The religion of Wilkie Collins: Three unpublished documents', *Huntington Library Quarterly*, 52:3 (1989), 389–402; Kirk H. Beetz, 'Wilkie Collins and the *Leader*', *Victorian Periodicals Review*, 1:15 (1982), 20–9 (pp. 23–5).

10 Collins's adaptations necessarily condense the plots of the novels in order to place them on the stage; family relationships are simplified and the action takes place in fewer locations. In *The Woman in White* alterations include the early revelation of information (such as Pesca's membership of the Brotherhood and Sir Percival's illegitimacy) and the means of Sir Percival's and Count Fosco's deaths (respectively, drowning, and assassination in England rather than France). See Wilkie Collins, *The Woman in White: A Drama in a Prologue and Four Acts* (London: published by the author, 1871).

11 Wilkie Collins, *No Name: A Drama in Four Acts* (London: published by the author, 1870), p. 16 (cf. *No Name*, p. 236).

12 In Collins's dramatic adaptation of *Armadale*, *Miss Gwilt* (1875), the change between novel and play, and specifically the leading females, is even more striking. Advising Collins on his initial attempt at dramatising *Armadale*, Dickens warned that Miss Gwilt would not do for the stage, as drama required '*interest in some innocent person*', preferably '*a young woman ... in peril*' (*Letters*, 10 July 1866). In *Miss Gwilt*, she subsequently becomes the toy of the evil Dr Downward, who, unlike in the novel, is responsible for planning her marriage to Allan. Miss Gwilt is at one point reduced to pleading 'Oh, Doctor, Doctor, don't expect too much of me! I'm only a woman after all!' (Wilkie Collins, *Miss Gwilt: A Drama in Five Acts* (printed for performance in the theatre only, not published, 1875), p. 30).

13 Norman McCord, *British History: 1815–16* (Oxford: Oxford University Press, 1991) p. 287.

14 John Bale, 'Anti-sport: Victorian examples from Oxbridge', *Sport in History*, 34:1 (2014), 34–48 (p. 36).

15 Originally printed as Herbert Spencer, 'Physical training', *British Quarterly Review*, 58 (April 1859), 362–97.

16 For the ambivalent Victorian reception of muscular Christianity see Donald E. Hall (ed.), *Muscular Christianity: Embodying the Victorian Age* (Cambridge: Cambridge University Press, 1994), esp. Part III.

17 [E. L.], 'On quacks', *Temple Bar*, 2 (May 1861), 268–75 (p. 272).

18 M. J. Higgins ['Paterfamilias'], 'On some points of the Eton report', *Cornhill Magazine*, 10:55 (July 1864), 113–28 (pp. 113–14).

19 Thomas Henry Huxley, 'A liberal education; and where to find it', in *Collected Essays*, Vol. III, pp. 76–110 (p. 79).
20 Charles Kingsley, *Glaucus: The Wonders of the Shores* (Cambridge: Macmillan, 1855), pp. 47–8. Cited in Bale, 'Anti-sport', p. 38.
21 Anon., 'Monomania', *Chambers's Edinburgh Journal*, 595 (June 1843), 177–8 (p. 177).
22 In Barlow's thinking, therefore, Hester can only truly be classified as insane when she finally succumbs to her impulse.
23 Harrington Tuke, 'Monomania and homicide', *Lancet*, 90:2302 (12 October 1867), 472–3 (p. 472).

6

Lost for Love

> There must be a soul lurking in this neglected form—a soul of wider capabilities than common souls—a mind that lacked only the light of education ... What a glorious thing it would be to illumine the outer darkness in which this poor child lived—to redeem this imprisoned soul from its bondage—or, in plain words, to educate Jarred Gurner's daughter![1]
>
> (Mary Elizabeth Braddon, *Lost for Love*, 1874)

The previous chapter on Wilkie Collins's *Man and Wife* focused on the negative outcome of a bad educational experience, the brutal Geoffrey Delamayn. However, for Victorians thinking about the best way to cultivate desirable members of society, education was seen as a tool that, if skilfully wielded, could go some way (how far exactly was arguable) to preventing the manifestation of negative characteristics and also to developing natural potential that might otherwise remain dormant. In this sense, education could be a counteraction or an aid to biological determinism and a means of manipulating innate characteristics for socially desirable ends.

Interest in good education in the second half of the nineteenth century contributes to the history of debate about how to manage the nurture of individuals and social groups, a history that includes such works as Jean-Jacques Rousseau's *Emile; or, On Education* (1762). Victorian fiction frequently explored the dangers of mismanaged education, perhaps most didactically and famously in Dickens's *Hard Times* (1854), which depicts the harmful consequences of a utilitarian education. Chapter 3 showed how *The Lady Lisle* depicts education as an improving force on Rupert Lisle, and Braddon touches upon educational themes in many of her other novels. Some of Braddon's most famous heroines are poorly or irregularly educated and subsequently jeopardise their domestic environments. For example, Aurora Floyd's undisciplined childhood culminates in her abandoning a finishing school in France in order to elope with her father's groom. Isabel Gilbert in *The Doctor's Wife* (1864) has had 'no friendly finger to point a pathway in the intellectual forest', and so she 'rambled as her inclination led her'.[2] Inclination leads Isabel from romantic fiction, to impossible fantasies, to a dangerous attraction to the dashing Roland Lansdell.

This chapter considers Braddon's more extensive representation of education as a means of cultivating character in her largely overlooked novel *Lost for Love* (1874). Like *John Marchmont's Legacy*, *Lost for Love* engages with mid-Victorian debates over the role of women in society and female intellectual capabilities, but this novel speculates more optimistically about the potential for intelligent and talented women to find personal fulfilment. Whereas Olivia Marchmont's fearsome intellect is given no suitable outlet and prevents her from finding contentment in life, *Lost for Love*'s two heroines, Flora Chamney and Louisa Gurner, find happiness in part *because* of their intellectual abilities. Both heroines have received inadequate, although very different, educational experiences, but rather than portraying the disastrous consequences of a poor education, *Lost for Love* depicts the heroines' experiences of informal "higher" educations under the instruction of the men who eventually become their husbands, and their development into intellectually and socially accomplished women. In this way the novel contributes to the debates concerning the value and purpose of female higher education that arose in the last half of the nineteenth century. In doing so it invites the reader to make inferences regarding both biological and environmental determinism in relation to women, presenting them as having vast inherent intellectual potential that requires education to fulfil its promise.

Flora and Louisa are moulded intellectually in accordance with the desires of their husbands, who consciously contribute to the formation of their wives' adult personalities. Education lifts Flora and Louisa out of their former narrow worlds, but this is done at the will of the men who fall in love with them; they are inescapably defined by their ability to fulfil their roles successfully as companions to men. This could be read as a similar strategy on Braddon's part to that adopted by some feminist campaigners who used the promise that educated women would be improved helpmates to men as an incitement to reform. However, in this novel Braddon seems genuinely to promote the benefits to marriage of educated and intellectually fulfilled wives. This does mean that Braddon's endorsement of female intellectual ability and call for improved female education remains largely within the bounds of Victorian gender conventions, but she is also promoting the value of education as a privately (in relation to both the domestic sphere and the individual) fulfilling pursuit, and not merely as a means to practical or public ends (such as a qualification or job). Flora and Louisa, as the novel closes, are not making the best of a bad job, using their intellectual skills in the domestic environment because that is the only option open to them; they are portrayed as genuinely content women. Moreover, as Flora and Louisa reap the benefits of education, female influence is shown to be a potent and restorative force upon their husbands. *Lost for Love* therefore asserts that both men and women (and relations between them) will be better off if women are raised to be intelligent, interesting and competent individuals whose personalities are influenced by, but not entirely subsumed into, those of their husbands. The implication is that a woman can and should be more than 'a mere appendage to a man, allowed to have no interests of her own', as Taylor Mill complained was often the assumption in Victorian gender relations (p. 301).

Braddon draws further distinctions between types of female companion in her depiction of Flora and Louisa. Flora's intellectual development is coupled with a first stunted, and then painful, emotional maturation. It is initially painful because her first love, the artist Walter Leyburne, disappears; it is more so, however, because she later discovers that the man she marries during the course of the novel, Dr Cuthbert Ollivant, is actually responsible for Leyburne's disappearance, having accidentally pushed him from a cliff during a scuffle (caused by Ollivant's discovery that Leyburne has been making love to Louisa Gurner when he is engaged to Flora). By showing the psychological and emotional damage done to Flora by Ollivant, and coupling this with his dictation of the direction her learning takes, Braddon emphasises the fact that Flora has married before she is ready to do so; her representation of Flora as a typical product of the Victorian educational system suggests that young women are not being adequately prepared for life. By contrast, Louisa has a far less traditional education and is the more mature of the two girls, and although her interest in poetry is awakened by Leyburne, she is more naturally inclined to it than Flora is to the classics that Ollivant teaches her. Louisa also marries *after* becoming intellectually and emotionally developed, following her own inclinations in life and learning, rather than having those of others imposed upon her. In both cases Braddon demonstrates how in Victorian society the cultivation of women is, for better or worse, very much in the hands of the men who, legally, financially and socially, have control over their lives, but she also implies that a woman should be mature enough to know her own mind and interests before marriage, that she should allow that knowledge to inform her choice of husband, and that better education will help women to achieve this.

'What do we want in the woman when we have educated her?' Victorian debates about female education

As mentioned in the previous chapter, the results of the Schools' Inquiries Commissions of the 1860s sparked new debate about the quality and purpose of education. After four years of visits to middle-class schools around the country, the results of the Taunton Inquiry in 1868 (some of which are discussed below) brought renewed attention to female education, and were generally seen as proof that educational reform was urgently required. There was less consensus, however, about exactly what a woman should know, what the depth of her learning should be, and what ends she should be able (and expected) to put her learning to. Assumptions about nature and nurture often underpinned the debates. For example, Henry Maudsley's controversial article 'Sex in mind and in education', published in April 1874 at the same time as *Lost for Love* was being serialised in *Belgravia* (November 1873–November 1874), argued that periods of intensive study would endanger both women's general health and their delicate reproductive systems, meaning that women's educational opportunities were not predominantly limited by their mental capacity, but by their 'foreordained work as mothers and nurses of children'.[3] Herbert Spencer similarly argued that educated women more often were sterile or prematurely menopausal and had trouble breastfeeding (see Burstyn, p. 94).

Others arguments centred less on what women were capable of and more on the social roles they were expected to fulfil, and invoked the image of woman as companion, as Eve was to Adam. In 1856 the *Oxford and Cambridge Magazine* asserted that women were under a necessity 'of understanding, appreciating and assisting their male friends (especially wives their husbands) in their intellectual pursuits'.[4] Montagu Burrows, writing for the *Quarterly Review*, asked 'What do we aim at? What do we want in the woman when we have educated her?', and concluded that 'such a cultivation as will make a really good wife, sister, or daughter, to educated men, is the thing to be aimed at'.[5] With this in mind, Burrows advised that 'woman' ought not to be 'brought up to the same point as man by education, and taught to be his rival; but rather as the complement of man, perfect in herself, and intended to hold an entirely different place in the world' (Burrows, pp. 465–6). John Ruskin similarly explained that woman was 'made to be the helpmate of man' (p. 50). Whilst his assertion that woman is *made* a helpmate may suggest a divinely ordained, innate role for women, Ruskin insisted that good education was necessary to help women achieve this goal. He claimed that a woman 'ought to know whatever her husband is likely to know', but added that such knowledge need only stretch 'so far as may enable her to sympathise in her husband's pleasures, and in those of his best friends' (Ruskin, pp. 64–5). Braddon depicts the benefits of being such a woman in *John Marchmont's Legacy*'s universally admired Belinda, but also suggests that not all women can find satisfaction in being 'only just clever enough to be charming' (p. 378). *Lost for Love* depicts a more deliberate moulding of the female intellect for male satisfaction but also implies that women's learning should not be curtailed by men's intellectual limitations, and demands that it should be satisfying for them as well as for their husbands.

Much emphasis was also placed on the moral influence of women over men, a belief bolstered by the ideal of the "Angel in the House", which presented women as the moral hearts of the domestic sphere. James Davies, also writing for the *Quarterly Review* in 1866, favourably reviewed Ruskin, agreeing that 'the primary and divine idea of woman is "a help meet for man"', and added that a woman needed to be educated so as to 'fit her to exercise her proper influence as a wife over her husband, or as an unmarried woman over society', and to 'make her a model mother to her boys and girls. In each sphere, if she realises her mission, she has it in her power to be *"vainqueur des vainqueurs de la terre"* ["conqueror of the conquerors of the earth"]; the more cultivated her mind and heart, the more complete her spell in whatsoever state of life she finds herself occupying' (p. 500). Davies recognised that women do have influence over those they are close to, and felt that education was the key to developing each woman's potential to be the ideal wife, mother or spinster.[6] These definitions of the female vocation as companion concur that women should be educated in keeping with an ideal defined by the needs of those around them.

It was not only advocates of separate spheres and conservative conceptions of women's role who employed the image of companion and ideas of female influence. In the 1860s women's rights campaigners were fighting, with increasing success, for opportunities for women to enter higher educational courses and to achieve professional qualifications.[7] These campaigners appropriated the concept of woman as companion 'as a means of legitimating' their movement for changes that 'seemed to contradict conventional definitions of femininity'.[8] For example, in 1851 Taylor Mill, argued that 'Those who are associated in their lives, tend to become assimilated in character', and that because women's faculties are only exercised on 'petty subjects and interests ... the companionship of women ... so often exercises a dissolvent influence on high faculties and aspirations in men' (pp. 303–4). In 1868 Millicent Garrett Fawcett, who came to lead the women's suffrage movement, made similar arguments to call for equal educational opportunities for both sexes:

> constant companionship with a person of inferior and ill-developed capacities must deteriorate the most powerful mind ... A woman whose whole life is bounded by her own domestic circle, and who has no thought or care for anything outside it, is certain to infect her husband with this sort of selfishness, to damp, and perhaps destroy his public spirit and sense of public duty.[9]

These early feminists describe female influence not only as something that can be elicited and enhanced through education in order to benefit the family and society, but as something that *must* be cultivated to useful ends for fear that it may otherwise have a detrimental effect, actually weakening the husband's commitment to appropriate "masculine" pursuits. Fawcett observes (like Davies and Burrows) that women cannot necessarily assume that they are to become wives and mothers; she insists that a 'woman who commences life with a soundly-trained mind and well-developed capacities, will be fitted to perform, with far greater efficiency than had she been badly trained, whatever duties, public or private, may devolve upon her' (p. 569). Education for Fawcett is to be put to practical ends, helping women not only to support themselves should they be unable to marry, but to contribute to society. The idea of duty is important here, as is the insistence that this may take a 'public or private' form; Fawcett presents women as socially responsible beings, and therefore requiring more than training as a domestic companion to men.

Other critics, falling somewhere between the extremes of advocating separate spheres and calling for sexual equality, drew on similar arguments to campaign for improved female education. In 1865 T. H. Huxley, for example, assumed that 'the female type of character is neither better nor worse than the male, but only weaker', and added that women are 'meant neither to be men's guides nor their playthings, but their comrades, their fellows, and their equals, so far as Nature puts no bar to that equality'.[10] He therefore argued that women should be given the same educational opportunities, partly because with their natural disadvantages they needed all the help they could get, and partly because they were meant to be men's companions. Huxley reassured his (inferably male) readers, however, that even with these opportunities the 'big chests, the massive brains, the vigorous muscles and stout frames of the best men will carry the day' when they 'contest the prizes of life with the best women' (pp. 73–4). Huxley also points out that because at least some women are required to bear children, they will always 'be found to be fearfully weighted in the race of life' (p. 75).

Fraser's Magazine for Town and Country avoided advocating higher education for women on the basis that even if they did end up working towards careers, it would not be until some point in the 'millennium'; or, as expressed in another article, a women's college could not 'generally be made to fit into the present arrangements of society' beyond providing training for teachers and governesses.[11] Yet the magazine also presented women as being in desperate need of better educations for the good of individual families and the nation. Once again, the concept of female influence was key: one critic argued that if readers really thought about how much influence women already had over those around them they would no longer 'consent to leave the preparation for such a sphere of action in the hands of the worst educated of human beings ... the governesses and schoolmistresses of England' (Varney, pp. 377–8). From these examples it is apparent that whilst there was undoubtedly disagreement as to what constituted a good education, it was generally conceded that a good education was precisely what was needed if women were to fulfil effectively their roles as wives, mothers, companions and members of society. *Lost for Love* takes up these ideas of companionship and influence as central themes.

The 'common boarding-school type': the dangers of standard Victorian female education

Of the two heroines in *Lost for Love*, Flora receives the more conventional education, being described as of the 'common boarding-school type' (I, p. 115). Standard female education tended to focus on the obtaining of 'social rather than intellectual skills ... girls were taught how to behave as contenders in the marriage market, and as social hostesses; most were given neither systematic intellectual training, nor instruction in the skills of housekeeping and childcare' (Burstyn, p. 22). This sort of education drew frequent criticism. In 1862, for example, Benjamin Brodie argued that because of women's influence over their children 'it is to the wellbeing of society that the education of the female sex should include studies of graver interest, and not be exclusively devoted, as it too often is, to the acquirement of those accomplishments which are merely graceful and ornamental' (p. 342). Spencer also complained about the 'immense preponderance of "accomplishments"', which proved that 'use' in girls' education was 'subordinated to display. Dancing, deportment, the piano, singing, drawing – what a large space do these occupy!' (p. 3).

There was already an established literary history critiquing the superficial nature of female education. Mary Wollstonecraft's *A Vindication of the Rights of Woman* (1792) rebukes society's contentment with women displaying merely 'superficial accomplishments'.[12] On a less serious note, the Misses Musgrove in Jane Austen's *Persuasion* (1817) leave school with 'all the usual stock of accomplishments, and were now, like thousands of other young ladies, living to be fashionable, happy, and merry'.[13] Although content and affable young women, they are not trained for any practical ends beyond giving pleasure to themselves and others. Jane Eyre famously insists that women should not be confined to 'making puddings and knitting socks, to playing on the piano and embroidering bags'.[14]

The Schools' Inquiries Commissioners' reports of 1868 noted a 'want of thoroughness and foundation, want of system, slovenliness and showy superficiality, inattention to rudiments, undue time given to accomplishments, and those not taught intelligently or in a scientific manner' (quoted in Fawcett, p. 559). Burrows also cited the commissioners' reports, and their claim that there was a 'sacrifice of everything else to "accomplishments", and the pitiful character of those "accomplishments" when acquired – the poverty of the French, the worthlessness of the music, the absence of any training and strengthening of the mind' (p. 450). Such superficial training did not, commentators argued, develop any critical or reasoning faculties, and 'even where female education goes beyond mere accomplishments, it is of its very essence that it should be superficial' (anon., 'Women's education', p. 545). Despite his opinions on women's capacities for study, Maudsley also criticised 'the trivial and defective character of female education', which fitted them 'only for the frivolous purposes of the present fashion in female life' ('On some of the causes', p. 492).

Braddon's descriptions of Flora and her educational background are reminiscent of these disparaging accounts. When the novel commences, she has little grasp of intellectual subjects, but a basic grounding in the accomplishments expected of a young lady, such as painting, playing the piano and singing. As Flora's first fiancé, the artist Walter Leyburne, puts it, she 'doesn't know a great deal of anything, but she knows a little of everything'; he pronounces her to be 'a dear little thing, and clever too in her feminine way; she's essentially feminine' (I, p. 175). Read in the context of contemporary critiques of female education, it seems that Flora's broad but superficial knowledge is not "essential" to her, but mass-produced; Braddon's engagement with educational themes in the rest of *Lost for Love* confirms such an assessment.

Despite the objections made to a preponderance of accomplishments, such skills were not entirely disparaged in Victorian society: whilst lamenting the 'pitiful character' of female accomplishments, Burrows maintained that 'society requires some power in the sex of pleasing others, yes, and of being useful to others in social life, over and above what it requires of men, who are necessarily trained to earn their bread or to govern' (p. 469). This qualifies Spencer's distinction between 'use' and 'display' in relation to education: in the context of both the marriage market and social engagements, female accomplishments were useful. Different notions of utility are therefore under examination in these debates. Flora's vocal skills are certainly put to use in social situations, as she entertains her father and his guests (I, p. 35). In fact, Leyburne is enchanted by Flora's singing: when he first hears her, he fancies that Flora is to prove 'the perfection and completion of his lot' (I, p. 47). Flora and her accomplishments are useful here *because* they are ornamental and provide pleasure to the men who observe them. Leyburne and Flora soon end up singing duets together, and when his affections for her are wavering, Flora's singing remains 'the one fascination which Walter could not resist' (I, p. 213).

Whilst Flora's natural vocal talent has been successfully cultivated, it is evident that she is typical of the young ladies described in the commissioner's reports, full of superficial, half-developed abilities. For example, Flora admits that, whilst she likes to paint, she rarely finishes her pictures, as they 'look beautiful at first', but 'then somehow they go wrong' (I, p. 34). Her artistic attempts create an opportunity to develop her relationship with Walter Leyburne; he is 'enraptured' when he discovers that she paints, and immediately offers to help her with her studies (I, p. 48). Yet when his feelings for Flora are waning he becomes disenchanted; her artistic aspirations, unlike her singing, inspire only pity, as he imagines 'little Flora, who was struggling up the steep mountain of art, with a box of crayons, chalking Gulnares and ancient beggarmen *ad nauseam*' (I,

p. 172). Flora's painting does not give the same personal satisfaction or provide the same social leverage as the singing she excels in.

Indiscriminate teaching of accomplishments regardless of talent or efficacy, such as Flora has received, was a common area for complaint in the press throughout the 1860s. In 1861, a *Temple Bar* contributor claiming to be a woman, and possibly Braddon herself (see Chapter 2, n. 11) complained that women are

> wofully [*sic*] brought up from the beginning. Few, very few of us are ever properly and steadily and judiciously educated, with a view to our capacities, our individualities, and the talents or qualities it is probable we shall be afforded opportunity to turn to the best account in our maturity. We rarely learn anything thoroughly; we are made smatterers; our faculties are half cultivated, our minds, not at all.
>
> ('A word to women', p. 55)

After this damning claim that girls' education is meagre, irregular and impersonal, making no attempt to cultivate individual proclivities, the article proceeds to give a depiction of poorly educated women who cannot act as successful companions to their husbands, being intellectually incapable of conversing with them. Davies similarly asks if it would 'not be well to take a little more trouble in ascertaining the various bents of girlish capacity', because 'the struggle to master too many accomplishments is apt to end in a superficiality, spreading over the more solid studies, and acting prejudicially on the whole mind' (p. 503). Both of these quotations express concern that by showing no discrimination in choosing what subjects are to be taught, educators not only fail to encourage inherent abilities, but have a negative impact upon the character of women: they grow up mentally "uncultivated", trained to think only in a superficial manner.

Moreover, the prevalence of superficial accomplishments in girls' curricula attracted criticism from objectors who felt that girls were being deliberately groomed in order that they might 'be at leisure to contemplate an eligible investment in the matrimonial market', whilst the 'resources' they would need in 'future life' were disregarded (Davies, p. 501). Flora (whose pet name is Baby) is no femme fatale; she has 'a sweetness, a freshness, a youthful innocence about her that are more winning than beauty' (I, p. 25), and 'the ways and works of coquetry were unknown to her simple soul' (I, p. 150), yet her vocal talents prove an enticement to Leyburne. Despite this, when he considers her as a potential life companion Leyburne worries that she 'might be but a childish helpmate for one who hoped to be distinguished by-and-by' (I, p. 221); the utility of accomplishments only goes so far, and an ability to enchant and entertain is only moderately desirable. Flora is an example of those young women who were brought up 'as if they were meant for sideboard ornaments' (Ruskin, p. 67), and Braddon implies that however dazzled men may be by an array of accomplishments, this may not suffice in the long run.

Dr Ollivant initially seems satisfied with Flora's superficial accomplishments. In their first conversation Flora, with a 'wry face', comments that science 'means steam-engines and cotton-looms and things, doesn't it?' in a 'winning childish way, which made even her foolish speeches pleasant to hear' (I, p. 31). Ollivant is unsurprised by Flora's lack of knowledge, assuming that 'one can hardly expect a young lady to be interested in [science], any more than one can expect the flowers to know their own Latin names, or be learned in botany' (I, p. 31). This initial interest in Flora's superficial merits, rather than her mental aptitude, appears to support the views of those writers who argued that women pursuing higher education would 'not be popular with men' (Burrows, p. 465).

But as *Lost for Love* progresses it both discredits the superficial, indiscriminate teaching of accomplishments and suggests that women have a huge intellectual potential that will ultimately prove desirable to potential partners. Despite his lack of wonder or concern at her ignorance, soon after meeting Flora, Ollivant fantasises about 'how he might improve her education ... and enlarge her mind', and imagines that 'his own old love of poetry ... might revive in this Indian summer of his life' (I, p. 115). Importantly, Ollivant intends not to teach Flora about science, but to use her as a connection to his earlier life and interests. This is not because she shares those interests, but because he believes that she may be made to do so.

Ollivant is given the opportunity to make his fantasy a reality after he pushes Leyburne off of the cliff. Distraught at Leyburne's disappearance, Flora will have nothing to do with art and music (which remind her of him), and so Ollivant seeks 'some occupation which would beguile her from this brooding sorrow', and determines to 'develop this poor child's intellect, to teach her something' (II, p. 29). Significantly, the narrator comments that Ollivant turns to 'that literature which he knew best', the classics (II, p. 29); he begins to teach her Latin so that she can read the Roman poets. Rather than being immediately charmed by her subject, Flora works to please her father and Ollivant – this new educational phase in Flora's life is to be shaped regardless of her own tastes and talents. Instead, her educational experience is moulded according to the tastes and understanding of the man who intends to be her future husband.

Flora proves both capable and, as her interest is stimulated, eager to learn. Huxley likened learning the classics to 'toiling up a steep hill, along a bad road', so that only a 'strong man ... can appreciate the charms of [the] landscape' ('A liberal education', p. 97). Braddon (using a similar metaphor) shows that Flora's progress is partially due to the fact that Ollivant is a good teacher who 'did his utmost to make the road easy' (II, p. 31). Importantly, however, rather than doing this by making things simpler for her, Ollivant does 'not bind her down to the dry details of grammar ... He gave her a Horatian ode almost at the beginning, and by that one lyric showed her the genius of the language, and awakened her interest in the study' (II, p. 31). Braddon leaves no doubt that Flora is perfectly capable of tackling more advanced aspects of the language and of appreciating the quality of the poetry.

Ollivant is 'careful not to overtax the young student's brain, yet stretched the cord to its fullest tension' (II, p. 32). Here, Braddon alludes to concerns about the dangers of overwork that received much attention throughout the Victorian period. Spencer, for example, wrote against the dangers of 'excess of mental application', which could lead to mental and physical illnesses (p. 174). Maudsley argued that women attempting to compete intellectually with men would be especially vulnerable to overexertion because of the 'the nature of [their] organization' – i.e. their reproductive capacity – and 'the demands which its special functions make upon its strength' ('Sex in mind', p. 466). The following number of the *Fortnightly Review* featured Dr Elizabeth Garrett Anderson's rebuttal of Maudsley's article, which accused him of exaggerating the enervating effects of both puberty and menstruation in women, and insisted that so 'far as education is concerned it is conceivable, and indeed probable that, were they ten times as unlike as they are, many things would be equally good for both [boys and girls]'.[15] Significantly, Flora is not portrayed as vulnerable to the dangers of overwork because of her sex. Ollivant is careful not to 'fatigue her or exhaust her interest' (II, p. 31), but rather than reducing her learning, he varies it, teaching her astronomy, botany and later politics (II, pp. 31–2, 88); the concern is primarily about maintaining intellectual engagement. At one point Flora, reeling from the revelation that Leyburne had been pursuing a relationship with Louisa as well as herself, becomes too eager to study, and Ollivant must 'recommend less devotion to Horace and Linnæus, the flowers and the stars' (II, p. 66), but there is no indication that her gender plays a significant part in this decision, and her learning continues. In the same paragraph we are told that 'the mighty world of natural science opened before her', allowing her to forget the loss of Leyburne (II, p. 66). In *Lost for Love*, rigorous intellectual exertion is a cure (or at least a palliative) for emotional trauma, which leads to physical regeneration.

Flora undertakes a demanding (and traditionally male) learning process, which benefits her mental and physical well-being.[16] Her initial intellectual shortcomings are shown to be a result of her previous inadequate education, rather than of natural mental limitations. Fawcett commented that although the Schools' Inquiries Commissioners complained about the 'deplorably bad' state of girls' education, it was 'cheering to see that all the causes which produce the inferiority are removable either by social or legislative reform', rather than girls being 'naturally unfitted to receive and benefit by the highest mental culture'. In fact, she added, 'in classics and mathematics, girls, when properly taught, were found quite as proficient as boys' (Fawcett, p. 565). Braddon tacitly supports this description of female ability.

Under Ollivant's tuition, Flora's 'mind ripened rapidly in this intellectual forcing-house' (II, p. 66). Botanical metaphors were a well-established means of discussing the cultivation of young women. For example, Wollstonecraft complains that, owing to defective educations, women are 'like the flowers which are planted in too rich a soil[;] strength and usefulness are sacrificed to beauty' (p. 2). In the Victorian period, references to hot- or forcing-houses were used (like Wollstonecraft's rich soil) to refer negatively to the premature mental and social development imposed upon girls. Davies, for example, complained that a boy of seventeen would be 'entering the most telling years of his mental culture. At the very same age the hot-house plant, his sister, is transferred from the school-room, where every appliance has been used to facilitate precocious ripeness of mind and manners' into society where she will begin her hunt for a husband. Davies felt 'that this kind of forcing is physically as well as morally hurtful' (p. 501).

In *Lost for Love*, contrastingly, the image of the forcing-house is a positive one in connection to Flora, as Ollivant proves to be a competent "gardener" who does not allow her to develop too quickly. Whereas Wollstonecraft condemned the way women are forced into roles as beautiful flowers too soon, with the result that 'the flaunting leaves, after having pleased a fastidious eye, fade, disregarded on the stalk, long before the season when they ought to have arrived at maturity' (p. 2), Ollivant does not cultivate Flora for immediate gratification over long-term benefits.

Flora learns to acquire 'stronger command over herself' (II, p. 68), and acquits herself admirably at the social gatherings Ollivant begins to hold for her 'well-being' (II, p. 99): 'the light-hearted schoolgirl [develops] into a thoughtful woman, self-contained, self-possessed, accomplished, well-informed ... There were few subjects of which she could not talk, and talk well' (II, p. 101). Ollivant's careful tuition creates a suitable companion, but also an admirable and intelligent member of society in her own right, which is exactly what many campaigners for improved female education wanted to see in educated women. Nevertheless, Braddon's use of the forcing-house metaphor, not to mention the symbolism of Flora's name, maintains a sense of women as flowers to be cultivated and brought to bloom (intellectually as it may be) for the pleasure of others, particularly their husbands.

The concern over the quality of education that had led to the launching of the Schools' Inquiries Commission was associated with questions about the benefits of different forms of education. For example, the merits of studying the classics (for boys, let alone girls) generated much debate. Spencer felt that the Greek and Latin learnt by schoolboys did not prepare them for their practical working lives, and were merely a 'badge marking a certain social position', making the classics as much for show as women's accomplishments (p. 2). Burstyn notes that although many advocates of women's higher education (such as Emily Davies) wanted equality between the sexes, others were opposed to women receiving a classical education the same as men because it was seen as outdated (p. 152). Contrastingly, James Davies (a classical scholar) urged that girls should learn Latin, because it encouraged 'accuracy', improved the 'English style' and was 'helpful to familiarity with the grammar and syntax of most European tongues' (Davies, p. 504). In addition to these arguments, however, Davies quoted Ruskin's comments that women should know whatever their husbands are likely to know (Davies, p. 505). For Flora the real benefits of her course of study are initial distraction from dwelling on Leyburne's disappearance (II, p. 31) and, more significantly in the long term, the provision of a common interest with her husband. She and Ollivant honeymoon in Rome and 'talk about Virgil and Horace, and the Rome they knew, before the old gods were dead' (II, p. 202). On the one hand, education is presented as a determining tool that does not just prepare a person for work or the achievement of social standing, but can bring about personal fulfilment and improved personal relations; moreover, women are equally as able to benefit from advanced education as men. On the other hand, and more problematically from a modern feminist perspective, women's characters are portrayed as pliable under male influence: Ollivant becomes the 'the master and guide who had *formed* her mind, and filled her dreams with fairest fancies' (II, p. 203, my emphasis); rather than finding a wife who is already a suitable match for him, he has the opportunity of tailoring one to his own tastes.

Braddon's portrayal of female education as a personally fulfilling experience for use in the domestic sphere engages with mid-Victorian arguments over the function of female higher education. Laura Morgan Green observes that in the mid-1860s 'the reformist view of women's educational needs encompassed two somewhat different emphases – on "cultivation" and on "action"' (p. 15). Some (such as Emily Shirreff) saw education as a means of developing 'self-culture',[17] and others (represented in the *English Woman's Journal*, which aimed to increase opportunities for female employment) saw it as having more practical ends. Green argues that George Eliot's *Middlemarch* (1871–2) shows a distrust of 'institutionalized knowledge systems', and 'takes moral development to be at the heart of the educational project' (p. 72). Whereas Dorothea Brooke at least wants to improve the lot of those around her, *Lost for Love* exhibits even less desire for women to partake of learning for practical ends. Intellectual development is a means of finding fulfilment and of helping to establishing a happy marital union; it is not necessary for learning to lead to professional or constructive occupation.

Although *Lost for Love* shares some of the thematic elements of *Middlemarch*, Dorothea's relationship with Mr Casaubon is strikingly different from the relationships in *Lost for Love*. Dorothea is thirsty for knowledge and imagines that a 'really delightful marriage must be where your husband was a sort of father, and could teach you even Hebrew, if you wished it'; she believes that 'those provinces of masculine knowledge', Latin and Greek, must be 'a standing-ground from which all truth could be seen more truly', and she wishes not only for 'a wise husband', but 'to be wise herself'.[18] Unfortunately, Casaubon is neither as learned as Dorothea believes, nor willing to share his knowledge; the result is a marriage of emotional boundaries and disappointments. Contrastingly, Flora does not initially wish to be 'wise', and does not choose her husband based on this criteria, and Ollivant *does* desire to share his learning with her; this is key to the success of their developing relationship.

Despite the beneficial nature of Flora's intellectual forcing-house, her affective and social development is also being forced in a detrimental manner. On his deathbed, Mark Chamney tells his daughter to be 'useful to others, as a woman should be', and to fulfil 'a woman's fairest destiny – loving and beloved – happy wife, happy mother' (II, pp. 74–5). Female happiness in Chamney's eyes is inextricable from female duty and reflects the conventional ideal of womanhood; but the context of this speech means that it must be read ambivalently. Chamney goes on to voice his desire that Flora marry Ollivant. Whilst the doctor undoubtedly loves her, and will protect her, she does not love him, and the reader is aware that Ollivant is responsible (albeit accidentally) for the violent removal of his rival, Leyburne. Also, Flora is not prepared for the death of her father (telling him 'if I lose you, I lose all' (II, p. 77)), nor for marriage and motherhood. As an indication of her unreadiness for womanhood, Chamney's death prompts an attack of brain fever that returns Flora's mind to 'her girlish, nay even childish, days at the Notting-hill academy' (II, p. 80), and from which Ollivant nurses her by carefully reinstating her educational development, stimulating her mind, but paying little heed to her emotional maturity.

On account of Chamney's deathbed wish, Ollivant is now Flora's guardian with the understanding that they will marry. She finally accepts his proposal by unromantically promising him 'I will give you all I can – fidelity and obedience' (II, p. 107). In the same issue of *Belgravia* that Flora consents to marry Ollivant, a light-hearted article asserted that in courtship 'the girl' in particular (as she had no public duty to occupy her otherwise) should 'surrender her whole soul'.[19] This suggests by contrast how far from the romantic ideal Flora and Ollivant's relationship is. Flora's appreciation of Ollivant's feelings for her, as well as mutual respect, partially compensate for the lack of love on Flora's part, and on returning from the honeymoon she is 'to all appearances as bright and happy a bride as a man could desire to give gladness to his days' (II, p. 114). The narrator's description of the impression Flora conveys, rather than her actual inner state, serves as a warning to the reader that things are not perfect; Flora's development is far from complete.

As a new bride, Flora's girlishness remains her dominant quality, and despite claiming that she does not want to be 'treated quite as a child', she concedes to Ollivant that 'it is very nice to be so petted by you and mamma' (II, p. 119). Mrs Ollivant, Flora's mother-in-law, continues to manage the house, and if Flora 'had lived in a fairy palace, where all the household work was performed by enchantment, she could not have been more free from household cares' (II, p. 120). The fairy-tale imagery indicates Flora's childishness and that, as is often the case with fairy tales, there may be a loss of innocence for her yet to encounter. The servants regard Flora as an 'ornamental addition to the household' (II, p. 120), recalling those previously quoted criticisms of accomplished, yet useless, young ladies raised to be ornaments. This actually shows a regression in Flora's development into a mature wife. Chamney's ill health had meant that Flora started to learn the 'mysteries' of housekeeping (II, p. 70), and after his death (but before her marriage) Flora experiences a gradual awakening to her own naivety; she remembers her 'bright holiday life' when she was simply 'playing at housekeeping' (II, p. 92). As Ollivant's wife she is relieved of any immediate need to continue with this practical education or growing self-awareness, and no longer even needs to play housekeeper.

Whilst women's movement campaigners such as Fawcett tended to be rather dismissive of practical housekeeping skills, insisting that 'women cannot really be good wives and mothers if charming accomplishments *and domestic tastes* are to be considered their highest virtues' (p. 567, my emphasis), Braddon's novels involving heroines who marry prematurely or foolishly often place intrinsic value upon domestic skills, making them a measure of maturity. Isabel Gilbert, for example, is described as being without any 'of the common distractions of a young matron', having relinquished all household tasks to the housekeeper, Mrs Jeffson (*The Doctor's Wife*, p. 116). Similarly, Aurora Floyd frankly tells her husband 'Heaven help your friends if they ever had to eat a dinner of my ordering', and hands all responsibility over to her ex-governess, Mrs Powell, who plots her downfall (p. 132). The shirking of domestic responsibility symbolises at best immaturity, at worst moral laxity.

The importance of housekeeping skills can be traced to the fact that, while the Angel in the House needed to possess moral purity and maternal instinct, she also needed the practical ability to ensure the household ran smoothly, making the home a pleasant place for working men to return to. Isabella Beeton opened her successful *Book of Household Management* (1861) by assuring her readers that those feminine 'acquirements' that 'enter into a knowledge of household duties' are especially important because 'on these are perpetually dependent the happiness, comfort, and well-being of a family'.[20]

Mrs Ollivant is an important figure here, because of her outstanding household management; as her husband declares on his deathbed, 'there never was such a woman to save money' (I, p. 9). After her husband's death, Mrs Ollivant moves into her son's new London residence, and becomes 'the careful mistress of his house' (I, p. 11). Whilst not allowing for the waste of 'a stale crust of bread or a basin of dripping', she manages to provide her son with every comfort he requires; his 'simple dinners ...

could hardly have been exceeded at a West-end Club' (I, p. 12). Her ability to achieve this and 'retain the respect of her servants' is also a sign of domestic capability; Beeton notes that if a mistress can inspire respect and affection in her servants 'they will be still more solicitous to continue to deserve her favour' (p. 15).

Equally importantly for this discussion, Mrs Ollivant is also 'the intelligent companion of [Ollivant's] brief intervals of leisure' (I, p. 11), making it 'her business to be interested and well informed in everything that interested her son' (I, p. 12). She even adapts her own tastes to his: 'his opinions were her opinion. For him to dislike or disapprove was enough for her' (I, p. 62). Mrs Ollivant is, therefore, an estimable housewife and companion, wife and mother, who has willingly spent her life caring for the men in it. The narrator claims that it 'would have been hard to imagine a face which indicated a more tranquil existence, a serener soul' (I, p. 55). Coexisting with this ostensible serenity, however, is 'an indefinable melancholy in the countenance, as of a woman who had only half lived, whose life had been rather like the winter sleep of hibernating animals than the ardent changeful existence of warm-blooded mankind' (I, p. 55). Mrs Ollivant's years of devotion to her husband and child have imbued her with a sense of incompleteness: Ollivant's own life has been 'a solitary and sequestered life, and she had lived only for him' (I, p. 63). A woman, it seems, may be a good companion whilst being an incomplete person, but Mrs Ollivant belongs to 'an age gone by' (I, p. 55), and in the younger generation Braddon suggests that a more mutually fulfilling model of companionship is possible. Nevertheless, housekeeping skills are valued in their own right (the anonymous writer of 'A word to women' asserted they should be studied before marriage, p. 59), and used by Braddon as a metaphor for, and indication of, mature womanhood.[21]

Flora's immaturity is emphasised when Ollivant buys a country house at Teddington as 'a toy for his wife' (II, p. 121). It is here, in the place where she can once again "play" at being in charge, that Flora suffers her greatest loss of innocence when she discovers the truth about Ollivant's involvement in Leyburne's disappearance. When Ollivant admits that he struck Leyburne the shock forces her towards a realisation of her own naivety, and we are told that 'the anguish of these moments had transformed her. She was no longer the gentle girlish wife he had known an hour ago' (II, p. 166). Flora subsequently loses the baby she has been carrying, which she had previously thought of 'as a child thinks of its first doll' (II, p. 212). The symbolism of this is made explicit when the doctor attending her miscarriage explains to Ollivant that 'all had happened prematurely, and in the dead of night' (II, p. 175). The practical and physical aspects of marriage (from housework to reproduction) cannot be achieved, in this novel, without the analogous mental and emotional maturity.

One benefit of women completing higher education before marriage was that, as Anderson argued, they would enter 'society at a somewhat less immature age', and therefore be better prepared to take 'an intelligent part in it' and to 'get more real pleasure from the companionship it affords'. Moreover, such a woman would be 'less apt to make a hasty and foolish marriage' (p. 591). Flora's "higher education" may be intellectually beneficial, but it cannot help her to make a more mature marital choice because it only happens through Ollivant who, as both he and her father have already decided, is to be her husband. The events of Flora's love life happen in the wrong order, causing her great emotional distress along the way: she first marries, then learns to love Ollivant, *then* discovers his part in Leyburne's disappearance, and eventually forgives him, at which point they are finally described as 'utterly happy' (II, p. 302). Braddon implies that girls such as Flora, with 'common boarding-school educations', are run through a forcing-house of accomplishment learning so that they may take their place in the marriage market as soon as possible. Rather than waiting and taking a husband with whom they share mutual interests and inclinations, such girls will make immature brides and only begin their personal development after they have chosen their future husbands (to the extent that it *is* their choice), a decision that they, with no real sense of self, are ill-equipped to make.

'A mind that nature had attuned to his': a model for mutually fulfilling companionship

Louisa Gurner is the barely educated child of Jarred Gurner, a poor picture- and violin-restorer, who lives in shabby lower-middle-class Voysey Street, an environment that has had a definite impact on the formation of her character:

> Neither selfishness nor vanity found a congenial soil in the flower-gardens of Voysey-street. Other vices might spring up there and thrive apace; but for these delicate flowers of evil there was but scanty nutriment. Louisa, having never known what it was to find her inclinations studied or her desires ministered to, had resigned herself, even before she turned up her back hair and lengthened the skirts of her shabby gowns, with advancing womanhood, to take life as she found it.
>
> (I, p. 85)

The botanical imagery here works very differently from that used to describe the hot-house flower Flora. The metaphor merges Louisa with her environment – Voysey Street is a soil in which vices may (or may not) grow, but Louisa, as the possessor (or otherwise) of these vices, may also be seen as the soil or garden in which they grow. Louisa cannot disassociate her sense of self from her home environment, and feels that she and her family are irrevocably degraded because of the time they have spent there. For example, Leyburne declares that 'it is only education that constitutes [Flora's] present superiority' and that education could 'raise' Louisa to Flora's 'level', but then adds that Flora's 'sweetness is the sweetness of a refined nature which has never been degraded by vulgar associations'. Louisa bitterly replies that her 'nature has been so degraded' by life in Voysey Street that 'you couldn't wash the vulgarity out' (I, p. 160).

It is true that the 'vulgarity' of her home environment means that Louisa has an 'early-acquired knowledge of life's darker side', which makes her seem 'to be ten years older than Mark Chamney's daughter' (I, p. 131). This knowledge of the 'darker side' of life affects Louisa's behaviour, but not necessarily in a negative sense. For example, when Leyburne declares his feelings for her, she assures him 'I know too much of the world for that' (I, p. 185) and will not allow him to desert Flora, showing 'more firmness and wisdom than her lover' (I, p. 186). When shut out of doors by her father after returning late from a daytrip with Leyburne (Gurner hopes to prompt a proposal of marriage), Louisa refuses to be given lodgings by Leyburne, prompting the narrator to declare that Louisa is 'not a wild-wood blossom by any means, this young woman; not a snowdrop, whose petals no poisonous breath had ever polluted; but stanch and pure after her own fashion' (I, p. 191). Once again the botanical imagery is in clear contrast to that used with Flora. Louisa is explicitly not likened to a flower; while she may not be as 'pure' in the sense of the innocent (and ignorant) Flora, nor is she so easily dismissed as decorative.

Louisa does not only take a moral stance against Leyburne and her father's behaviour; she is practical in her actions. Even when she has nursed Leyburne back to health after his fall, and his affections are no longer divided, she makes him wait three months before consenting to marry him.[22] Whereas Flora enters into a union she is unready for, Louisa's increased independence of mind and maturity stop her from rushing into (or being rushed into) marriage until she is certain of her own and her lover's readiness. Louisa is a rarity amongst Braddon's heroines in that she gains and keeps her first love untarnished: perhaps this is because she has suffered somewhat before she meets him; perhaps because, unlike other heroines (including Flora), she is already mature in a number of ways. Her experiences and heartaches mark a passage not to womanhood, but to refinement. Louisa's more successful negotiation of life and marriage is symbolised by the fact that she ends the novel not only as a happy wife but, unlike Flora, a happy mother.

Louisa has received some sporadic education in the 'small academies' that are occasionally run in the 'front parlours' of her neighbours' houses (I, p. 78) and has 'managed to pick up some shreds and patches of education from her father' that make her 'not quite as ignorant as the majority of young women in Voysey-street' (I, p. 87), but she is painfully aware that her learning is incomplete and unrefined. When Gurner reproaches her for remaining silent during a conversation, Louisa reacts indignantly: 'I suppose it's nature's fault if I'm stupid ... and I don't see that it's my fault if I'm ignorant. I'd have been glad enough to learn if any one would have taken the trouble to teach me' (I, p. 97). Louisa's bitterly witty retort (showing a quickness of mind that is anything but stupid) acknowledges a distinction between innate intelligence and knowledge acquired through learning. As the novel progresses, Louisa is shown to have plenty of the former, which is drawn out through her relationship with Leyburne.

Initially, however, Louisa's meagre education is only 'enough, at least, to teach her the sordid misery of her existence, and the bare fact that there is a higher kind of life somewhere beyond the regions of Voysey-street' (I, p. 87). As a young woman with no financial prospects, no useful education, and nobody (until Leyburne's arrival) who is willing to help her improve her lot in life, Louisa 'has learned to be angry with destiny for casting her lot in this back slum', unlike the other, less aware, locals, 'who talk as if Voysey-street were the world ... education had removed Louisa from this Arcadian simplicity, and to her vitiated mind Voysey-street was hateful' (I, pp. 87–8). Education, at this point, cannot bring personal satisfaction or practical improvement.

Louisa's resignation to her lot is echoed by her father, who fleetingly wonders whether Louisa could ensnare Leyburne, but then dismisses this thought, believing that 'the girl's surroundings were too much against her' (I, p. 98). He looks at her 'untidy hair, worn gown, and listless attitude' and concludes that even if there might be 'some capability in her that might be worth cultivation ... it was too late now; the chance was gone. There the girl was, unkempt, untaught, uncared for—a weed instead of a flower' (I, p. 98). Gurner's musings entertain the possibility of cultivating people through education and upbringing, but he assumes an individual must be raised in a certain way from the start; weeds cannot be transformed into more desirable plants. The aspects of Louisa that are mentioned, however, are all external and alterable, and indeed are entirely altered by the end of the novel when Louisa, married to Leyburne, possesses all the appearances of a lady to the extent that when Flora sees her, she not only perceives her as a social equal, but envies her appearance (II, p. 213). This transformation is the result of an educational process initiated by Leyburne that, although different in detail, is similar to Ollivant's education of Flora as it results in Louisa being Leyburne's ideal wife.

Leyburne initially wants Louisa to be able to support herself financially, optimistically assuming that a 'woman with a good education may do so many things. She may turn governess or companion ... or she may go in for book-keeping, and earn a handsome living in some commercial establishment' (I, p. 123); he later adds that 'there are telegraph-offices and houses of business, and goodness knows what, open to the weaker sex nowadays' (I, p. 159). In light of this, Leyburne intends to send Louisa to a boarding school where she will learn the skills necessary for self-sufficiency. However, Louisa never gains any of those modes of employment suggested by Leyburne; she is saved from her unsatisfactory existence by the more standard option open to Victorian women – marriage.

Louisa's entrance to boarding school is intended as a gift of thanks for acting as Leyburne's model. During the sittings, however, he takes it upon himself to begin Louisa's education by reading her poetry, including Shakespeare and the Romantics. Already bitter at the world, Louisa is deeply moved by what she reads, but experiences a new level of dissatisfaction with her life: 'now I feel restless, and there's a fever in my mind sometimes, and I have such wishes and longings for a brighter life' (I, p. 170). Yet she remains resolute that nothing can extricate her from the 'degradation' in which her family is mired, and even Leyburne begins to feel 'that he had done her disservice by raising her ideas above the dull level of her most prosaic surroundings' (I, p. 171).

Popular periodicals often discussed what kind of education was appropriate and useful for different social levels. In 1861, for example, two *Temple Bar* articles included discussions about educational opportunities for the working classes. Blanchard Jerrold's 'Our pet social doctor' advocated better education for the poorer classes as a way to a better lifestyle: 'education opens new ways of life to the poor. The man in rags, who has culture, even of the simplest description, sees chances, and can invent remunerative employment.'[23] However, the anonymous 'The management of servants' was more concerned that the kind of 'culture' people received be appropriate to their prospects in life, and advised that in the case of servants, 'reading, writing, arithmetic, geography, and history' are 'all very good, nay indispensable, but very incompetent and insufficient if used as substitutes for industrial training'; after all, the article asks, 'what connection is there between the multiplication-table and boiling potatoes?' (pp. 545–6). Whereas Flora's initial learning of the classics at least helped her to overcome her grief, Louisa's newfound love of poetry is emotionally disruptive and difficult to integrate into her daily life. Although Braddon is not necessarily devaluing a knowledge of poetry on an intellectual level (as Louisa enjoys reading it for its own sake), if she had not married Leyburne she would have found Keats and Shakespeare of little practical or economic use in terms of either her current lifestyle or her likely future occupations (this is not to say that Flora's education is any more practical, but she is an heiress who need not work for her living). A career on the stage may spring to the reader's mind but, perhaps strangely considering Braddon's theatrical background, no one suggests this.[24]

Even though Louisa declares 'I couldn't sit quiet to teach children grammar and geography if it was my only chance of escaping starvation' (I, p. 159), she finds herself with little choice after Gurner shuts her out of doors. Under Leyburne's sponsorship, Louisa attends 'Miss Tompions [sic] of Thurlow House, Kensington' (I, p. 218) in order to be 'thoroughly grounded in all the branches of a useful modern education' so that she may be 'able to impart instruction in music to girls of twelve after three years' painstaking study on her own part' (I, pp. 218–19). In this section of the novel Braddon offers a satirically comic depiction of 'common boarding-school' educations. Not only is the ultimate aim of her education detestable to Louisa, but Miss Tompion's opinions about what constitutes an appropriate syllabus for a young lady differ fundamentally from Leyburne's. Miss Tompion does not approve of a 'taste for poetry' unless 'acquired under the guidance of a cultivated understanding, after education has formed the mind', and declares that she would consider 'an ignorant undisciplined love of poetry in an ill-regulated mind … a fatal tendency' (p. 219); she finds Shakespeare particularly objectionable from a moral perspective (I, p. 302). Louisa's introduction to poetry has certainly not been a good grounding for the type of education she is expected to undergo.

At Miss Tompion's Louisa receives the kind of indiscriminate teaching, regardless of talent or inclination, that Victorian critics of education complained about. Although she has 'an intellect keen enough to have grappled with the difficulties of serious study' (II, p. 5), Louisa is placed in the lowest class with the youngest children 'because she too was a beginner' (I, p. 300). The narrator points out the error in this reasoning by explaining that an educational challenge 'would have inspired this vigorous nature', and 'her ardent longing for enlightenment would have given zest to toil' and 'develop[ed] the latent power of her mind' (I, p. 303). More specifically, by building on Louisa's existing interests, her learning could have been accelerated: if Louisa had been given 'Schiller and a German dictionary, the eager desire to know a new poet might have overcome all difficulties'; instead she is given 'infantine lessons, which she repeated parrotwise, in common with girls in pinafores and plaited hair' (I, p. 303). This is a clear contrast to Flora's classical education under Ollivant where he does, successfully, use poetry in order to spur on her language study. It is also the kind of out-of-date learning that mid-century educational writers such as Herbert Spencer were rejecting. Spencer felt that rote learning (repeating facts 'parrotwise') sacrificed 'the spirit to the letter' (Spencer, p. 29), and promoted what has come to be known as enquiry-based learning. He asserted that children should be 'led to make their own investigations, and to draw their own inferences. They should be *told* as little as possible, and induced to *discover* as much as possible'(Spencer, p. 77). It was important to get the method right, and to cater to the right level of mental development, Spencer argued, because the intellect will naturally crave the material it is ready for and children who enjoy learning will be inclined to keep improving, whilst those who are chastised and forced will simply cultivate a dislike of education and teachers, becoming generally sullen and unenthusiastic (Spencer, pp. 68, 102–3). Louisa's mind craves knowledge appropriate to its level of maturity and personal inclination; the lack of it dissuades her from education generally, as Spencer predicts will be the case.[25]

As well as receiving a negative educational experience, Louisa is appalled by the manners and ignorance displayed by the pupils at Miss Tompion's. The girls share (unsympathetically) Louisa's conviction that one cannot escape one's family and antecedents, claiming that Louisa has visibly 'low instincts' and that she is 'out of place' at the school (I, p. 306). However, the girls do not live up to Louisa's expectations of the products of good breeding; they are 'boastful and arrogant, loud-voiced and shrill of laughter', and their 'various claims to distinction were alike based upon the material advantages of their "people"'(II, p. 6). Critics of middle-class education often deplored the '"school-girl" type' as not being 'a favourite one in good English society. The mischief learnt so often at school is only too well known' (Burrows, p. 460). Education within the home could be preferable, as there are 'greater facilities in girls' schools for pettiness, deceit, and frivolity' (Davies, p. 510). The girls at Miss Tompion's are based on quite another stereotype of the boarding-school student to gentle Flora, but they share her inadequate education. Miss Portslade, the head girl, is supposedly finishing off her education in 'Latin, chemistry, and Italian singing', but Louisa, having talked to her about 'poets and painters', is 'surprised by the narrow views of the damsel, whose acquaintance with the world of imagination had never gone beyond the choice morsels in a gift-book or selection for recitation, and who knew about as much of art as the great grey cockatoo on the brazen stand in the ballroom' (I, p. 304). Miss Portslade is the product of the rote learning begun in the lowest class, capable only of 'recitation', literally compared to a parrot. Impractical and brief as Louisa's education under Leyburne may have been, it has been far more enriching than the years that girls such as Miss Portslade have spent at Miss Tompion's.

Whilst Louisa responds so well to Leyburne's teaching because of her brilliant natural grasp of poetry, the lack of a conventional education also contributes to the fresh and original manner in which she reacts to literature: on hearing Shakespeare she responds to the texts as 'no young woman who had been spoon fed with "Gems of Shakespeare" at school could have' (I, p. 132). The combination of her keen mind and special circumstances – coming to poetry as an adult from an imaginatively barren life – results in a startling intellectual development:

> An education such as this—the world of poetry suddenly unveiled to an intelligence sharpened by privation and the bitter experiences of Voysey-street—effected a strangely rapid transformation in this ardent undisciplined nature. This girl's mind was empty of all those objects which distract the attention, or even absorb the mind, of the happier portion of womanhood. Dress, pleasure, society, had for her no existence. Half the dreariness of her past life had arisen from the fact that, except cares and troubles, she had nothing to think of. Her mind was a virgin soil, ripe to receive the new seed that fell upon it—the seed of grand thoughts and of melodious verses full of deep meaning.
>
> (I, p. 134)

Once again Braddon employs botanical imagery, and again Louisa is not a flower but the soil in which flowers may grow, making her appear a site of more organic potential than 'forcing-house' Flora. Although Gurner thinks of Louisa as a 'weed' rather than a 'flower' (above), he is mistaken in his metaphor, and meanwhile the narrator presents Louisa as intellectually fertile. It is partly because of her lack of education that Louisa becomes so interesting to Leyburne, who early on discovers that hers is 'a mind hid in darkness, but with infinite capacity' (I, p. 132). As Leyburne tells her: 'when I think how little you know and how much you understand, I'm absolutely thunderstruck' (I, p. 177). As Ollivant does with Flora, Leyburne consciously decides to become Louisa's teacher, and chooses poetry based on his own tastes. Yet unlike Flora, Louisa's interest is spontaneous and unforced.

Moreover, Louisa offers a very different type of companionship from Flora. Leyburne talks to Louisa 'as if she were on an intellectual level with himself' and 'as he had never ventured to talk to Flora—with a certain Bohemian recklessness, but no shadow of evil thought' (I, pp. 130–1). Leyburne's ease is partly due to Louisa's social status and Bohemian environment. He does not feel constrained to act within the conventions of polite society and is not 'particularly anxious to retain her good opinion'. Louisa does not hold the 'sacred character in his mind' that Flora (at this point his fiancée) does (I, p. 131). Importantly, this lack of restraint does not lead Leyburne to act disrespectfully or condescendingly towards Louisa. Instead it allows him to address her as an intellectual equal, something he finds particularly attractive, as he tells Louisa:

> [Flora] hasn't so bold a mind as yours, Loo: she's not such a companion to a man as you are. One must sing duets, or talk about the last book she has read, to get on with her; but you seem to understand and sympathize with me about everything; you follow my thoughts everywhere, even when you have to grope through the dark. When I talked to you about Æschylus just now, I could see that you went with me into the dark hall where Agamemnon lay groaning in his bath. Flora would only have shuddered, and said 'How dreadful'.
>
> (I, pp. 174–5)

Flora's accomplishments and decorous upbringing restrict, as far as Leyburne is concerned, her thoughts and imagination. This speech of Leyburne's advocates something approaching equality between spouses, but it also reveals another issue at the heart of this novel: it is not merely that Louisa can match Leyburne imaginatively and intellectually, it is that she can do so on his terms: *he* talks about Aeschylus, *she* follows him. Burrows, writing against higher education for women, argues that 'sensible men will always like sensible and cultivated women; but they will always prefer that their good sense and cultivation should have come through channels which they recognise as suitable for the womanly character' (p. 465). Louisa's unconventional learning and lifestyle may not be what Burrows had in mind, but the 'channels' her learning travels through are far more 'suitable' for making her the kind of woman that Leyburne desires.

Leyburne favours a challenging and inspiring companion, but one who is moulded to his own needs and interests. Unlike Flora, who labours to appreciate the classics to please Ollivant, Louisa immediately astounds Leyburne with her ability both to understand and to sympathise with him. It is reiterated many times in the novel that Leyburne feels an intellectual and emotional release when he is with Louisa: 'How he talked! pouring out every thought and fancy as freely as if Loo were his second self, his twin-born spirit, with a mind that nature had attuned to his— she seemed to understand him so thoroughly, and all she said chimed in so well with his own thoughts' (I, pp. 173–4). Louisa is the perfect complement to Leyburne, and implicitly his equal. Her ability to learn what he knows so quickly and effortlessly suggests she may even be his superior, but this is never openly acknowledged. Braddon draws a picture of extreme female capability that is still compatible with male authority, as it is Leyburne who dictates the direction of Louisa's learning. Finally, Louisa and Leyburne end up as the happiest of couples because she adores him and he loves her in return, but even more, he loves to be adored: he is 'perfectly happy in the companionship of a wife who worshipped him' (II, p. 236). Indeed, after their marriage his "creation" of Louisa is an endless source of pride to Leyburne, who feels 'as Pygmalion the sculptor might have felt if his animated statue had been a clever woman instead of a non-entity' (II, p. 291). She has been a muse to, and is a creation of, Leyburne, who has worked with her inherent abilities to produce his ideal wife. Flora, piqued by the revelation that Leyburne loved another, believes that he cared for Louisa 'with a low common love for her handsome face' (II, p. 44), but the reader has been shown differently. Leyburne's love for Louisa is not 'common' but bespoke.

After she is married, Louisa, leading a 'wandering life' with Leyburne, continues to benefit from her experiences in such a way as to make her an even more suitable companion for him: 'the communion with all that is loveliest and grandest in nature, the study of all that is purest and noblest in art, had been a higher educational process than any formal scholastic routine ever devised by mortal teacher, and Loo had profited by her opportunities of culture' (II, p. 263). Louisa's response to 'culture' is strikingly different from James Gilbert's in *The Lady Lisle*. James's inability to be improved by his European tour is one of the signs that he is perhaps inherently incapable of acting like a gentleman. For Louisa, travel is an educational experience, but it is also a sign that she is inherently capable of learning and benefiting from exposure to art and nature. Her innate intelligence and sensitivity allow her to respond to her experience and are in turn heightened by it.

Significantly, Flora, pursuing the accomplishments she learnt at school, dabbles weakly in watercolours, whereas Louisa is a muse who inspires "powerful" art, happily sitting for Leyburne's paintings: 'always Loo; that most patient and devoted of models was never weary' (II, p. 291). Whilst in a coupling of Flora and Leyburne one would be the poor shadow of the other, trying to create her own art rather than inspiring his, Leyburne and Louisa more fully realise the Victorian ideal of woman as support and companion to man: complementary, not the same.

Both Leyburne and Ollivant profit from the efforts they put into educating their wives: Ollivant finds himself finally enjoying life, redecorating his old-fashioned town house, and imbibing some of Flora's youthfulness; Leyburne finds in Louisa the grounding and inspiration he needs to begin building a serious career as a painter. The "influence" of these females (Flora's girlishness, Louisa's common sense) is not a direct outcome of their learning, but their learning allows them to build relationships with their husbands in such a way as to let them exert that influence. Comparison with *Middlemarch* is again fruitful here: Dorothea is unable to cater to Casaubon's needs, or alleviate his anxieties, and in contrast he cannot give her the intellectual stimulation she requires. Braddon offers a more optimistic portrayal of married life than Eliot's depiction of Dorothea and Casaubon (or indeed Rosamond and Lydgate, whose temperaments are equally unsuited), but this is because she lowers the expectations of her heroines, and aligns those expectations to fit in with their husbands' desires. Part of the "problem" for *Middlemarch*'s Dorothea and Rosamond is that they have a preconceived idea of what a husband should be like, and what he should be able to offer his wife (education and material comforts respectively). Both Flora and Louisa are, by comparison, blank canvases on which their husbands may paint at will.

The personalised developments of Flora and Louisa, in line with the tastes and needs of their husbands, are made apparent towards the end of the novel when Flora sees Louisa (whom she has never met) arranging Leyburne's artist's paraphernalia. For Flora this reminds her of what she now feels to be a foolish affection for Leyburne, whilst for Louisa it is the fulfilment of her wifely duty and a source of pleasure (II, pp. 213–15). When Flora finally sees Leyburne alive and well she sees him with new eyes: his 'old lightness', which had 'been a charm in the past, an attribute of that careless sunny nature which had seemed so bright and fair to the girl's fancy ... jarred upon the woman now' (II, p. 222). Each woman has developed in accordance with her husband's tastes and mode of life.

This novel celebrates female intellectual potential, but it also portrays men as responsible for dictating the lines along which intellectual development will progress. Braddon's advocacy of female ability is embedded almost unresistingly within the tenets of domestic ideology, and her claims about the satisfaction that can be gained from learning are enmeshed with her implication that women may find happiness and intellectual stimulation through devotion to their roles as wives. *Lost for Love* acknowledges Victorian women's reliance on the men who governed their lives, whether or not those men were dependable and responsible guardians; neither Leyburne nor Ollivant is entirely reliable throughout, and they cause much suffering, particularly for Flora. In an 1869 article for *Belgravia* entitled 'Whose fault is it?' Braddon castigated men for not realising the power they hold over women. She argued that young men had set a bad example by ridiculing 'everything virtuous as "spoony", and everything domestic as "slow"', and had consequently encouraged young ladies to mimic the loose women whom the men they hoped to marry seemed to find so exciting. Braddon insisted that the 'cure must begin where the disease began—amongst the stronger, not amongst the weaker sex'.[26] Kate Mattacks points out that any 'claims to feminism' in this article are 'problematically undercut ... by the relegation of the feminine to that of an automaton who is passive and reflective rather than assertive' (p. 218). Such sentiments are reflected in *Lost for Love*, in which, despite being intellectually capable and improving influences, women are pliable and the role of creation lies with the men who marry them. Moreover, whilst there may be plenty of predetermined potential in young women, *Lost for Love* shows that conducive circumstances are vital to bringing it out, and that a good education is one of the best means of ensuring this happens. On the other hand, in *Lost for Love* (and more tragically in *John Marchmont's Legacy*), Braddon is unwilling to perceive female biology or psychology as a restriction on female intellectual achievement; it is patriarchal society that holds women back, and its male representatives who have the power to lift those restrictions. *Lost for Love* goes some way to suggesting how this could happen and, while she adheres to, and reflects, many of the gender conventions of her age by granting so much power to the husbands who form their wives' characters, Braddon also insists that the happiest marriage is one in which a woman is neither pushed into matrimony before knowing her own mind, nor restrained from achieving her full intellectual potential.

Notes

1 Mary Elizabeth Braddon, *Lost for Love*, 2 vols ([n.p.]: Elibron Classics, 2005 [1874]), Vol. I, p. 122.
2 Mary Elizabeth Braddon, *The Doctor's Wife* (Oxford: Oxford University Press, 1998), p. 29.
3 Henry Maudsley, 'Sex in mind and in education', *Fortnightly Review*, 15:88 (April 1874), 466–83 (p. 471). Maudsley controversially made explicit references to the female reproductive system, menstruation and puberty, treating readers 'to a discussion which, however appropriate to the pages of a medical publication, is a novelty in English current literature' (Cowell, p. 737).
4 Anon., 'Woman, her duties, education, and position', *Oxford and Cambridge Magazine*, 1 (August 1856), 462–77 (p. 464).
5 Montagu Burrows, 'Female education', *Quarterly Review*, 126:252 (April 1869), 448–79 (pp. 452, 465).
6 Davies's acknowledgement that not all women were necessarily going to marry in life was not a recognition that some women might prefer not to, but a response to the fact that an 'increasing number of women in mid-Victorian Britain had to remain unmarried' as there was a 'surplus of women over men' that increased by 42 per cent between 1851 and 1871. There was greater infant mortality in boys, and more men emigrated; also, men tended to wait until they were older to marry so that they could keep their wives in the manner to which they had been accustomed in their parents' homes (Burstyn, pp. 34–5). The anxiety about "surplus" women could also be used to campaign for 'women's education and entry into the professions', as Jennifer Phegley has shown in relation to the *Cornhill Magazine* (Jennifer Phegley, 'Clearing away "the briars and brambles": The education and professionalization of the *Cornhill Magazine*'s women readers, 1860–65', *Victorian Periodicals Review*, 33:1 (2000), 22–43 (p. 36)).
7 For example, the College for Women at Benslow House, Hitchin (later Girton College, Cambridge) was established in 1869. For women's higher education debates see Burstyn, and Laura Morgan Green, *Educating Women: Cultural Conflict and Victorian Literature* (Athens: Ohio University Press, 2001).
8 Ellen Jordan, '"Making good wives and mothers"? The transformation of middle-class girls' education in nineteenth-century Britain', *History of Education Quarterly*, 31:4 (Winter 1991), 439–62 (p. 443).
9 Millicent Garrett Fawcett, 'The medical and general education of women', *Fortnightly Review*, 4:23 (November 1868), 554–71 (p. 569).
10 Thomas Henry Huxley, 'Emancipation – black and white' (1865), in *Collected Essays*, Vol. III, pp. 66–75 (p. 72).

11 Anon, 'Women's education', *Fraser's Magazine for Town and Country*, 79:473 (May 1869), 537–52 (p. 548); F. P. Varney, 'Female education in France', *Fraser's Magazine for Town and Country*, 80:477 (September 1869), 366–79 (p. 379).
12 Mary Wollstonecraft, *A Vindication of the Rights of Woman: With Strictures on Political and Moral Subjects* (London: [n. pub.], 1792), p. 67.
13 Jane Austen, *Persuasion* (London: Headline, 2006), p. 41.
14 Charlotte Brontë, *Jane Eyre* (1847) (Oxford: Oxford University Press, 1998), p. 115.
15 Elizabeth Garrett Anderson, 'Sex in mind and education: A reply', *Fortnightly Review*, 15:89 (May 1874), 582–94 (p. 584).
16 Isobel Hurst's *Victorian Women Writers and the Classics: The Feminine of Homer* (Oxford: Oxford University Press, 2006) discusses how and why Victorian women learned the classics, as well as how female authors used them in their work.
17 Maria Shirreff Grey and Emily Shirreff, *Thoughts on Self-Culture, Addressed to Women* (London: Edward Moxon, 1850).
18 George Eliot, *Middlemarch* (Oxford: Oxford University Press, 1997), pp. 10, 59.
19 Sidney H. Blanchard, 'Courtship', *Belgravia*, 3 (June 1874), 511–15 (p. 513).
20 Isabella Beeton, *Mrs Beeton's Book of Household Management* (Oxford: Oxford University Press, 2000), p. 7.
21 This attitude makes a lot of sense in the light of Braddon's own personal and professional relationship with her partner and publisher, John Maxwell. Braddon's commitment to being a successful wife (although, despite being together for almost fifteen years, they did not officially marry until *Lost for Love* had almost finished its run in *Belgravia*) and mother became an important part of her public image in later years. An 1897 article on Braddon's home life described her as never allowing 'her special work as a novelist to crowd out of her life her everyday work as a woman' and responding 'as the simplest matter of course, to all the demands made upon a wife and a mother', whilst also highlighting her love of, amongst other things, history, languages and collecting china (Mary Angela Dickens, 'Miss Braddon at home', *Windsor Magazine*, 6 (June 1897), 415–18 (p. 416)). In his autobiography, Braddon's son admiringly cites her ability 'actively [to conduct] the domestic affairs of two households' with 'scarcely any help from a housekeeper' as a sign of her merits, and also describes her as an attentive mother and 'companion' to his father (W. B. Maxwell, *Time Gathered* (London: Hutchinson, 1937), pp. 281–2). For Braddon's conservative leanings see Kate Mattacks, 'Mary Elizabeth Braddon's secret: An antifeminist amongst the new women', in Tamara S. Wagner (ed.), *Antifeminism and the Victorian Novel: Rereading Nineteenth-Century Women Writers* (Amherst, NY: Cambria Press, 2009), pp. 216–33.

22 Readers of sensation fiction will be unsurprised to discover that Leyburne is in fact not dead, but fails to convey this fact to Flora.
23 Blanchard Jerrold, 'Our pet social doctor', *Temple Bar*, 3 (October 1861), 329–39 (p. 333).
24 For Braddon's theatrical career see Jennifer Carnell, *The Literary Lives of Mary Elizabeth Braddon* (Hastings: Sensation Press, 2000), pp. 11–86.
25 Spencer prioritised forms of knowledge useful to duty and livelihood over accomplishments and classics (including poetry), so Louisa's education certainly does not proceed along his ideal route. However, he also believed that humanity has 'a more worthy aim' than 'to be drudges', and knowledge of poetry was, for him, one of the things that made life worthwhile (p. 87).
26 Mary Elizabeth Braddon, 'Whose fault is it?', *Belgravia*, 9 (August 1869), 214–16 (pp. 214, 215).

Conclusion

The whole character of the man then as we find him may be said to have been built up by the following processes. He comes into the world as an infant, with a nervous system in a comparatively undeveloped state. This nervous system as it exists in infancy is the result of the combination of the two original constitutions of its parents, plus the effects of their life-experience upon them; life-experience meaning the modifications effected in the original constitution by the whole circumstances of the whole existence of the individual. And having come into the world thus constituted, the man's character is modified again by circumstances as he also grows from infancy to manhood, and the final result is *the sum of the effects which these modifications are capable of producing on his original constitution*. That a conclusion such as this is that to which the present state of physiology seems not indistinctly to point, we think can hardly be denied.[1]
(G. W. Child, 'Physiological psychology', *Westminster Review*, 1868)

In his 1868 review of Henry Maudsley's *The Physiology and Pathology of the Mind* (1867) for the *Westminster Review*, G. W. Child took the opportunity to bring readers up to date with 'the present position of our knowledge of mental physiology' (Child, p. 38), and the above passage formed part of his conclusion. Child's account of each individual as the result of a multitude of pre- and post-congenital factors includes many of the determinants that, as we have seen throughout *Creating Character*, were debated, contested and theorised in a variety of Victorian writing, including sensation fiction. Braddon and Collins explicitly and implicitly engage with these determining factors in their fiction; their work contains numerous instances, but also frequent questioning, of the influence of biological transmission of physical, mental and moral characteristics, and of environmental stimuli such as education, social environment and upbringing.

211

Conclusion

Reading a range of Braddon's and Collins's texts reveals that neither author has a consistently favoured form of determinism; they are sensitive to the complex mass of context-dependent circumstances that build the chain of cause and effect that drives people through life, and characters through plots. Moreover, Braddon and Collins are willing to employ one form of character formation over others if it serves their literary, social or moral purpose. Different novels employ types of nature and nurture in different ways and to different ends: to provide an explanation for a character's behaviour, engineer particular plot developments or make a particular point. Hester Dethridge's monomaniacal murder of Geoffrey Delamayn, for example, is a means both of doing away with the novel's villain, and of showing the awful consequences of domestic abuse and unjust marriage laws. Part of this willingness is because Braddon and Collins are also extremely aware that ideas of what makes (and makes up) character are crucial to how people are perceived. To imply that someone is a certain way by nature or nurture can damn or excuse them, or both, and Braddon and Collins take advantage of this as they manage the sympathies and understanding of their readers: neither Geoffrey Delamayn, nor James Gilbert, nor Magdalen Vanstone can help their behaviour, but only the last can be forgiven (and allowed to live) because of the insistence that she is inherently a good person.

Both authors implicitly believe in a core personality, or 'original constitution', but how much later *'modifications are capable'* of altering that constitution varies from novel to novel and character to character. It is notable that Collins and Braddon write stories about the power of heredity (*The Lady Lisle*, 'Mad Monkton' and *Armadale*) in the 1860s, and novels advocating the power of education to form and improve or ruin the individual in the 1870s (*Man and Wife* and *Lost for Love*). Although the latter are in part responses to popular concerns about the state of education, it is significant that Braddon and Collins were writing these novels at a time when scientific theories and social policies were tending towards more deterministic, less optimistic conceptions of heredity, and beginning to consider eugenics as the means of halting social degeneration. Both authors are asserting the ability and responsibility of society to raise good citizens, and are to at least some extent buffering the individual from blame. Reading the novels collectively, there is also an evident reluctance (with a few notable exceptions) to portray the individual as so much at the mercy of either inherent constitution or uncontrollable environmental influences that *all* possibility of self-improvement and, even more, personal responsibility is effectively excluded. In the work of

Conclusion

both authors the individual is a site of great potential: Collins's faith in the forces of both Good and Evil within each person means that victory over the latter is always possible; Braddon's interests centre more on the intellect, and her characters often have the capacity for greatness or the makings of genius. In each case, though, the individual needs a supportive and flexible social framework in which to develop.

Braddon and Collins experiment imaginatively and speculatively with the combinations of nature and nurture that will allow innate potential to flourish or perish in a given situation, focusing on those moments when someone's core nature clashes with their external circumstances – circumstances that are ideological as much as physical, financial, accidental and so on. This allows them space to question and challenge, but also to perpetuate, various prejudices and stereotypes of their age. And so, in *Lost for Love*, Braddon promotes a conception of womanhood that includes intrinsic intellectual ability, even as she harnesses that ability to the serving of men's pleasure. And Collins makes a mixed-race murderer's son the hero of *Armadale*, but unquestioningly associates his 'hot African blood' (p. 35) with violence, and does not go so far as to grant him the traditional literary prize of a wife and children. Sensation fiction as a genre is both controversial and strangely conventional. Despite the many and varied forms of transgressive behaviour that occur in these novels, the endings tend to reassert class hierarchies and gender divisions, and purge (often through death, occasionally through rehabilitation) immoral elements. Deborah Wynne suggests that we should focus on the centre of these novels as much as the end because 'although sensation novelists usually provided conservative solutions at the ends of their novels, their complex depictions of subversive possibilities are prominently placed for most of the narrative, suggesting alternatives without necessarily endorsing them'.[2] Some conservative readers may well have found themselves wishing, at least for a moment, that Miss Gwilt and Midwinter's marriage had been a success, even if they were more comfortable with the ending as it stands.

To look at the sometimes frustrating assumptions about class, race, gender and sexuality embedded in the Victorian literature (fictional and otherwise) covered in *Creating Character* could give modern readers a sense of superiority. It is easy to think that we have grown beyond prejudices in which our society is still, in actuality, enmeshed. Moreover, notions of nature and nurture continue both to prompt cultural debates and to be used as powerful rhetorical tools within them. Writing as I am in 2016, campaigners for African American rights are still resisting negative preconceptions about black "nature". The Black Lives Matter movement, for example, draws attention to the environmental factors that result in increased crime rates in 'black communities', and 'refuses to locate that crime problem as a problem of black pathology. Black people are not inherently more violent or more prone to crime than other groups. But black people are disproportionately poorer, more likely to be targeted by police and arrested, and more likely to attend poor or failing schools.'[3] The near impossibility of buying a card for a new-born baby that is not pink or blue shows that we are still labouring under facile conceptions of what it means to be a boy or a girl, and books that (only semi-humorously) play on gender stereotypes, such as *How to Mow the Lawn: The Lost Art of Being a Man*, reveal continued anxiety about how to teach gender roles.[4] Meanwhile, debates concerning feminism and transgender rights frequently turn on conceptions of what it means, fundamentally, to be a woman or a man.[5] Media debates over access to healthcare often hinge on whether unhealthy behaviour is the result of genes, illness or poor lifestyle choices, and come loaded with allocations of blame and guilt directed towards individuals, parents and society.[6] On a different note, the rapid progress being made in the field of genetics is sparking concern that the possibility of "designer babies" could lead to a new form of eugenics.[7] If reading Victorian literature can make us aware of what was wrong in Victorian society, and how concepts of nature and nurture were used to sustain and challenge those problems, it can also help us to be aware of what continues to be wrong in our own.

Notes

1 G. W. Child, 'Physiological psychology', p. 63, emphasis in original.
2 Deborah Wynne, *The Sensation Novel and the Victorian Family Magazine* (Basingstoke: Palgrave, 2001), p. 149.
3 Anon., '11 major misconceptions about the Black Lives Matter movement', *Black Lives Matter*, http://blacklivesmatter.com/11-major-misconceptions-about-the-black-lives-matter-movement/ (accessed 18 September 2016).
4 Sam Martin, *How to Mow the Lawn: The Lost Art of Being a Man* (London: Bloomsbury, 2003).
5 See, for example, Katy Guest, 'When it comes to transgender rights, there's nothing feminist about being a bigot', *Independent* (30 January 2016), www.independent.co.uk/voices/when-it-comes-to-transgender-rights-there-s-nothing-feminist-about-being-a-bigot-a6843811.html (accessed 21 October 2016).

Conclusion

6 See, for example, Amanda Platell, 'Sorry, why should the NHS treat people for being fat?', *Daily Mail Online* (27 February 2009), www.dailymail.co.uk/debate/article-1156678/AMANDA-PLATELL-Sorry-NHS-treat-people-fat.html (accessed 18 September 2016).

7 See, for example, 'UN panel warns against "designer babies" and eugenics in "editing" of human DNA', UN News Centre (5 October 2015), www.un.org/apps/news/story.asp?NewsID=52172#.WAnLMSTtX20, (accessed 21 October 2016).

Bibliography

For unsigned articles I have used the attributions of the *Wellesley Index to Victorian Periodicals: 1824–1900*, excepting *Athenaeum* articles, for which I have drawn on *The Athenaeum Index of Reviews and Reviewers: 1830–1870*.

Abercrombie, John, *Inquiries Concerning the Intellectual Powers and the Investigation of Truth*, 2nd edn (Edinburgh: Waugh and Innes, 1831 [1830])

Acton, William, *The Functions and Disorders of the Reproductive Organs in Childhood, Youth, Adult Age, and Advanced Life: Considered in Their Physiological, Social, and Moral Relations*, 6th edn (London: J. & A. Churchill, 1875)

Adams, Joseph, *A Treatise on the Supposed Hereditary Properties of Diseases: Containing Remarks on the Unfounded Terrors and Ill-Judged Cautions Consequent on Such Erroneous Opinions* (London: Callow, 1814)

Allan, Janice M., 'Sensationalism made real: The role of realism in the production of sensational affect', *Victorian Literature and Culture*, 43 (2015), 97–112

Anderson, Elizabeth Garrett, 'Sex in mind and education: A reply', *Fortnightly Review*, 15:89 (May 1874), 582–94

Anon., 'Cases of monomania', *Chambers's Edinburgh Journal*, 2:63 (April 1833), 88

—— 'The degeneration of race', *Lancet*, 76:1947 (22 December 1860), 619–20

—— '11 major misconceptions about the Black Lives Matter movement', *Black Lives Matter*, http://blacklivesmatter.com/11-major-misconceptions-about-the-black-lives-matter-movement/ (accessed 18 September 2016)

—— 'The force of habit', *Chambers's Edinburgh Journal*, 294 (August 1849), 105–7

—— 'The houseless poor', *Temple Bar*, 1 (March 1861), 225–9

—— 'Insanity and its treatment', *Belgravia*, 10 (February 1870), 467–78

—— 'Labour', *London Journal*, 12:290 (July 1889), 47

—— '*Man and Wife*', *Saturday Review*, 30:767 (July 1870), 52–3

—— 'The management of servants', *Temple Bar*, 1 (March 1861), 545–57

—— 'M.D. and M.A.D.', *All the Year Round*, 6:148 (22 February 1862), 510–13

—— 'Miss Martineau and her master', *British and Foreign Medico-Chirurgical Review*, 8 (1851), 538–40

—— 'Monomania', *Chambers's Edinburgh Journal*, 595 (June 1843), 177–8

Bibliography

—— On the physical and mental characters of the Negro', *Reader*, 2 (1863), 324

—— 'Physical and moral heritage', *British Quarterly Review*, 29:57 (January 1859), 3–56

—— 'Preface', *Welcome Guest*, 4 (May 1861), iii

—— 'The progress of fiction as an art', *Westminster Review*, 60:118 (October 1853), 342–74

—— 'Religious monomania; self-mutilation', *Lancet*, 58:1472 (15 November 1851), 456

—— 'Responsibility of monomaniacs', *New Monthly Magazine and Humorist*, 89:356 (August 1850), 404–8

'UN panel warns against "designer babies" and eugenics in "editing" of human DNA', UN News Centre (5 October 2015), www.un.org/apps/news/story.asp?NewsID=52172#.WAnLMSTtX20 (accessed 21 October 2016])

—— 'Woman, her duties, education, and position', *Oxford and Cambridge Magazine*, 1 (August 1856), 462–77

—— 'Woman in her psychological relations', *Journal of Psychological Medicine and Mental Pathology*, 4 (1851), 18–50

—— 'Women's education', *Fraser's Magazine for Town and Country*, 79:473 (May 1869), 537–52

—— 'A word to women, by one of themselves', *Temple Bar*, 2 (April 1861), 54–61, repr. *Sixpenny Magazine*, 2:10 (March 1868), 423–31

Antinucci, Raffaella, '"Not another like him in the world": Wilkie Collins and the gentleman within', in Mariaconcetta Costantini (ed.), *'Armadale': Wilkie Collins and the Dark Threads of Life* (Roma: Aracne, 2009), pp. 133–54

Atkinson, Henry George, and Harriet Martineau, *Letters on the Laws of Man's Nature and Development* (London: John Chapman, 1851)

Austen, Jane, *Persuasion* (London: Headline, 2006)

Bachman, Maria K., '"Furious passions of the Celtic race": Ireland, madness and Wilkie Collins's *Blind Love*', in Andrew Maunder and Grace Moore (eds), *Victorian Crime, Madness and Sensation* (Aldershot: Ashgate, 2004), pp. 179–94

Bachman, Maria K., and Don Richard Cox, 'Wilkie Collins's villainous Miss Gwilt, criminality, and the unspeakable truth', *Dickens Studies Annual*, 32 (2002), 319–37

Baker, William, *Wilkie Collins's Library: A Reconstruction* (London: Greenwood Press, 2002)

Bale, John, 'Anti-sport: Victorian examples from Oxbridge', *Sport in History*, 34:1 (2014), 34–48

Barlow, John, *On Man's Power over Himself to Prevent or Control Insanity*, 2nd edn (London: W. Pickering, 1849 [1843])

Barnett, Richard, 'Education or degeneration: E. Ray Lankester, H. G. Wells and *The Outline of History*', *Studies in History and Philosophy of Biological and Biomedical Sciences*, 37:2 (June 2006), 203–29

Beecher, Ward, 'Self-control', *Bow Bells*, 9:230 (December 1868), 531

Bibliography

Beer, Gillian, 'Beyond determinism: George Eliot and Virginia Woolf', in Mary Jacobus (ed.), *Women Writing and Writing about Women* (Beckenham: Croom Helm, 1979), pp. 80–99

—— *Darwin's Plots: Evolutionary Narrative in Darwin, George Eliot and Nineteenth-Century Fiction*, 2nd edn (Cambridge: Cambridge University Press, 2000)

Beeton, Isabella, *Mrs Beeton's Book of Household Management* (Oxford: Oxford University Press, 2000)

Beetz, Kirk H., 'Wilkie Collins and the *Leader*', *Victorian Periodicals Review*, 1:15 (1982), 20–9

Beller, Anne-Marie, 'Detecting the self in the sensation fiction of Wilkie Collins and Mary Elizabeth Braddon', *Clues*, 26:1 (2007), 49–61

—— 'Sensation fiction in the 1850s', in Andrew Mangham (ed.), *The Cambridge Companion to Sensation Fiction* (Cambridge: Cambridge University Press, 2013), pp. 7–20

—— 'Sensational *Bildung*? Infantilization and female maturation in Braddon's 1860s novels', in Jessica Cox (ed.), *New Perspectives on Mary Elizabeth Braddon* (Amsterdam: Rodopi, 2012), pp. 113–32

Birch, Dinah, and Francis O'Gorman (eds), *Ruskin and Gender* (Basingstoke: Palgrave, 2002)

Blanchard, Sidney H., 'Courtship', *Belgravia*, 3 (June 1874), 511–15

Bowen, John, 'Collins's shorter fiction', in Jenny Bourne Taylor (ed.), *The Cambridge Companion to Wilkie Collins* (Cambridge: Cambridge University Press, 2006), pp. 37–49

Braddon, Mary Elizabeth, *Aurora Floyd* (Oxford: Oxford University Press, 1996)

—— *Birds of Prey* (Whitefish, MT: Kessinger Publishing, 2004)

—— *The Captain of the Vulture* (London: Simpkin, Marshall, Hamilton, Kent, 189[?])

—— *The Doctor's Wife* (Oxford: Oxford University Press, 1998)

—— *John Marchmont's Legacy*, ed. Tōru Sasaki and Norman Page (Oxford: Oxford University Press, 1999)

—— *Lady Audley's Secret* (Oxford: Oxford University Press, 1998)

—— *The Lady Lisle*, *The Welcome Guest*, 4 (July 1861), 239–43

—— *The Lady Lisle* (London: Ward and Lock, 1862)

—— *Lady Lisle* (London: Simpkin, Marshall, Hamilton, Kent, 189[?])

—— *Lost for Love*, 2 vols ([n.p.]: Elibron Classics, 2005 [1874])

—— *The Lovels of Arden* (Teddington: Echo Library, 2006)

—— 'Whose fault is it?', *Belgravia*, 9 (August 1869), 214–16

Brantlinger, Patrick, 'What is "sensational" about the "sensation novel"?', *Nineteenth-Century Fiction*, 37:1 (1982), 1–28

Brodie, Benjamin Collins, *Psychological Inquiries, Part II* (1862), in *The Works of Sir Benjamin Collins Brodie: With an Autobiography*, 3 vols (London: Longman, Green, Longman, Roberts and Green, 1865), Vol. I, pp. 259–385

Bibliography

Brooks, Peter, *The Melodramatic Imagination: Balzac, Henry James, Melodrama, and the Mode of Excess* (New Haven: Yale University Press, 1976)
Brontë, Charlotte, *Jane Eyre* (Oxford: Oxford University Press, 1998)
Browne, Charles Thomas, 'Criminal lunatics', *Temple Bar*, 1 (December 1860), 135–43
Bucknill, John Charles, 'The law and the theory of insanity', *British and Foreign Medico-Chirurgical Review*, 13 (January 1854), 76–93
Bulwer-Lytton, Edward, 'On self-control', in *Caxtoniana* (London: Routledge and Sons, 1875 [1863]), pp. 206–14
—— 'Self-control', *Reynolds's Miscellany*, 32:835 (June 1864), 397
Burgess, Joshua, 'The policy and pathology of insanity', *Lancet*, 58:1463 (13 September 1851), 246–7
Burrows, Montagu, 'Female education', *Quarterly Review*, 126:252 (April 1869), 448–79
Burstyn, Joan N., *Victorian Education and the Ideal of Womanhood* (London: Croom Helm, 1980)
Caleb, Amanda Mordavsky, 'Questioning moral inheritance in *The Legacy of Cain*', in Andrew Mangham (ed.), *Wilkie Collins: Interdisciplinary Essays* (Newcastle: Cambridge Scholars Publishing, 2007), pp. 122–35
Carnell, Jennifer, *The Literary Lives of Mary Elizabeth Braddon* (Hastings: Sensation Press, 2000)
Carpenter, William Benjamin, 'On the hereditary transmission of acquired psychical habits', *Contemporary Review*, 21 (December 1872), 295–314
—— 'The physiology of the will', *Contemporary Review*, 17 (April 1871), 192–217
—— *Principles of Human Physiology: With Their Chief Applications to Psychology, Pathology, Therapeutics, Hygiene and Forensic Medicine*, 5th edn (London: J. Churchill, 1855)
—— *Principles of Mental Physiology: With Their Applications to the Training and Discipline of the Mind, and the Study of Its Morbid Conditions* (London: H. S. King, 1874)
Ceraldi, Gabrielle, 'The Crystal Palace, imperialism, and the "struggle for existence": Victorian evolutionary discourse in Collins's *The Woman in White*', in Maria K. Bachman and Don Richard Cox (eds), *Reality's Dark Light: The Sensational Wilkie Collins* (Knoxville: University of Tennessee Press, 2003), pp. 173–94
Child, G. W., 'Physiological psychology', *Westminster Review*, 33:1 (January 1868), 37–65
Chorley, H. F., '*Armadale*', *Athenaeum*, 2014 (June 1866), 732–3
—— '*No Name*', *Athenaeum*, 1836 (January 1863), 10–11
Collins, Wilkie, *Armadale* (Oxford: Oxford University Press, 1999)
—— *Basil* (Oxford: Oxford University Press, 2005)
—— *The Legacy of Cain* (Stroud: Sutton Publishing, 1993)
—— *The Letters of Wilkie Collins*, ed. William Baker and William M. Clarke, 2 vols (London: Macmillan, 1999)

—— *'Mad Monkton' and Other Stories*, ed. Norman Page (Oxford: Oxford University Press, 1994)
—— *Man and Wife* (Oxford: Oxford University Press, 1998)
—— *Miss Gwilt: A Drama in Five Acts* (printed for performance in the theatre only, not published, 1875)
—— 'Miss or Mrs?', in *'Miss or Mrs?', 'The Haunted Hotel', 'The Guilty River'* (Oxford: Oxford University Press, 1999), pp. 1–83
—— *The Moonstone* (London: Pan, 1967)
—— 'The Monktons of Wincot Abbey', *Fraser's Magazine for Town and Country* 52:311 (November 1855), 485–502; 52:312 (December 1855), 662–78
—— *No Name* (London: Penguin, 2004)
—— *No Name: A Drama in Four Acts* (London: published by the author, 1870)
—— *Poor Miss Finch*, ed. Catherine Peters (Oxford: Oxford University Press, 2000)
—— *The Woman in White* (Oxford: Oxford University Press, 1998)
—— *The Woman in White: A Drama in a Prologue and Four Acts* (London: published by the author, 1871)
—— 'The twin sisters: A true story', *Bentley's Miscellany*, 29 (March 1851), 278–91
Conolly, John, *An Inquiry Concerning the Indications of Insanity, with Suggestions for the Better Protection and Care of the Insane* (London: John Taylor, 1830)
—— *The Treatment of the Insane without Mechanical Restraints* (London: Smith, Elder, 1856)
Cope, Ellie, 'Undoing a "symmetrical existence": Boldwood's monomania in *Far from the Madding Crowd*, *Thomas Hardy Journal*, 26 (2010), 35–42
Corbet, K., 'The degeneration of race', *Lancet*, 78:1981 (17 August 1861), 170
Costantini, Mariaconcetta, *Venturing into Unknown Waters: Wilkie Collins and the Challenge of Modernity* (Pescara: Tracce, 2008)
Cowell, Herbert, 'Sex in mind and education: A commentary', *Blackwood's Edinburgh Magazine*, 115 (June 1874), 736–49
Curtis, Jeni, 'The "espaliered" girl: Pruning the docile body in *Aurora Floyd*', in Marlene Tromp, Pamela K. Gilbert and Aeron Haynie (eds), *Beyond Sensation: Mary Elizabeth Braddon in Context* (Albany: State University of New York Press, 2000), pp. 77–92
Darwin, Charles, *The Origin of Species* (Oxford: Oxford University Press, 1998)
Daston, Lorraine J., 'British responses to psycho-physiology, 1860–1900', *Isis*, 69:2 (1978), 192–208
Dawson, Gowan, *Darwin, Literature and Victorian Respectability* (Cambridge: Cambridge University Press, 2007)
Davies, James, 'Female education', *Quarterly Review*, 119:238 (April 1866), 499–515
Davis, Lennard J., *Obsession: A History* (Chicago: University of Chicago Press, 2008)

Bibliography

Delafield, Catherine, *Women's Diaries as Narrative in the Nineteenth-Century Novel* (Farnham: Ashgate, 2009)
Dennis, John, 'Only a Clod', *Fortnightly Review*, 1 (July 1865), 511–12
Dickens, Charles, *Bleak House* (Oxford: Oxford University Press, 1998)
—— *The Letters of Charles Dickens*, ed. Graham Storey *et al.*, 11 vols (Oxford: Clarendon Press, 1965–99)
Dickens, Mary Angela, 'Miss Braddon at home', *Windsor Magazine*, 6 (June 1897), 415–18
Dolin, Tim, and Lucy Dougan, 'Fatal newness: *Basil*, art, and the origins of sensation fiction', in Maria K. Bachman and Don Richard Cox (eds), *Reality's Dark Light: The Sensational Wilkie Collins* (Knoxville: University of Tennessee Press, 2003), pp. 1–33
Duffy, W. L., 'Monomania and perpetual motion: Insanity and amateur scientific enthusiasm in nineteenth-century medical, scientific and literary discourse', *French Cultural Studies*, 21 (2010), 155–66
During, Simon, 'The strange case of monomania: Patriarchy in literature, murder in *Middlemarch*, drowning in *Daniel Deronda*', *Representations*, 23 (1988), 86–104
Eliot, George, *Middlemarch* (Oxford: Oxford University Press, 1997)
Ellis, Havelock, *The Criminal* (New York: Scribner and Welford, 1890)
Esquirol, J. E. D., *Mental Maladies: A Treatise on Insanity*, trans. E. K. Hunt (Philadelphia: Lea and Blanchard, 1845)
Fancher, Raymond E., 'Scientific cousins: The relationship between Charles Darwin and Francis Galton', *American Psychologist*, 64:2 (February–March 2009), 84–92
Fawcett, Millicent Garrett, 'The medical and general education of women', *Fortnightly Review*, 4:23 (November 1868), 554–71
Fisch, Audrey, 'Collins, race, and slavery', in Maria K. Bachman and Don Richard Cox (eds), *Reality's Dark Light: The Sensational Wilkie Collins* (Knoxville: University of Tennessee Press, 2003), pp. 313–28
Galton, Francis, 'Hereditary talent and character', *Macmillan's Magazine*, 12:68 (June 1865), 157–66; 12:70 (August 1865), 318–27
—— *Inquiries into Human Faculty and Its Development* (London: Macmillan, 1883)
Garrison, Laurie, *Science, Sexuality and Sensation Novels: Pleasures of the Senses* (Basingstoke: Palgrave Macmillan, 2011)
Gatens, Moira, 'Freedom and determinism in *Middlemarch*; or, Dorothea, the lunatic', *Sidney Studies in English*, 29 (2003), 31–8
Gerard, Jessica, 'Lady Bountiful: Women of the landed classes and rural philanthropy', *Victorian Studies*, 30 (1987), 183–210
Gilbert, Pamela K., *The Citizen's Body: Desire, Health, and the Social in Victorian England* (Columbus: Ohio State University Press, 2007)
—— *Disease, Desire, and the Body in Victorian Women's Popular Novels* (Cambridge: Cambridge University Press, 1997)

Bibliography

Goldstein, Jan, *Console and Classify: The French Psychiatric Profession in the Nineteenth Century* (Cambridge: Cambridge University Press, 1987)

Green, Laura Morgan, *Educating Women: Cultural Conflict and Victorian Literature* (Athens: Ohio University Press, 2001)

Greenslade, William, *Degeneration, Culture, and the Novel, 1880–1940* (Cambridge: Cambridge University Press, 1994)

Grey, Maria Shirreff, and Emily Shirreff, *Thoughts on Self-Culture, Addressed to Women* (London: Edward Moxon, 1850)

Guest, Katy 'When it comes to transgender rights, there's nothing feminist about being a bigot', *Independent* (30 January 2016), www.independent.co.uk/voices/when-it-comes-to-transgender-rights-there-s-nothing-feminist-about-being-a-bigot-a6843811.html (accessed 21 October 2016)

Hall, Donald E. (ed.), *Muscular Christianity: Embodying the Victorian Age* (Cambridge: Cambridge University Press, 1994)

Hannigan, D. F., 'The tenacity of superstition', *Westminster Review*, 154:1 (July 1900), 69–72

Hartley, Lucy, *Physiognomy and the Meaning of Expression in Nineteenth-Century Culture* (Cambridge: Cambridge University Press, 2001)

Harwood, John Berwick, 'The servant's hall', *Belgravia*, 9 (January 1873), 331–9

Haynie, Aeron, '"An idle handle that was never turned, and a lazy rope so rotten": The decay of the country estate in *Lady Audley's Secret*', in Marlene Tromp, Pamela K. Gilbert and Aeron Haynie (eds), *Beyond Sensation: Mary Elizabeth Braddon in Context* (Albany: State University of New York Press, 2000), pp. 63–76

Healey, T. P., 'Shall we marry her?', *Welcome Guest*, 1 (January 1860), 228–9

Heller, Tamar, *Dead Secrets: Wilkie Collins and the Female Gothic* (New Haven: Yale University Press, 1992)

Hensley, Nathan K., '*Armadale* and the logic of liberalism', *Victorian Studies*, 51 (2009), 607–32

Higgins, M. J. ['Paterfamilias'], 'On some points of the Eton report', *Cornhill Magazine*, 10:55 (July 1864), 113–28

Hingston, Kylee-Anne, '"Skins to jump into": The slipperiness of identity and the body in Wilkie Collins's *No Name*', *Victorian Literature and Culture*, 40 (2012), 117–35

Holland, H. W., 'Thieves and thieving', *Cornhill Magazine*, 2:9 (September 1860), 326–44

Holland, Henry, *Chapters on Mental Physiology* (London: Longman, Brown, Green and Longman, 1852)

Hughes, Winifred, *The Maniac in the Cellar: Sensation Novels of the 1860s* (Princeton: Princeton University Press, 1980)

Hurley, Kelly, *The Gothic Body: Sexuality, Materialism, and Degeneration at the 'Fin-de-Siècle'* (Cambridge: Cambridge University Press, 1996)

Bibliography

Hurst, Isobel, *Victorian Women Writers and the Classics: The Feminine of Homer* (Oxford: Oxford University Press, 2006)

Huskey, Melynda, '*No Name*: Embodying the sensation heroine', *Victorian Newsletter*, 82 (1992), 5–13

Huxley, Thomas Henry, 'A liberal education; and where to find it', in *Collected Essays*, 9 vols (London: Macmillan, 1895), Vol. III, pp. 76–110

—— 'Emancipation – black and white', in *Collected Essays*, 9 vols (London: Macmillan, 1895), Vol. III, pp. 66–75

—— 'On the study of biology', in *Collected Essays*, 9 vols (London: Macmillan, 1895), Vol. III, pp. 262–93

—— 'The school boards: What they can do, and what they may do', in *Collected Essays*, 9 vols (London: Macmillan, 1895), Vol. III, pp. 374–403

—— 'Scientific education', in *Collected Essays*, 9 vols (London: Macmillan, 1895), Vol. III, pp. 111–33

Ifill, Helena, 'Wilkie Collins's monomaniacs in *Basil*, *No Name* and *Man and Wife*', *Wilkie Collins Journal*, 12 (2013), http://wilkiecollinssociety.org/wilkie-collinss-monomaniacs-in-basil-no-name-and-man-and-wife/ (accessed 21 October 2016)

Japp, A. H. [H. A. P.], '*Man and Wife*', *Contemporary Review*, 15 (August 1870), 317–19

Jerrold, Blanchard, 'Our pet social doctor', *Temple Bar*, 3 (October 1861), 329–39

Jones, David W., 'Moral insanity and psychological disorder: The hybrid roots of psychiatry', *History of Psychiatry* (10 April 10 2017), 1–17, DOI 10.1177/0957154X17702316 (accessed 10 May 2017)

Jordan, Ellen, '"Making good wives and mothers"? The transformation of middle-class girls' education in nineteenth-century Britain', *History of Education Quarterly*, 31:4 (Winter 1991), 439–62

Kingsley, Charles, 'Heroism', in *Sanitary and Social Lectures* (London: Macmillan, 1880), pp. 225–54

—— 'The science of health', in *Sanitary and Social Lectures* (London: Macmillan, 1880), pp. 21–45

[L., E.], 'On quacks', *Temple Bar*, 2 (May 1861), 268–75

Lankester, Edwin Ray, *Degeneration: A Chapter in Darwinism* (London: Macmillan, 1880)

Larkin, Maurice, *Man and Society in Nineteenth-Century Realism: Determinism and Literature* (London: Macmillan, 1977)

Law, Graham, and Andrew Maunder, *Wilkie Collins: A Literary Life* (Basingstoke: Palgrave Macmillan, 2008)

Lawrence, Keith, 'The religion of Wilkie Collins: Three unpublished documents', *Huntington Library Quarterly*, 52:3 (1989), 389–402

Levine, George, 'Determinism and responsibility in the works of George Eliot', *PMLA*, 77:3 (1962), 268–79

Lewes, George Henry, 'Hereditary influence, animal and human', *Westminster Review*, 66:129 (July 1856), 135–62

—— 'The principles of success in literature', *Fortnightly Review*, 1 (May 1865), 85–95

—— 'The two aspects of history', *Cornhill Magazine*, 9:51 (March 1864), 292–6

Liggins, Emma, 'Her mercenary spirit: Women, money and marriage in Mary Elizabeth Braddon's 1870s fiction', *Women's Writing*, 11:1 (2004), 73–87

Lombroso, Cesare, 'Introduction', in Gina Lombroso-Ferrero, *Criminal Man: According to the Classification of Cesare Lombroso* (New York and London: Knickerbocker Press, 1911), pp. xi–xx

Lonoff, Sue, *Wilkie Collins and His Victorian Readers: A Study in the Rhetoric of Authorship* (New York: AMS Press, 1982)

Lycett, Andrew, *Wilkie Collins: A Life of Sensation* (London: Random House, 2013)

Maddyn, Daniel Owen, '*Basil: A Story of Modern Life*', *Athenaeum*, 1310 (December 1852), 1322–3

Mangham, Andrew, *Violent Women and Sensation Fiction: Crime, Medicine and Victorian Popular Culture* (Basingstoke: Palgrave Macmillan, 2007)

Martin, Sam, *How to Mow the Lawn: The Lost Art of Being a Man* (London: Bloomsbury, 2003)

Mason, Diane, 'Latimer's complaint: Masturbation and monomania in George Eliot's *The Lifted Veil*', *Women's Writing*, 5:3 (1998), 393–403

Mattacks, Kate, 'Mary Elizabeth Braddon's secret: An antifeminist amongst the new women', in Tamara S. Wagner (ed.), *Antifeminism and the Victorian Novel: Rereading Nineteenth-Century Women Writers* (Amherst, NY: Cambria Press, 2009), pp. 216–33

Maudsley, Henry, *Body and Mind: An Inquiry into Their Connection and Mutual Influence, Specially in Reference to Mental Disorders* (London: Macmillan, 1870), in Jenny Bourne Taylor and Sally Shuttleworth (eds), *Embodied Selves: An Anthology of Psychological Texts 1830–1890* (Oxford: Oxford University Press, 2003 [1998]), pp. 326–9

—— 'On some of the causes of insanity', *Journal of Mental Science*, 12 (January 1867), 488–502

—— *The Physiology and Pathology of Mind*, 2nd edn, rev. (London: Macmillan, 1868)

—— 'Practical observations on insanity of feeling and of action', *Lancet*, 87:2234 (23 June 1866), 679–80

—— *Responsibility in Mental Disease*, 2nd edn (London: H. S. King, 1874)

—— 'Sex in mind and in education', *Fortnightly Review*, 15:88 (April 1874), 466–83

Maunder, Andrew, '"Stepchildren of nature": *East Lynne* and the spectre of female degeneracy, 1860–1861', in Andrew Maunder and Grace Moore (eds), *Victorian Crime, Madness and Sensation* (Aldershot: Ashgate, 2004), pp. 59–71

Maunder, Andrew, and Grace Moore (eds), *Victorian Crime, Madness and Sensation* (Aldershot: Ashgate, 2004)

Bibliography

Maxwell, W. B., *Time Gathered* (London: Hutchinson, 1937)

McCarthy, Justin, 'Novels with a purpose', *Westminster Review*, 26:1 (July 1864), 24–49

McCord, Norman, *British History: 1815–16* (Oxford: Oxford University Press, 1991)

Melville, Herman, 'Benito Cereno', in Nina Baym and Robert S. Levine (eds), *The Norton Anthology of American Literature, Volume B, 1820–1865*, 8th edn (New York: W. W. Norton, 2012), pp. 1526–82

Mill, Harriet Taylor, 'The enfranchisement of women', *Westminster Review*, 55:2 (July 1851), 289–311

Millingen, John Gideon, '*The Passions; or Mind and Matter*' (London: J. and D. Darling, 1848), in Jenny Bourne Taylor and Sally Shuttleworth (eds), *Embodied Selves: An Anthology of Psychological Texts 1830–1890* (Oxford: Oxford University Press, 2003 [1998]), pp. 169–70

Mivart, St George, 'Darwin's *Descent of Man*', *Quarterly Review*, 131 (July 1871), 47–90

Monro, Frederick T., 'Truth is stranger than fiction', *Belgravia*, 9 (July 1869), 103–8

Morgan, T. C. ['μ'], 'Monomaniacs and monomania', *New Monthly Magazine and Humorist*, 68:269 (May 1843), 43–51

Morgentaler, Goldie, *Dickens and Heredity: When Like Begets Like* (Basingstoke: Macmillan, 2000)

Nayder, Lillian, 'The empire and sensation', in Pamela K. Gilbert (ed.), *A Companion to Sensation Fiction* (Chichester: John Wiley and Sons, 2011), pp. 442–54

—— 'Science and sensation', in Andrew Mangham (ed.), *The Cambridge Companion to Sensation Fiction* (Cambridge: Cambridge University Press, 2013), pp. 154–67

Odden, Karen M., '"Reading coolly" in *John Marchmont's Legacy*: Reconsidering M. E. Braddon's legacy', *Studies in the Novel*, 36 (2004), 21–40

Oliphant, Margaret, 'New books', *Blackwood's Edinburgh Magazine*, 108:661 (November 1870), 607–31

—— 'Novels', *Blackwood's Edinburgh Magazine*, 102:623 (August 1863), 168–83

Olson, Greta, *Criminals as Animals from Shakespeare to Lombroso* (Boston: De Gruyter, 2013)

Oppenheim, Janet, *Shattered Nerves: Doctors, Patients and Depression in Victorian England* (New York: Oxford University Press, 1991)

Pal-Lapinski, Piya, 'Chemical seductions: Exoticism, toxicology, and the female poisoner in *Armadale* and *The Legacy of Cain*', in Maria K. Bachman and Don Richard Cox (eds), *Reality's Dark Light: The Sensational Wilkie Collins* (Knoxville: University of Tennessee Press, 2003), pp. 94–130

Paul, Diane B., *Controlling Human Heredity: 1865 to the Present* (New York: Humanity Books, 1998)

Pedlar, Valerie, *'The Most Dreadful Visitation': Male Madness in Victorian Fiction* (Liverpool: Liverpool University Press, 2006)

Peters, Catherine, *The King of Inventors: A Life of Wilkie Collins* (London: Secker and Warburg, 1991)

Peterson, M. Jeanne, 'Dr Acton's enemy: Medicine, sex, and society in Victorian England', in Patrick Brantlinger (ed.), *Energy and Entropy: Science and Culture in Victorian Britain* (Bloomington: Indiana University Press, 1989), pp. 248–69

Phegley, Jennifer, 'Clearing away "the briars and brambles": The education and professionalization of the *Cornhill Magazine*'s women readers, 1860–65', *Victorian Periodicals Review*, 33:1 (2000), 22–43

—— *Educating the Proper Woman Reader: Victorian Family Literary Magazines and the Cultural Health of the Nation* (Columbus: Ohio State University Press, 2004)

Pick, Daniel, *Faces of Degeneration: A European Disorder, c. 1848–c. 1918* (Cambridge: Cambridge University Press, 1989)

Platell, Amanda, 'Sorry, why should the NHS treat people for being fat?', *Daily Mail Online* (27 February 2009), www.dailymail.co.uk/debate/article-1156678/AMANDA-PLATELL-Sorry-NHS-treat-people-fat.html (accessed 18 September 2016)

Poovey, Mary, *Uneven Developments: The Ideological Work of Gender in Mid-Victorian England* (London: Virago, 1989)

Prichard, James Cowles, *On the Different Forms of Insanity in Relation to Jurisprudence* (London: Hippolyte Ballière, 1842)

—— *A Treatise on Insanity and Other Disorders Affecting the Mind* (London: Sherwood, Gilbert and Piper, 1835)

Pykett, Lyn, 'Collins and the sensation novel', in Jenny Bourne Taylor (ed.), *The Cambridge Companion to Wilkie Collins* (Cambridge: Cambridge University Press, 2006), pp. 50–64

—— *The Sensation Novel: From 'The Woman in White' to 'The Moonstone'* (Plymouth: Northcote House, 1994)

Rae, W. Fraser, 'Sensation novelists: Miss Braddon', *North British Review*, 43:85 (September 1865), 180–204

Reed, John R., *Victorian Will* (Athens: Ohio University Press, 1989)

Reitz, Caroline, 'Colonial "Gwilt": In and around Wilkie Collins's *Armadale*', *Victorian Periodicals Review*, 33:1 (2000), 92–103

Ribot, Théodule A., *Heredity: A Psychological Study of Its Phenomena, Laws, Causes and Consequences*, 2nd edn (London: King, 1875), in Jenny Bourne Taylor and Sally Shuttleworth (eds), *Embodied Selves: An Anthology of Psychological Texts 1830–1890* (Oxford: Oxford University Press, 2003 [1998]), pp. 306–8

Richardson, Coke, 'Extenuating circumstances', *Cornhill Magazine*, 9:50 (February 1864), 210–18

Bibliography

Rimke, Heidi, and Alan Hunt, 'From sinners to degenerates: The medicalization of morality in the 19th century', *History of the Human Sciences*, 15:1 (2002), 59–88

Robinson, Solveig C., 'Editing *Belgravia*: M. E. Braddon's defence of "light literature"', *Victorian Periodicals Review*, 28:2 (1995), 109–22

Rowell, George, *Nineteenth-Century Plays* (London: Oxford University Press, 1953)

Ruskin, John, 'Sesame and lilies', in *'Sesame and lilies', 'The two paths' and 'The king of the golden river'* (London: J. M. Dent and Sons, 1907), pp. 1–79

Rylance, Rick, *Victorian Psychology and British Culture, 1850–1880* (Oxford: Oxford University Press, 2000)

Sala, George Augustus, 'The cant of modern criticism', *Belgravia*, 4 (November 1867), 45–55

Schroeder, Natalie, and Ronald A. Schroeder, *From Sensation to Society: Representations of Marriage in the Fiction of Mary Elizabeth Braddon, 1862–1866* (Newark: University of Delaware Press, 2006)

Sheppard, Nathan, 'Genesis', *Temple Bar*, 41 (May 1874), 175–93

Shuttleworth, Sally, 'Demonic mothers: Ideologies of bourgeois motherhood in the mid-Victorian era', in Linda M. Shires (ed.), *Rewriting the Victorians: Theory, History, and the Politics of Gender* (London: Routledge, 1992), pp. 31–51

—— '"Preaching to the nerves": Psychological disorder in sensation fiction', in Marina Benjamin (ed.), *A Question of Identity: Women, Science, and Literature* (New Brunswick, NJ: Rutgers University Press, 1993), pp. 192–222

Smith, Alexander, 'Novels and novelists of the day', *North British Review*, 38:75 (February 1863), 168–90

Smith, Andrew, *Victorian Demons: Medicine, Masculinity and the Gothic at the 'Fin de Siècle'* (Manchester: Manchester University Press, 2004)

Spencer, Herbert, *Education: Intellectual, Moral and Physical* (London: Routledge, 1993 [1861])

—— 'Physical training', *British Quarterly Review*, 58 (April 1859), 362–97

Stepan, Nancy, 'Biological degeneration: Races and proper places', in J. Edward Chamberlin and Sander L. Gilman (eds), *Degeneration: The Dark Side of Progress* (New York: Columbia University Press, 1985), pp. 97–120

Sturrock, June, 'Murder, gender, and popular fiction by women in the 1860s: Braddon, Oliphant, Yonge', in Andrew Maunder and Grace Moore (eds), *Victorian Crime, Madness and Sensation* (Aldershot: Ashgate, 2004), pp. 73–88

Summerscale, Kate, *The Suspicions of Mr Whicher: or, The Murder at Road Hill House* (London: Bloomsbury, 2008)

Swinburne, Algernon Charles, 'Wilkie Collins', *Fortnightly Review*, 46:275 (November 1889), 589–99

Bibliography

Talairach-Vielmas, Laurence, *Wilkie Collins, Medicine and the Gothic* (Cardiff: University of Wales Press, 2009)

Taylor, Jenny Bourne, *In the Secret Theatre of Home: Wilkie Collins, Sensation Narrative, and Nineteenth-Century Psychology* (London: Routledge, 1988)

Taylor, Jenny Bourne, and Sally Shuttleworth (eds), *Embodied Selves: An Anthology of Psychological Texts 1830–1890* (Oxford: Oxford University Press, 2003 [1998])

Thomson, J. B., 'The hereditary nature of crime', *Journal of Mental Science*, 15 (January 1870), 487–98

Tomaiuolo, Saverio, *In Lady Audley's Shadow: Mary Elizabeth Braddon and Victorian Literary Genres* (Edinburgh: Edinburgh University Press, 2010)

Trollope, Anthony, '"Sesame and lilies"', *Fortnightly Review*, 1 (July 1865), 633–5

Tuke, Harrington, 'Monomania and homicide', *Lancet*, 90:2302 (12 October 1867), 472–3

Turner, Trevor, 'Henry Maudsley – psychiatrist, philosopher and entrepreneur', *Psychological Medicine*, 18:3 (August 1988), 551–74

Tytler, Graeme, 'Heathcliff's monomania: An anachronism in *Wuthering Heights*', *Brontë Society Transactions*, 20:6 (1992), 331–43

Van Zuylen, Marina, *Monomania: The Flight from Everyday Life in Literature and Art* (Ithaca, NY: Cornell University Press, 2005)

Varney, F. P., 'Female education in France', *Fraser's Magazine for Town and Country*, 80:477 (September 1869), 366–79

Waller, John C., 'Ideas of heredity, reproduction and eugenics in Britain, 1800–1875', *Studies in History and Philosophy of Biological and Biomedical Sciences*, 32:3 (September 2001), 457–89

Walsh, Dermot, 'The birth and death of a diagnosis: Monomania in France, Britain and in Ireland', *Irish Journal of Psychological Medicine*, 31 (2014), 39–45

Wiener, Martin J., *Reconstructing the Criminal: Culture, Law, and Policy in England, 1830–1914* (Cambridge: Cambridge University Press, 1990)

Willan, J. N., 'Extremes', *Belgravia*, 2 (January 1874), 298–302

Williams, [?], '*The Lovels of Arden: A Novel*', *Athenaeum*, 2294 (October 1871), 487–8

Wolff, Robert Lee, 'Devoted disciple: The letters of Mary Elizabeth Braddon to Sir Edward Bulwer-Lytton, 1862–1873', *Harvard Library Bulletin*, 22:1–2 (January and April 1974), 5–35, 129–61

—— *Sensational Victorian: The Life and Fiction of Mary Elizabeth Braddon* (New York: Garland, 1979)

Wollstonecraft, Mary, *A Vindication of the Rights of Woman: With Strictures on Political and Moral Subjects* (London: [n. pub.], 1792)

Wood, Mrs Henry [Ellen], *St Martin's Eve* (London: Macmillan, 1907)

Wood, Jane, *Passion and Pathology in Victorian Fiction* (Oxford: Oxford University Press, 2001)

Wynne, Deborah, *The Sensation Novel and the Victorian Family Magazine* (Basingstoke: Palgrave, 2001)

Index

Note: 'n.' after a page reference indicates the number of a note on that page. The six texts with their own chapters are indexed individually, other texts are listed under authors' names.

accident *see* chance
acquired characteristics 20, 114, 128, 134, 145
Adams, Joseph 125–7
agency 12, 37, 155, 164
ancestry 101–2, 130, 165
Anderson, Elizabeth Garrett 84, 190
Angel in the House *see* womanhood, the ideal woman
Armadale 22, 111, 121n.28, 122–5, 133–47, 177n.9
  Armadale, Allan 135–6, 140–4, 146
  Armadale Senior 134–6
  Brock, Mr 136–7, 139
  Gwilt, Miss 123–4, 136, 144–6
  Midwinter, Ozias 123–4, 135–6, 137–46, 164, 213
atavism 21, 126–7, 138, 151n.40, 164
athletics and athleticism *see* physical development
Austen, Jane
  Persuasion 186

Barlow, John 15, 42, 55, 57, 174, 178n.22
Basil 17–18, 33–48
  Basil 43–7
  Mannion, Robert 33–6, 38–42
  Ralph 46
Beeton, Isabella 195–6
blame *see* responsibility

Braddon, Mary Elizabeth 9–10, 92, 156, 209n.21, 211–13
  Aurora Floyd 84, 113, 121n.29, 179–80, 195
  criticism of 5, 7
  Doctor's Wife, The 180, 195
  Lady Audley's Secret 17, 84, 98–9, 117, 169
  letters to Bulwer-Lytton ('Devoted disciple') 7–8, 11, 72, 119n.6, 169
Brodie, Benjamin 103, 141, 155, 166–7, 186
Brontë, Charlotte
  Jane Eyre 186
Bulwer-Lytton, Edward 1–2, 28n.44, 45
  see also Braddon, Mary Elizabeth, letters to Bulwer-Lytton ('Devoted disciple')

Carpenter, William Benjamin 4, 12–13, 43, 51–3, 55–9, 77, 81, 97, 100, 112, 164
  unconscious cerebration 12, 66n.32
chance 6, 33, 112, 137, 147, 169–71
Christianity 75–7, 80, 88, 136–7, 177n.9
  and science 10–13
  see also muscular Christianity
circumstance 4, 6, 13, 18, 22–3, 36–7, 41, 53–4, 112, 147, 155–6, 167, 169–71, 207, 211
  see also education; environment; upbringing
civilisation 21, 144, 151n.39, 156, 164

Index

class 3, 22, 101, 110–11, 113, 116–18
   aristocratic decline 101–5, 142
   middle-class attributes 101, 106–7
coincidence *see* chance
collective development 166
Collins, Wilkie 9–10, 92, 156, 176, 211–13
   criticism of 5, 7
   Legacy of Cain, The 124, 148n.8
   'Mad Monkton' 22, 123–5, 130–3, 135
   Miss Gwilt 177n.12
   New Magdalen, The 159
   No Name (1870) 161
   'twin-sisters, The' 43
   Woman in White, The (1860) 17, 43, 99, 119n.13, 120n.23, 121n.30, 143, 169
   Woman in White, The (1871) 160, 177n.10
companionship *see* women's role
Conolly, John 44–5, 47
   see also moral management
consanguinity 126, 130–1
criminality 15, 144–5
   and heredity 97–8, 109, 127–8
   and insanity 16, 61–2, 175
cultivation 37, 165, 181, 193, 199

Darwinism 11, 12, 13, 126
   social Darwinism 13, 91, 143
degeneration 20–2, 105, 123–4, 135–7, 141–7, 163, 171, 212
   hereditary 117, 122–30, 134–5, 148n.8, 155
delusion *see* monomania and delusion
destiny *see* fate
Dickens, Charles 33, 131, 177n.12
   Bleak House 76, 102
   Hard Times 157, 179
dominant idea *see* monomania

education 22–4, 57, 79, 97–9, 106, 131, 156, 158, 162, 164–7, 179, 181–2, 192, 198–203, 212
   the classics 189–90, 192
   physical 162
   see also female education
Eliot, George 6, 24, 91
   Adam Bede 83
   Middlemarch 193, 206
Ellis, Havelock 138
England *see* nation, the
environment 22, 89, 106, 112, 142–3, 156–7, 198
   environmental determinism 78, 86, 110, 118, 165, 172, 175, 180
Esquirol, J. E. D. 16, 38, 50, 173
eugenics 20, 104–5, 107, 122–3, 127–9, 147, 156, 166, 171, 212
   literary eugenics 129–30
evolution *see* Darwinism
exercise *see* physical development

fate 39, 130, 136–7, 167, 169–70
Fawcett, Millicent Garrett 184, 191, 195
female education 182–3, 187–8, 192–3
   accomplishments 185–9, 194–5
   boarding-school 185, 200–3
   forcing-house metaphors 191–3
   higher education 180, 183, 189, 197, 208n.7
female influence 181, 183–6
   see also women's role, companionship
female intellectual ability and potential 86, 180, 189–91, 199, 201–2, 203–5
free will *see* will, the

Galton, Francis 20, 105, 107, 122, 127–8
   see also eugenics
Gaskell, Elizabeth
   Mary Barton 157
   Ruth 160
gout 97, 102, 126

habit 4, 100, 107, 128–9
hallucination *see* monomania and delusion
Hardy, Thomas 125
   Far from the Madding Crowd 77
   Tess of the D'Urbervilles 160
heredity 20–1, 86, 97, 103–4, 108–9, 113, 117, 125–30, 156, 167–8, 212
   hereditary disease 103, 125–7, 146
   see also gout; syphilis
   moral heredity 22, 73, 98, 125, 127, 135–7, 167, 133–4, 148n.8

see also ancestry; criminality, and heredity; degeneration, hereditary; insanity, hereditary
homosexuality 137
Huxley, Thomas Henry 10–11, 13, 23, 163, 184–5, 190

ideal woman *see* womanhood
identity *see* the self
illusion *see* monomania, and delusion
inborn personality *see* innate characteristics
incest *see* consanguinity
inherent personality *see* innate characteristics
inheritance (financial) 103, 142
  biological, mental and moral inheritance *see* heredity
  see also ancestry
innate characteristics 9, 37, 53–5, 56–7, 60, 67–8, 70, 75, 78, 86–7, 89, 100, 132–3, 144, 159, 161, 165, 199, 205–6, 211–13
insanity 15, 106
  causes of 40–2, 50, 56, 130–3
  distinction from sanity 42, 43, 61–2
  hereditary 40–1, 124, 126, 130–3
  moral alienation 50–1
  moral insanity 39–40, 55
  partial insanity 39–40, 61, 173
  see also monomania

John Marchmont's Legacy 19–20, 67–8, 70–92, 102
  Lawford, Belinda 72, 88–90, 183
  Marchmont, Mary 72, 85–8
  Marchmont, Olivia 19–20, 67–8, 70–85, 87

Kingsley, Charles 137–8, 141–2, 163

Lady Lisle, The 21, 98–118, 119n.7
  Arnold, James 98, 108–18
  Lisle, Claribel 99–101, 104–5, 110–11, 114
  Lisle, Rupert 98, 101–8, 117
Lamarck, J. B. *see* acquired characteristics
Lankester, Edwin Ray 142, 144, 147n.3

Lewes, George Henry 5, 109, 126–7, 133, 149n.21
Lombroso, Cesare 138
Lost for Love 23, 179–208, 213
  Chamney, Flora 180–1, 187–97, 200, 205–6
  Gurner, Louisa 180–1, 197–206
  Leyburne, Walter 187–9, 198, 200, 204–6
  Ollivant, Cuthbert 189–94, 196–7, 206
  Ollivant, Mrs 194–6

Man and Wife 23, 113, 156–76
  Brinkworth, Arnold 157, 159, 171
  Delamayn, Geoffrey 157–8, 160, 162–5, 170
  Dethridge, Hester 157–8, 163, 173–5, 212
  Lundie, Blanche 157, 159, 169–70, 172
  Lundie, Patrick 160, 165–6, 170–2
  Silvester, Anne 157, 159–62, 168, 170, 175
marriage 168, 181–2, 198–200, 205
  laws 157–8, 162, 175
  market 185, 187–8
  premature 194, 196–7
  see also women's role, companionship
Maudsley, Henry 18, 20, 80–1, 82, 105, 107, 109, 114–15, 122, 128–9, 144, 146–7, 149n.14, 174, 182, 186, 190
melodrama 34, 160–1
Melville, Herman
  'Benito Cereno' 139
Mill, Harriet Taylor 158, 181, 184
modernity 172
  see also civilisation
monomania 16–19, 35–52, 68, 130–2, 173–5
  and delusion (including hallucination) 16, 38–40, 131, 173–4
  dominant idea 18, 53
  instinctive (also homicidal, impulsive) 173–4
  literary examples 16
  as obsession 16, 42, 44, 48–9, 81–2, 131–2
  see also Basil; Mannion, Robert; criminality and insanity; *John Marchmont's Legacy*, Marchmont, Olivia; *No Name*, Vanstone, Magdalen

Index

moral management 15, 47, 55, 92
muscular Christianity 163

nation, the 129, 172, 185
  England 165
  national decline 134, 149n.21
  national fitness 171
natural selection *see* Darwinism
nature 4, 100, 113
  nature and nurture 3–4, 113–16, 127–8, 143–4, 165, 182, 211–14
No Name (1862) 17–19, 35–8, 48–63, 119n.13, 127–8, 159–76
  Vanstone, Magdalen 18–19, 35–6, 48–51, 54–7, 159, 175
Nordau, Max
  Degeneration 156
novels with a purpose 157
nurture *see* education; nature, nature and nurture; upbringing

obsession *see* monomania
Oliphant, Margaret 61, 157, 160, 162
original constitution *see* innate characteristics
overwork 190

parental influence *see* heredity; upbringing
passions, the 14–15, 42, 44–8, 131
physical development 158, 162, 166
  physical deterioration 165
physical fitness *see* physical development
Prichard, James Cowles 15, 39–40, 43–4, 58, 131, 173

race 138–41, 144
Rae, W. Fraser 25n.8, 68
realism 6, 8, 26n.17, 33–5
religion *see* Christianity; womanhood, sexual repression
responsibility 19, 24, 37–8, 41, 55–8, 61, 112, 127, 134, 155, 165–7, 175, 214
  of society 156, 165–7, 172, 212
Ruskin, John 69–70, 183, 189

savages (and savagery) 138, 140, 144, 162, 164–5

scientific developments 10–11, 13–14
self, the 1–2
  in sensation fiction 8–9
self-control 3, 14–15, 17, 42–3, 45–6, 51–2, 57–9, 77, 131, 139, 164
self-determination 166
self-determinism 101
selfhood *see* self, the
self-improvement and modification 2–3, 54, 97, 117, 156, 166, 212
sensation fiction 5–10, 17, 145–7, 169
sins of the father 134
social policy 3
Spencer, Herbert 14, 91, 162–4, 182, 186, 190, 192, 202
sport *see* physical development
sterility 21, 105, 135
Stevenson, Robert Louis
  Strange Case of Dr Jekyll and Mr Hyde 77, 156
Stoker, Bram 125, 156
superstition 45, 136–7, 151n.39, 168
sympathy 161
syphilis 133–4

upbringing 22–3, 58–9, 90, 97–9, 100, 104, 108, 112–13, 142–5, 156, 166, 199

will, the 3, 14–15, 51–3, 55–9, 77, 173–4
  free will 1–2, 13, 97, 155, 166–7, 170–1
willpower *see* will, the
Wollstonecraft, Mary 186, 191
womanhood 74–5
  conceptions of female physiology (physical and mental) 19, 71–2, 80
  the ideal woman 69–71, 74, 85–92, 183, 195, 205–6
  sexual repression 80–1
  see also female education
women's role 70, 74, 180, 182–3, 187, 192
  companionship 182–5, 192, 196–7, 204–6, 209n.21
  housekeeping 194–7, 209n.21
Wood, Mrs Henry [Ellen]
  St Martin's Eve 103

EU authorised representative for GPSR:
Easy Access System Europe, Mustamäe tee 50,
10621 Tallinn, Estonia
gpsr.requests@easproject.com

www.ingramcontent.com/pod-product-compliance
Ingram Content Group UK Ltd.
Pitfield, Milton Keynes, MK11 3LW, UK
UKHW021840140426
5217IPUK00022B/1534